GOSPEL OF THE GODDESS

A Return to God The Mother

by

William Bond and Pamela Suffield

With illustrated Tarot and Quabalah

ARTEMIS CREATIONS PUBLISHING

First edition published 1994.

Cover design by Mario Gould

Printed in the U.S.A.

1. Religion—Female God. 2. Sex role identity. 3. Title

LC 94-71080

ISBN 0-9640963-4-X

ARTEMIS CREATIONS PUBLISHING
3395 Nostrand Avenue, Suite 2J
Brooklyn, New York USA 11229

"The modern woman stands before a great cultural task, which means perhaps, the beginning of a new Era."

—C. G. Jung, *Women in Europe*

Preface

Gospel of the Goddess is a book with the potential to raise our collective consciousness to a new level and initiate revolutionary new concepts and ideas that can provide guidance to a world desperately seeking positive change. It contains the blueprints for a new social structure that promises to restore the balance to our lives that is in harmony with Nature because it acknowledges and restores the feminine side of our Creator to Her rightful place. The Gospel of the Goddess is an outline for a peaceful, loving, harmonious world of tomorrow.

Our male-god, male-dominated, patriarchal society has deliberately eliminated the feminine principle from our spiritual consciousness in order to elevate the male to a position of godlike supremacy over women and Nature. In so doing it has reduced women to the role of a dominated domestic slave and attempted to control Nature so that both could be used and abused in providing pleasure for males in whatever form and fantasy the male desired. Such male behavior is condoned by the patriarchal male gods and is sanctioned in the holy religious scriptures that were created and written by men. From these holy scriptures men then validated the rules and regulations of society that would become the laws of the land giving the religious and legal justification for their acts and behavior.

By nature men are aggressive, dominate, competitive and logical in their approach to solving problems. These are not negative qualities when properly channeled and focused, but when they are not balanced by feminine qualities of nurturing, unconditional love, forgiveness, justice and fair play, and intuition to do what is best for the community instead of the individual, it leads to the unjust warring, uncompassionate, intolerant society that we live in and have almost come to accept as "normal". It is not normal and has brought the human race and the world to the brink of chaos.

Gospel of the Goddess, like many other books, correctly identifies our patriarchal structure as the root cause of all our social, political, spiritual and economic illnesses. But, unlike those other books, Gospel of the Goddess also provides constructive, imaginative and revolutionary

iv

new concepts to deal with and correct the problems of our present society.

To correct the problems we must eliminate our patriarchal conditioning and rediscover the feminine side of our Creator and ourselves. Only in this way can we become whole human beings and restore the balance that is presently missing.

At present our patriarchal conditioning with its many rules and regulations, intolerance and aggression, gives immense advantages to men because it reflects a male dominant viewpoint, has been so ingrained into our psyche it is impossible for women or men to achieve equality without taking this necessary step. *Gospel of the Goddess* advocates this essential move toward a matriarchal society as the only method that will swing the pendulum, which has been moved to the extreme right by the patriarchy, back to center. In order to restore balance, the pendulum must now swing in the opposite direction.

Gospel of the Goddess is essential reading for anyone who is seriously interested in bringing about positive change in themselves and our society. It is a book that provides real hope for the future of our planet and the human race.

—*Femina Society Worldwide*

CONTENTS

INTRODUCTION

God the Mother

In the Western world, we are all familiar with the concept of a male god, whether the idea comes from Christianity, Judaism or Mohammedanism. When we think of a male god, at the back of our minds is a picture of an old man in the sky, who has a certain set of laws, rules and regulations we must all obey. If we follow these rules we will be loved and approved of by god, but if we disobey, we will be condemned and punished. Even today, when the power of this belief has been weakened, and many do not believe in a god at all, the image of Jehovah from the Old Testament is still very strong. Though we may consciously reject this view of god, subconsciously and within the structures of our society, the idea lives on. When we feel we have done the wrong thing, or "sinned", we tend to feel guilty or unworthy in some way, and expect punishment. It is so ingrained in us, that to a large extent the "Jehovah" figure is the only way we can envisage God. We appear to have only two choices; either this male god exists or there is no God at all.

Jesus Christ, through the teachings that have come down to us in the New Testament, attempted to offer an alternative by describing a God of Love who loves us all no matter what we do or who we are. Unfortunately, even though Christianity attempts to uphold the teachings of Christ, we find when we discuss the nature of God with many Christians, that they are still heavily influenced by the Jehovah of the Old Testament and see God as wrathful, judgmental and punishing unless you "get it right".

However, in the second half of the Twentieth Century another concept of God has appeared. This time God is not a man but a woman. Its promulgators talk about "the Great Goddess" or "the Great Mother", who existed in the Western World before the advent of male-centered religions and before Christianity achieved its dominance of the whole of Europe. Many books have been written on the necessity for our society to turn towards the Great Mother, who has been ignored in the Western world for millennia.

On the face of it, assessing the idea of a female Creator in a purely intellectual way, it seems quite ridiculous. Why should it matter whether God is male or female? Surely a supreme deity is beyond being male or female at all. Eastern religions like Buddhism and Taoism already accept the genderlessness of God. In Taoism, we are presented with the concept of the "Tao", which means "The Way". There is no entity or image which can be worshipped or appealed to. Buddhism is similar, but since its ideas were taught by an historical man, Gautama Buddha, he is the one worshipped, despite the fact that he insisted he was not a god.

If we were assessing the nature of God in an entirely logical way, the concept of "The Tao" would be the truest representation, since it perceives of a supreme entity as pure energy, beyond all ideas of human form and character. The trouble with this idea is that human beings find it difficult to grasp what the Tao is really like. It is ever mysterious, and beyond the comprehension of our limited minds. We seem to need an image that we can relate to, that we can understand in human terms. The truest representation of God which we can grasp, and which fits in with our growing ideas of a loving deity, is of God as the Great Mother. A masculine god is omnipotent, but judges, condemns and gives only limited love. His power is used to punish transgressors and reward the faithful. Man does the same. However, when you think of a mother, the picture is different. An ideal mother gives her children unconditional love which never changes. No matter what the child does, it will always be loved, supported in its growth, and nourished by the mother. Even if the child abuses her or commits horrendous crimes within society, this love never disappears. A wise mother obviously encourages loving behavior, and discourages mistakes, but her love never wavers.

When we think of the Great Mother, we are thinking of an entity who will love us all, for ever, because we are her creations,— her children, to use the earthly metaphor. This is a completely different picture from the one drawn by belief in a male god, which relies on the threat of punishment, or withdrawal of love and rewards, to keep us in line. Since it is now time for the "feminine" side of our Creator to be accepted and valued by men, it makes sense to worship a female deity. Only in this way will we begin to balance our society, which has denigrated and denied The Great Mother's gifts for millennia.

As we all know, in our society there are many people who do not obey the rules of the Church and still escape punishment. Some of them seem to flout all of the laws of society and religion yet still prosper and thrive. Others obey all the rules, behave in a very humble and loving way, yet seem to receive no reward for their actions. They are often despised and taken advantage of. The Church avoids the implications of this by saying that such people will be happy in the afterlife, and the others will go to Hell. Since this is only a speculation, it is of little practical help to those suffering in the here and now. The priests of the god can only offer a better life when we are dead—what they cannot deliver is happiness and joy now. In contrast to this, the priestesses of the Great Mother can promise peace, joy and paradise on this Earth while we are alive.

To be in paradise does not require us to be disciplined and sacrificial for the sake of future rewards; all it requires is a change in attitude. In the world of the god, whether it is the one reflected to us through Christianity, Judaism, Mohammedanism or Science (which is our latest male religion) we are offered a world of conflict and fear. We have to accept rules and regulations to keep us in check; we have to accept the masculine world of aggression and conquest, whether it is conquest of ourselves or others. All harmonious ideas of joy and happiness are looked down on as impossible, leaving us with only suffering as the route to salvation. In this world view, we learn and achieve only through struggle and pain, so it becomes an inevitable and necessary part of existence.

When we look to the Feminine and the Great Mother, there is a different perspective. The Great Mother will always look after us, no matter what we do and no matter what we believe in or say. There is no requirement to subscribe to a particular religion or way of behaving to "earn" her love—she loves us all, and equally, anyway. The Feminine is a concept of harmony, of bringing together, of joy and peace. The priests of the god see a world that is out of harmony with itself, where only the strongest survive and the weakest go to the wall. This is not necessary.

The feminine world-view shows us harmony in everything—on Earth, and in the whole of Creation. This idea of the essential harmoniousness of creation was recently brought out very clearly in the book *Gaia* by James Lovelock. It is interesting that he named his book after the ancient Earth Goddess, who was worshipped as the original deity. Though she was at one time acknowledged as the first to emerge from the primeval state of Chaos, later male-dominated cultures devalued her and placed the sky gods like Uranus and Zeus above her.

The truth of existence is that how we see the earth we live on and our fellow human beings, shapes our lives. Our desires and fears act as magnets, drawing towards us the reality which we feel is the "true" one. If we believe in conflict and limited love, that if we do not behave in a certain way we will not be loved or rewarded, then this will be the reality we create. We will become aggressive or defensive towards other people because we expect them to hurt or exploit us. This in turn attracts to us the very aggression we fear, and confirms our beliefs. If we believe that only the strongest and most ruthless survive, and that this is by divine order, then we will have no qualms about exploiting the Earth and our fellow man. But always lurking will be the fear that someone even stronger or more ruthless will snatch everything we have won away from us. If we also allow ourselves to judge others and find them better or worse than us, stronger or weaker, then we live in fear of others judging us. We create a god who does this when we die, sending some to Heaven and the rest to Hell based on his judgement of our worth.

The history of our species for the last few thousand years has been centered on conflict. Our idea of "right" is based on force, which is a particularly male attribute. A good example of this can be seen if we look at the Falklands war. Britain sent a Task Force to the Falkland Islands to retake them from Argentina, who had snatched them from us. If we had not possessed a strong Navy and Army then the Islands would now belong to Argentina. Each side in the conflict believed that justice was on its side, yet it was superior strength which prevailed. Although in many ways we are more enlightened than in the past, our society is still based on the idea that "might is right." The boundaries of countries, the distribution of wealth and land and the use of a particular language, owe their existence to the use of force on weaker people. Within each country, an unwritten law states that the more powerful you are, the more you can ignore the law and the rights of others less powerful than you. Once you have accumulated wealth and power by the use of aggression, then you invoke the force of the Law, the police and religion to prevent other equally rapacious people from relieving you of your booty. In such a world, no-one can be happy. Even if you are strong and successful, there is always fear that one day your strength and aggression will fail and you will become prey to others.

But if we were to return to worshipping the Great Mother, our direction would inevitably be towards harmony. There would there- fore be less likelihood of aggression towards others, and even less likelihood of aggression towards ourselves. Since we would look for evidence of harmony, it would be there, and since no-one would be perceived as a threat to us, we would not provoke aggression in others or draw it to ourselves. We would be more likely to cooperate with our fellow man and have no reason to exploit him. In a harmonious universe there is no need to fight for what you need—all resources, whether material, emotional or spiritual, are available to everyone because they believe that this is the case. The idea of scarcity can only exist when there is fear that you may miss out on something that you need, and that only you can provide it, by right behavior, force or belonging to the "right"religion or group.

There would be no reason for anyone to feel unworthy, as we do now, because we would know that we are loved by the Great Mother. Though we may make mistakes, this in no way changes her love, and she is always ready to help and support us. We would no longer have the inner conflicts bequeathed to us by the male priests of the god, reflecting in the world as strife and struggle, thus allowing us to live at peace with ourselves and the world.

Unfortunately, throughout recorded history, we have only known a patriarchal society. Though there is some evidence that matercentric (guided by women) societies have existed, we have no real way of telling how they functioned. All evidence that these societies existed, and were harmonious, was ruthlessly suppressed by the male-dominated cultures who took over from them, and where it could not be eliminated, was reinterpreted to support the ideas of the prevailing religion and culture. However, there are stories of a Golden Age, which existed before recorded history, in many religions and mythologies. In the East, the *Tao Te Ching* talks of a time when everyone lived in harmony, and catalogues the changeover from this period of peace to the present patriarchal society. Initially, in this Golden Age, there was no conflict of any kind, nor any rules and laws. Gradually, these were introduced until we arrived by slow degrees at our present fear-ridden society.

Today, society is yet again changing, and we will in the future progress into another matercentric society. Obviously, there will be those who oppose this, some because they wish to retain patriarchy, and others because they believe that the ideal society is one in which men and women are equal. This is not yet possible, even if we could define what "equal" means. As recent research has shown, (in *Brain Sex* by Anne Moir and David Jessel) there is a fundamental difference between the male and female brain which manifests itself in the way men and women think and feel. While men can ignore feelings, and rely on "logic" to make decisions, it is necessary for our evolution to move into a female-centred society, one in which we worship a female deity and in which men can learn to care for others.

It is possible that in the far future we will have a society in which neither sex is dominant, but at our present stage of evolution it is spiritually necessary and inevitable that we move into a matercentric society, as we will explain in subsequent chapters. This will benefit both men and women. At the moment our patriarchal society with its many rules and regulations, intolerance and aggression, gives immense advantages to men, because it reflects their way of seeing the world. There is no real way that women, or men for that matter, can achieve equality in such a society. We are seeing a drive for freedom within many countries of the world, and a growing acceptance of other's ways of living. Many patriarchal structures which restrict freedom are being eroded or destroyed. In this climate women will be far less disadvantaged than before because they have less need for order and hierarchy than men, and because men will not be able to use aggression and logic in the same ruthless way they are accustomed to. As men see that women's ability to mobilize both intellect and feeling in decision-making leads to greater stability, they will no longer wish to dominate. They will see clearly that they will be far happier directed by women than by other men, and gladly allow them to guide society.

I

CHE PATH OF CHE GOD

All human beings on this earth are children of the Great Mother. Once, we all existed within her in a world of paradise. The story of the Garden of Eden is probably an echo of this world, which is also reflected in the state of bliss we experience before physical birth, in the womb.

But then there came a desire, both from ourselves and the Great Mother, for us to become gods and goddesses in our own right. We needed to be able to create independently. As a result, we were put onto this three-dimensional planet, so that we could grow and learn how to create for ourselves. This was a crucial step. As long as we lived within the Great Mother, we would always be overwhelmed by her Creation, so we had to live in a very limited world, one that was equal to our limited understanding, limited ability to create and limited ability to love.

Because the only way to grow is to do things for ourselves, make mistakes and bring about our own creations, we had to be in a situation completely outside the Great Mother, or at least appear to be. The Mother had to set us free, just as a baby with a mortal mother, on whom he is totally dependent, sooner or later has to be freed to learn to do things for himself and gain autonomy. A wise mother, of course, allows the baby independence, and encourages him to be as free of her as he is able, while remaining always at hand to answer calls for assistance.

This is what the Great Mother has done for mankind. She has given us both freedom and protection, in a kindergarten which is three-dimensional earth. Man, in his evolutionary infancy, lived in a form of paradise, still strongly connected to the Great Mother. When we look at primitive tribes in the rain forests of Brazil, the pygmies in Africa and the aborigines in Australia, we gain a sense of the leisurely and safe existence which man led. He was able to feed himself quite easily by gathering fruits, roots and vegetables, supplement his diet by hunting and build simple shelters using the materials he found around him. Unlike today, there were no encroaching aggressive cultures to threaten him, and disease was unknown because he was still in harmony with himself and the planet. Only later on in our history did life become "nasty, brutish and short."

Of course, in time, man wanted more than this, as his drive towards autonomy and self-realization asserted itself. He embarked on the path of the god, which involves the creation of a feeling of independence and self-worth at an individual level rather than a communal one. This moved him further and further away from the Great Mother. Gradually, he began to create the first simple societies, and later on, civilizations. More and more, he began to control the world about him, to control himself and to control women, because they were still connected to the Great Mother, and represented the symbiotic past he was attempting to leave behind. Slowly, he developed an ego, or sense of self as an individual, and this told him that the way forward was to use his energy for himself alone. In time, as the distance between him and his Creator increased, it convinced him that he was a totally separate entity from others, trapped inside a body which represented the limits of his being. An ancient myth which embodies this growing divergence of men and women relates to the Egyptian deities, Isis and Osiris. Osiris was chopped into thirteen pieces by his evil brother, Set, and Isis had to search the world to find his scattered remnants. She found all but the phallus, which had been eaten by a crocodile, and brought him back to life. This story illustrates the way that man began to divide the world into separate individuals, while women remained whole. Isis loves Osiris enough to reassemble him, and is the only one who can do this, because she remembers what the whole is. In terms of human evolution, woman is the only one who can unite the fragmented universe of patriarchal society, because she has never become totally disconnected from others.

As man moved further away from the Great Mother, his intuitive faculties diminished and he was left with only his growing intellect. He began to question the existence of intuition, and despise women because they seemed to rely on this illogical sense for guidance. Though he looked for devotion from woman, he gave her nothing in return. If he could have dispensed with her, he would have, but he needed her. So she became his slave, and gave him the space he required to further develop his ego, by taking care of many of his needs. She received only contempt and hatred for herself. Everything was owned and controlled by men. Even children, who clearly emerge from a woman, were seen as the property of males. The woman was merely the incubator for male seed. In some patriarchal religions, the child was seen as evil because he was "born of woman," and had to be ritually cleansed by baptism. In this way, he is reborn "of spirit," and can worship the male deity without the taint of woman defiling him.

As we said in the first chapter, men and women are very different, not only in their physical bodies but within the brain. Man has in fact two brains: one, on the left side, is the cold intellectual brain which belongs to him alone —the other, the right brain, is the intuitive, emotional and artistic side of him and is linked directly to the Great Mother. To enable man to go his own way and become independent of the Great Mother, there is only a very slender link between the two halves of the brain. Man can easily ignore his right brain and behave as if the intellect is the only part of him that exists. This is not true for women, who have a very strong bridge between the two halves. They can not ignore the presence of the Great Mother and disconnect the two sides of themselves so easily.

What this means is that woman has a continuing link to the Great Mother, and functions as Her representative on earth. She acts therefore as nourisher and protector of man. She gives birth to him on the physical plane, and looks after him until he is able to fend for himself, just as the Great Mother did earlier on in our racial history. This makes all relationships between men and women, in essence, one of mother and son. Although we may enumerate other relationships such as father/daughter, husband/wife and brother/sister, the root relationship is always mother/son, because woman is the embodiment of the Great Mother.

This fact, in patriarchal societies, has brought conflict between men and women. Man, in his striving to go forward on the path of the god, has often seen women as his enemy, interpreting her efforts to help him as holding him back. He does not wish to remember that he is a child of the Great Mother, and punishes woman for reminding him that this is the case. He has also often chosen to see woman as his servant, rather than his protector and guide, thus distorting her function in the world and restricting the help he can receive from her. Woman's function is also the reason why men find women completely mysterious, unfathomable and unpredictable. Simply because she is the representative of the Great Mother on earth, she is truly unlimited, and can impart wisdom, when she is allowed to, to help herself as well as others.

Women call on the wisdom of the Great Mother to bear children, to rear them, to look after husbands, and to keep the whole of society functioning. Without women, there would have been no human communities, merely a collection of individuals fighting to gain knowledge, power or pleasure for themselves. Women are in the position of looking in two directions at once. One way, they are looking back towards paradise, when all was harmonious, and are learning from the Great Mother. The other way, they look towards man, see him struggling to create for himself, and learn from him too. On the path of the god, man learns by doing and woman learns by observing and being.

Because man wanted to forget the Great Mother and go his own way, he created a deity in his own image—the god. Man began to move away from the Great Mother on to the path of the male god, to begin the first half of a cycle which culminates eventually in a return to the Great Mother. Unfortunately, the path of the god has also been the way of suffering, conflict and separation. Within the Great Mother everything is one, and that oneness rests within her unconditional love. Everything is accepted and nothing is rejected, leading to total harmony. Man desired independence and separation, so he originated the idea of conflict, in which it is possible for one idea, belief or person to oppose another. Each person began to be seen as separate from others. Having done this, man then arranged the whole of creation, in his mind, into a hierarchy. Some people and things became more valuable than others, leading to feelings of superiority and inferiority, and desires to possess and control. Although the Great Mother is able to give us freedom, unfortunately man on the path of the god is unable to give himself or any other man that same freedom. He fears that he will lose control of himself or others if he does not keep a tight rein on everything in his world.

Everyone is a unique individual, with characteristics which are different from anyone else's. Man on the path of the god cannot cope with this. He sees difference as a threat, to be eliminated by any means possible, rather than a reason to celebrate the incredible diversity of creation. From this attitude came intolerance, repression, violence and wholesale war. Men of similar ideas banded together, however temporarily, to impose their ideas on others. Control was exerted to force people to think, feel and behave in certain ways. Protest was met by the setting up of laws and moral codes so that dissent could be outlawed—whether it was religious or political.

The process of man's loss of innocence on the path of the god is clearly documented in the Tao Te Ching. It says,

As the Great Tao declines
Morality and laws come into being.
As wisdom and knowledge arise
They make way for lies and deceit.
When there is conflict in families,
There is obedience and duty.
When countries are in turmoil
Warriors are praised.
When Tao is, all is one,
When Tao is lost,
All is divided.

Unconditional love for all has been replaced by rules and structures of behavior within a society which sees some people as worthier than others. Intuitive knowledge has been replaced with intellectual learning, and harmony has been lost, leading to conflict between people who have forgotten their connection to each other.

All this has come about simply because mankind has only a very limited mind. The mind of the Great Mother is completely unlimited, and can accommodate all ideas and all people, without fear. She has given us parts of her wisdom, and everyone has access to this. But man only feels safe in a world where he understands and therefore can control everything. The unknown or the uncontrollable are very fearful to him, and women, as the representatives of the Great Mother, are the ones he wishes to control the most.

When we look at the beliefs of mankind in Medieval times, we can see how limited he was. The earth was seen as the center of the universe. The sun orbited the earth, and the moon and stars were seen as lights in the sky. It was a small safe cocoon. As man's knowledge of the cosmos has increased, the horizons of his universe have expanded, allowing him to see even more possibilities. He now accepts that the earth orbits the sun, (although even that fact is not entirely true,) that our planet is only one of several within the solar system, and that he inhabits a vast galaxy, only one of the millions

judgment and division. Heaven is the state of mind of the Goddess, in which harmony is so total that no conflict can occur. There are no decisions to be made, no idea can oppose another idea, and no-one can be hurt in any way. As unbelievable as it may seem to someone on the path of the god, we really do not have to struggle for our existence, for enlightenment or for love. We do not have to earn it by being "good", fight for it through sacrifice and competition, or strive to understand it. Love, the Great Mother's gift to us in its myriad forms, is freely given. We only have to allow it to happen. There is no effort involved, only acceptance.

So it is possible to have a life of complete joy if you accept the help of the Great Mother, and relinquish "trying."

> *Bill: I have found this to be true in my own life. I was brought up by my father to believe in struggle. I was told that I would never achieve anything unless I worked very hard towards my goals. But personal experience has taught me that whenever I struggle to make things happen, nothing ever works out. When I have merely "followed the flow" of whatever life brought towards me, then everything seemed to resolve itself in a harmonious way. My father had the same experience. He had worked hard all his life, as the god dictated he should, but for little result. Then he became too ill and depressed to continue. He gave up and surrendered. Suddenly life began to work out for him and he became happier and more successful than he had ever been before in his life.*

Though illness and depression are not inevitable precursors of surrender, we are sure that most people who have a deep spiritual understanding could tell a similar story. In Christian mysticism, it is called "The long dark night of the soul," the point of deepest despair when you realize you know nothing, followed by surrender and peace.

We can see the same theme repeated in the life of the Buddha. When the Buddha was a very young man, he questioned the need for the suffering he saw around him, and tried to understand why man felt he needed to suffer at all. He gave up his privileged position as a prince, and went on the road to find spiritual enlightenment. After trying various disciplines and spiritual philosophies, to find some understanding, he became so disenchanted with his search that he simply gave up and surrendered, despairing of ever finding an answer. At that moment he became enlightened.

The same idea is found in the New Testament. Here we see a spiritual man, Jesus Christ, on the path of the Goddess. It is obvious that this is so from his teachings about a God of Love, and from the whole symbolism of the New Testament. This never caught on particularly well with Christians, who largely worship the old Jehovah god of the Old Testament. Jesus is crucified, descends into Hell, then rises again after three days. This encapsulates the whole cycle of man's development. The agony which Jesus experiences is the path of the god, one in which sacrifice and suffering are necessary. His death on the cross is the death of this path, offered to all human beings, so that they will not need to embrace suffering any longer.

His resurrection on the third day follows his surrender to the Great Mother, which brings rebirth in a changed form. Our patriarchal way of thinking needs to die, as Jesus died on his cross, so that we can return to the Great Mother.

The story of the Prodigal Son continues the same theme. A man leaves his home and ventures out on his own, where he becomes more and more impoverished. His misery allows him to realize that he is far worse off now than when he was at home, so he returns. His fear that he will not be welcome is dispelled by the joy his father expresses when he arrives. The New Testament calls the parent "father," to satisfy the patriarchal society of the time, but nevertheless the point is clear. We journey away from the Great Mother, until, poor and unhappy, we realize we need Her. Then we surrender, give up the fight, and go home. We find that only love and acceptance are waiting to meet us. There is no punishment for our "sin" in leaving, or for our mistakes and failures along the way.

Also in the New Testament we have the Virgin Mary, who continues a long tradition from earlier religions of being both a virgin and a mother. Of course, the Great Mother is the only one who can give birth without a male, but Mary allows us to see a very watered-down form of Her power and love in a religion which in every other respect totally devalues the feminine. Though the Christian Church emphasizes Mary's sexlessness and celibacy as an inducement to women not to express their own sexuality, millions of people have prayed to her for help and compassion, thus reaching to the Great Mother through this action.

Mary Magdalene is another woman in the New Testament who represents a facet of the Great Mother. She was said to be a prostitute, one of the most despised occupations for a woman in patriarchal society. Jesus chose not to condemn her, and in fact she seems to have been one of his closest disciples. He is accepting of her because she, like the Great Mother, can give unconditional love to any man yet not be possessed by one. In the temples of the old matercentric religions were sacred prostitutes, or qadishtu, who saw sex as a celebration of life and creativity, not as something sinful. They might temporarily or permanently reside in the temple, and their children were not disparaged as "bastards." The idea that a woman should be restricted to sex with one man to ensure his property was left to his own children could not be important in a society which was matrilineal -i.e. titles and property came down through the mother, not the father.

Yet another trace of the Great Mother in the New Testament is the idea of the Holy Trinity - Father, Son and Holy Ghost. This represents the three aspects of the Great Mother found in the stages of a woman's life; the Mother, Daughter and Wise Woman. Many of the old matercentric religions had a triple Goddess who was "three in one" in the same way Christianity is. These three faces of the Goddess were represented when Christ was crucified as the three Marys. It is also interesting to note that when he became resurrected, he appeared firstly to a woman, Mary Magdalene, before showing himself to the male disciples.

The most important point we can make about the New Testament is that its teachings are more in line with the path of the Goddess than the path of the god. Later on, Christ's message was distorted by the Church to fit in better with patriarchal society, and to preserve the power of the Church hierarchy. Jesus, because he was connected to the Great Mother, attempted to help people avoid needless suffering and separation. He was crucified for this, because people wanted their full measure of sorrow, pain and humiliation, even if it happened to be someone else's.

If you find this difficult to believe, think of how many people today are fascinated by stories of violence, murder or rape; how many enjoy plots involving oppositions such as cowboys/indians, cops/robbers, or other variations on the goodies/baddies theme. Many films and TV. programs are minor variations on the old Roman circuses, with the difference being that we are not physically present to witness the bloodshed. News reports also concentrate on disaster and violence, and filter out the peaceful and harmonious events occurring everywhere. While we are fascinated by fear, conflict, suffering and hatred, we are on the path of the god, and likely to create these themes in our lives. We are bored by harmony, because it is not exciting in the way "fighting for right" is. To paraphrase Shakespeare, all the world's a stage, and while we are on the path of the god, we play the game of fear, aggression and hatred for real. Having forgotten that we all write our own scripts, we believe it is necessary.

Even on the path of the god, in the midst of the apparent conflict, there is an underlying harmony, which we cannot disrupt. Although newspapers present a picture of a world in constant turmoil, most of life is ordered, harmonious and balanced. Though we may choose to focus on disease and disharmony, the universe continues to operate in a perfectly balanced way. When we move on to the path of the Goddess, we begin to appreciate this. We see that Nature has an innate balance, that the world we see through our telescopes is as mysteriously ordered as the one glimpsed by sub-molecular physicists. An underlying yet invisible balancing mechanism exists, which ensures that everything works together in a continuous state of harmony. Even though an infinitesimally small sub-atomic particle appears to have an element of unpredictability surrounding it, something like our own free-will, at the larger level, there is always order.

The conflicts within the patriarchal system also show a drive towards harmony. Without this, society would be destroyed. Extremes of violence, deprivation and oppression cause their own reaction, and move inevitably towards their opposite. Within the larger cycle of human development are smaller ones, all of which show the same tendency to move towards eventual balance and harmony. If we have had a mini-era of sexual restraint, for example, then we swing back into a time of sexual freedom, which then moves into another era of repression, hopefully not as severe as the first.

Although harmony is real, we are free to believe otherwise, because the Great Mother has given us free-will. Until we choose to change our beliefs, no-one can alter them, and they continue to produce a world which inevitably proves them true. On the path of the god, it is pain which prizes us loose from our entrenched attitudes, and eventually forces us to grow, though we may endure a great deal of it before rebelling. On the path of the Goddess, joy and trust give us the confidence to welcome change and learn.

The conflict of ideas and beliefs which exists in patriarchal societies is not a true one. The Great Mother has given each of us a part of the truth, and since we are all unique, we each have a different part of the truth. All truths are true, and we have no right to tell another person that theirs is wrong. However, that is not the end of the story. All the pieces of truth given to us are part of a vast jigsaw puzzle, and we will never see a wider picture until we put the pieces together. This can only happen if we restore communication between the separate parts of the Great Mother's creation, this time with full consciousness. Each person will then have access to the truths possessed by others, and be able to see the whole picture instead of the tiny fragment of the totality which is his personal truth. Until we do this, we wander around with a little bit of sky, tree or earth, insisting that the whole puzzle is this piece.

The very limited truth available to patriarchal men is illustrated by the figure of The Hermit in the Tarot. The Hermit stands alone, like the patriarchal man who does not trust others, fears his god, and is trying to become completely divorced from the Great Mother. In his hand he holds a light, which represents his conscious mind, and with this feeble beam, he is attempting to see the whole of truth. Because the light is only a small one, he is very limited in what he can see.

Around the Hermit is a vast darkness, which symbolizes all he does not know, or does not want to look at. In the darkness is the Great Mother, because the Hermit no longer wishes to acknowledge Her existence. As he moves further away from Her, he begins to see darkness as frightening. There is so much of it, and he can neither understand it or control it. He also fears punishment by the Great Mother for leaving Her, which intensifies his determination to forget She exists. The darkness becomes peopled with evil spirits, which represent the parts of himself he has discarded as "bad." The further he moves away from the Great Mother, and the brighter his personal light becomes, the more menacing the darkness appears. His reaction is to dump more and more of himself into the darkness of non-acceptance; his fears, "sins," love for others, and women. His god becomes a god of light, and darkness is equated with evil. Women in particular are seen as "dark" and evil, which in a sense is true. Since they still often operate in an instinctive and intuitive way, despite patriarchal conditioning, they have very little "light" in them, in the sense of intellectual and ego development.

People on the path of the god have a very strong sense of what is right and what is wrong, what is good and what is evil. Like the Hermit with his tiny lamp, they illuminate a small part of All That Is, and call it "good." The variety of behaviors and beliefs designated as good by this process is fascinating. One man may see compassion and caring as "bad," because it is "unmanly," and weak, while another man sees it as a true Christian quality, and castigates "selfish" people as evil. Like the Hermit, we keep ourselves focused on the known, and avoid the darkness of the unknown. Even scientists, who could be considered explorers par excellence, will often avoid investigating areas which they fear might lead them into revising deeply entrenched beliefs.

We keep ourselves stimulated and "busy" because we fear that if we opened up to the unknown, all our unacceptable thoughts and feelings might come flooding back. What is worse, we might not be able to control them. This is one of the fears of men who refuse to look at the oppression of women. If women are given too many freedoms, where will it all end? They may no longer be susceptible to the control and domination of men. It seems safer by far to avoid looking into the darkness, since we cannot see that it has anything of value in it.

One of the accompanying phenomena of the refusal to accept our whole selves, by looking beyond the conscious mind, is scapegoating. We search for someone to blame for the evil in the world, or for our own personal deficiencies. If you look around you, you will inevitably see people who do this to an inordinate degree.

Pamela: One of the places I have found to be a rich source of "it's not my fault" is a prison. When I was working in one for a time, I was amazed at the number of crimes which were completely excused on this ground. Rape is an obvious one. Many men blamed their victims, who were "asking for it" in some way, and showed no recognition that a woman had any rights. Another favorite, and not quite so simple, was to defend a long list of burglaries, violence etc. on the grounds that "hard" drugs such as Heroin are illegal, and so you "have to" rob people to buy them from your dealer. As far as the men were concerned, this was the sole cause of their being in prison. One might argue that there is some substance in what they say, because the Law is what makes us criminals by designating certain acts as illegal, but they extended this maneuver into almost every area of life. The fact that they could never see their own failings in a given situation, which allowed them self-esteem in a degrading prison system, was also the reason why they could never abandon their patterns of behavior and the justifications they used for them.

The Jews traditionally practiced scapegoating in a ritual whereby the sins of the people were passed on to an animal. When the animal was freed, it ran away, taking the sins of the community with it. Christians use this mechanism too. They see Jesus as having absolved them from sin through his crucifixion. Later on, the Devil took the blame for all the temptations people had to commit sinful actions. Women too are scapegoats. Eve's disobedience of the god was seen as the reason for man's fall from a state of grace, and women have been punished for this ever since. Their carnal nature was often seen as particularly suspect. Their sexual magnetism drew men towards them, leading to lustful, corrupt and weakening sexual activity which was definitely not the fault of men. At times, women were not even seen as deserving of the status of human beings, and did not have a soul.

Today, we still have scapegoats, but the movement towards the Great Mother is well-advanced in many individuals. We are less afraid of the darkness, in all its forms, and more willing to look at our fears and inadequacies. The awareness and acceptance of what psychologists call "the unconscious" is now commonplace, though for some people it remains an intellectual toy rather than a tool for self-discovery. While many people are uneasy in the face of silence and darkness, others are beginning to listen to the voice of the Great Mother. The trouble is that the "still small voice" tends to reverse the accepted wisdom of patriarchal society. No wonder it has been seen by so many people as the voice of the Devil. This is unfortunate, because if we were to trust this inner link to the Great Mother, it would take us home again to Paradise.

III

FROM THE PATH OF THE GOD TO THE PATH OF THE GODDESS

In the Middle Ages, in Europe, the majority of people were on the path of the god. Most were involved in situations of suffering, conflict, intolerance and fear. Practically everyone had a belief that they lived in a hostile world, where co-operation was either impossible or ungodly. The separative aspects of human nature were at their height. However, in the last few hundred years, many new ideas have sprung up which have changed the status quo in patriarchal society. The concepts of freedom, liberty and equality have found wide acceptance, for example. These are all matercentric ideas, because they eventually produce a harmonious and cooperative society.

To make matters worse for patriarchal society, the concept of evil has been eroded. Back in the Middle Ages, everyone had a strong sense of evil. It was relatively easy to see your fellow man as being possessed by the Devil, which justified all sorts of cruel punishments in the name of the god. Naturally, those who held most power decided what was good and what was evil, and used both force and propaganda to reinforce the distinction between the two.

Nowadays, however, we have a society in which the demarcation lines between good and evil are far more blurred. We can consider criminals who persistently break the law in minor ways, for example, and see that they are merely misunderstood, inadequate or unhappy, rather than evil. We can accept them more and judge them less. Perhaps, we think, we should not merely punish them, but help them. Perhaps we should not beat our children when they disagree with us or disobey us, and instead, show them more understanding. Maybe we should be more tolerant towards people who are different from us, instead of condemning them out of hand. Even more radical is the thought that we could allow women greater equality within society, instead of confining them to a few roles chosen by men.

All these ideas are changing the face of society in the West, and bringing about a great deal of confusion, simply because there are two forces within society, moving in opposite directions. There is the force of the god, moving away from the Great Mother, and emphasizing men, the individual, and intellect, and there is the force of the Goddess, returning us to the Great Mother, emphasizing women, co-operation and intuition. These forces are colliding within present-day society at many levels—within the individual, within large organizations and between nations. As a result, we have structures and belief systems which attempt, totally unsuccessfully, to combine both matercentric and patriarchal ideas. For instance, within left-wing politics, we have the belief that everyone is equal, and should have equal rights and opportunities. This is a matercentric idea. Unfortunately, socialists and communists who gained power by promising to promote equality, frequently created vast bureaucracies with a leader at the top, who would, in theory, dish out the proceeds of society equally, and ensure fairness by multifarious rules and regulations. Because the socialists used patriarchal methods—control and hierarchies—to bring about a fair society, harmony did not result, and their opponents were able to accuse them of naiveté in believing that Utopia is at all possible, human nature being what it is. There is a similar story over on the right wing of politics, where the belief is in the freedom of the individual. Again, this is a matercentric idea. But at the same time as supporting freedom, the right wing politicians are also endorsing the status quo in patriarchal society. The result is selective freedom, given only to people who are acceptable to those in power, and a reinforcement of their freedom to exploit others, within the old hierarchical system. So we see an undermining of the very freedom which the politicians seem to be advocating.

Children come in for a confusing time because of the mixture of matercentric and patriarchal ideas within society. They may have a parent who firmly believes that children should be given the freedom to develop in an atmosphere with as few restrictions as possible. They explain everything to the child, coerce as little as possible, and never use corporal punishment. Then the child visits granny, or attends school, where another set of beliefs may be in operation. This time the child is told exactly what to do, and punished if he fails to comply. No explanations or consultations come into it. A totally patriarchal male child would be thrilled by the first situation, and run rings around his exhausted but "caring" parents, as he indulges in mind-boggling tantrums, and exhibits utterly selfish behavior. He will obey and grudgingly respect his granny or his schoolteacher, because these are the rules he knows about, however despicable they may seem to his parents. He has been given the opportunity to see both ways of being, but no-one can force him to become a co-operative and caring child if he doesn't want to be one. Another child may need the freedom of a matercentric environment in order to survive and develop. A home or school in which your opinion is never asked, and where you do as you are told, or else, does not fit them. Families in which everyone is different give us opportunities to grow. If we are the ultimate "caring, sharing" parent, and we have an utterly patriarchal child, male or female, then we are being faced with a part of the human community which is different from us, and represents that part of us which is still patriarchal. There are no accidents in who we get as parents, and the children we bear are also reflections of a learning opportunity we have given ourselves, however unconsciously.

However, despite all the confusion within society, there is no doubt that we are moving towards a matercentric society. There is no way that anyone can stop this, because it is the will of the Great Mother, and ours too. All we can do is to allow the transition to take place in a smooth and easy way rather than a painful and traumatic fashion. One of the factors which will help in the changeover is a recognition that men and women are fundamentally different, and have to be treated in entirely different ways. Women, for example, have no need of a pecking order, unless they have been brainwashed by patriarchal society. They do not need to be as closely controlled as men do, because they are more in tune with the Great Mother. Men, however, will still need guidance from women for some time, if they are not to harm themselves and others, until they learn unconditional love.

In a patriarchal society, men undoubtedly have a great advantage over women. The reverse will be the case in a matercentric one. To begin with, women may control society in much the same way men have done, using law, structure and morality. This is partly because they will still have some patriarchal values, and partly due to the numbers of patriarchal people still on the path of the god. It will not be possible, initially, to allow people complete freedom, simply because they will neither desire it or believe in its possibility. There will be many people who wish to continue living within a patriarchy, and it must be recognized that they have to be treated differently from those moving into a matercentric way of life. People on the path of the Goddess will respond to love, consideration and tolerance with acceptance. Although they may have parts of their belief systems still rooted in patriarchy, they have turned the corner, and are moving back to the Great Mother. People on the path of the god do not want tolerance and understanding in their lives. They are used to conflict, judgment and intolerance, and the drama of the patriarchal way of life. We must accept their continuing need for friction, control and aggression, until they choose otherwise.

The Women's Liberation Movement has attempted to achieve equality for women in our patriarchal society. But while the structure of our society is designed to fit the needs and desires of men, women will always be at a disadvantage. So for women to achieve equality, the whole structure of society needs to change. This is beginning to occur already, even though the motives of those accommodating women's needs and nature can often be selfish. An employer who is short of workers and introduces a creche to his workplace may be accused of opportunism, but nevertheless changes have been made to society by this action. As change continues and becomes less superficial, more and more women will come to the fore and begin to assume positions of control. Undoubtedly, many of these women will be largely patriarchal in attitude to begin with, but as time goes on, and fundamental change continues, they will be replaced by women who are truly matercentric in their strong connection to the Great Mother.

Since the whole of patriarchal society is built around concepts of control—through force, law and morality, it is inevitable that a matercentric society will weaken that control. This is already happening. During the Middle Ages and before, the kings and princes who controlled society were often worshipped as gods, and their word was law. Although ambitious men might challenge their power through insurrection, the majority of the common people accepted their rule, having been convinced through propaganda or the fear of punishment that this was a good idea. Times have changed, however, and we are now realizing that the people who lead us are not gods but fallible human beings. There is more desire on the part of many people to be in charge of their own lives, rather than handing it over to someone else who may make mistakes or simply not care. Alongside this, there is still wide acceptance of patriarchal values, leading to desires for a "strong" leader, repressive laws, and a return to former certainties about everyone's place within society.

When people turn on to the path of the Goddess, there can be a dramatic shock, resulting from the realization that they neither want nor need someone else to make decisions for them. They begin to see that politicians and other power figures cannot be relied upon to lead in a way which results in happiness for everyone. As a result, they begin to take charge of their own lives, and experience greater harmony and love.

Another facet of patriarchal society which is currently changing is inequality. At one time, it was relatively easy for a small group of people to own a high proportion of a country's wealth and land, without awkward questions being asked. The inheritance of privileges of all kinds, and the inequitable provision of opportunity within a society was seen as right and good. The god had decreed that every person had his station in life, and this was not to be questioned or changed. The common people were encouraged to defer to those above them, and even seen as sinful because they were poor, or of lowly birth. Those with inherited wealth, social status, or power, came to see themselves as god-like beings, more fitted to rule than those below them. Occasionally, the inequalities were moderated by a few men who saw their role as protectors of their inferiors. They ensured that there was no mistreatment of people within their sphere of influence, and behaved with kindness and tolerance towards them. Others simply accepted the advantages inequality had given them, and felt no compunction about continuing to promote it and exploit it.

It would be foolish to pretend that inequality has ended. In the UK. 95% of wealth and assets (land, property, etc.) is owned by 5% of the population. In many Muslim countries, repression of women is still very strong. In India, riots took place when the Government suggested giving some rights to the Untouchable caste. All over the world, people are being discriminated against in every conceivable way. But inequality is at least being questioned in some societies. The poor do not accept their lot quite so humbly as they once did. They are beginning to ask why society is not giving them a fair deal, and why it always appears to be their fault that they are not more successful. Women, of course, question the inequalities of a society which still sees them as inferior and second-rate. All sorts of "isms"—racism, ageism, sexism, etc., are being pointed at, with the result that those who are discriminatory are beginning to have to justify themselves, rather than having a totally free hand to practice their prejudices. Even some of those in power are beginning to wonder whether what they are doing is the right thing, and asking if there is a more co-operative way to run society. Conspicuously wealthy people, who at one time might have used their riches to impress others, are now finding that they receive more brickbats than bouquets. They find themselves having to justify their disproportionate consumption of the world's resources, and answering searching questions about the manner in which they acquired their money. It would no longer be acceptable, for example, for a society lady to exist on the revenues from slavery, as it was in the Eighteenth Century in Britain. As a result, many wealthy people are keeping quiet about their affluence, or even pretending to be poorer than they actually are.

In a patriarchal society, the aim is to have control of everything, up to and including, if possible, people's thoughts. In a matercentric society, we will control nothing. There will be no leaders, in the sense we know them at present, no policemen, no lawyers or law, no vast bureaucracies, no organized religion, with a fixed dogma, and no moral code except that love should be the key to all behavior. Even that will not be a rule, as such, but spring from connection to the Great Mother. All kinds of behavior will be possible which would be frowned on by present-day society, yet no-one will be in any way harmed by this, because the motivation for everything will be unconditional love.

Each person will have the freedom to choose a way of life which fulfills them, without encroaching on the freedom of others to do the same. This is not the same as the so-called freedom of patriarchal society, which is often a thinly disguised cover for oppressing others or behaving irresponsibly in the name of personal freedom. In a matercentric society, no-one will either desire to or be allowed to, override the personal will of another individual. Instead of looking to others for decision making, each individual will take the reins in his own life, and be responsible for it in complete freedom.

At first sight, this scenario appears to be totally anarchic. No rules, no laws, no leaders—surely society cannot function without them? We need them to make life safe for us. But the truth of the matter is that we need all of these structures and regulatory devices because of a lack of trust in ourselves and others. We believe that without law and order, chaos would result, leading to an appallingly uncivilized society in which everyone fights openly to grab what they want. Our opinion of human nature is very low. We feel we cannot stop our selfish behavior without punishment as a deterrent, and even more so, believe that other people would have great difficulty in restraining themselves. Our laws, unfortunately, do not work. Even though we are heavily socialized against crimes such as murder and theft, and there are severe penalties for being caught committing them, we have had no success whatsoever in wiping them out. This is simply because our patriarchal consciousness is responsible for the desire to steal and kill, and only an inner and outer change to a matercentric way of being will eliminate them, not bigger and better laws. Our laws are a substitute for love; there

would be no necessity for them in a world in which trust and love predominated. When we trust the Great Mother to provide us with all our needs and
make us happy, there will be no desire to take the property of others, if
indeed we have any wish to see anything as belonging specifically to one
person. We are surrounded by everything we could ever need. To steal from
another person when we realize this, is akin to grabbing a drink from a
person's hand when all around is an ocean of freely available water. Pointless.

The impulse to murder, which is the most heinous crime in society's eyes,
will similarly disappear in a matercentric society, without the necessity for
any laws regarding it. Since anger, greed, fear and possessiveness will no
longer exist, the motives for ending the life of someone will not be there
either. As with all of the changes in society, the elimination of crime, law and
the policing of people will not happen overnight. Not until there is enough
trust and love on the planet will those who cling to these things abandon
their faith in them. There will be a long slow evolution into a free yet secure
society, with many people continuing to invest their faith in patriarchal
structures until they are convinced that they are not necessary, either for
themselves or for others. Those who enjoy rules because it is exciting to
break them, for example, will take time to learn new ways of being. They
may see a female-led, free society not as anarchic and frightening, but as
boring. Currently, they need something to defy and outwit, and the structures and laws of our society fit the bill admirably.

So the solution to any difficulties within society is not to bring out new
laws, but to change mankind itself through the evolution of the soul, such
as is already happening. There is on earth today, an enormous number of
people who have completed the path of the god. They are no longer interested in violence, conflict, hatred and intolerance. Now changing to the path
of the Goddess, they are looking for harmony, love and peace. As more and
more people become willing to live together, guided by unconditional love,
all our patriarchal structures will deteriorate and die.

Although the seeds of the matercentric society have been sown over the
last few centuries, the "hippy" movement of the sixties was the first major
push towards it on a conscious level. Of course it did not last long, because
it was too far ahead of its time, and it was compromised by too many
patriarchal attitudes. However, another, similar movement is inevitable,
since the present generation of young people are more matercentrically
inclined than ever before. This will be very important, because there are so
many people today who are dissatisfied with the quality of society: they are
not happy with their lack of freedom, they are not willing to be told what
they can and cannot do, or how they should lead their lives. Those who
uphold the present structures of society are coming increasingly under pressure. No matter how they try, nothing seems to be right. Fundamentally,
movement towards the Goddess will erode and destroy all structures within
society. Finally, when a group of people can come together and demonstrate
that they can live together in peace and harmony without any patriarchal
structures, all systems will begin to disappear.

There are many well meaning religious cults today who are attempting to live in a loving way. Unfortunately, the mistake they are all making is that although they want to live in peace, they still build patriarchal structures to make it happen. There seems to be an underlying belief that without some form of organization or leader nothing can be achieved. They need to realize that the structure itself destroys any possibility of harmony, because it is always a form of limitation. All that is really required is recognition of and surrender to the Great Mother, and a realization that she is always there to give us unconditional love. We have to give or receive love from our fellow human beings and then get on with our own lives, without attempting to change or control ourselves or others. This sounds a radical and dangerous concept, but in truth it is not. If we truly believe in the unconditional love of the Great Mother, anyone on the path of the god will avoid us like a bucket of pig's offal. We will essentially be uncontrollable, and therefore of no interest. We will not be threatening to them, because we are not competitive or violent. Anyone on the path of the Goddess will realize the truth of what we are trying to do and cooperate.

The essential problem for the male ego, when the movement towards the Great Mother begins, is the acquisition of humility. Most patriarchal men are extremely arrogant. They believe that they can solve not only their own problems but every other person's too, usually by the use of control. When they begin to move on to the path of the Goddess, they have to learn to let go and recognize that they do not have a solution to all problems, that we have to look to the Great Mother for help and understanding. A patriarchal society embodies Murphy's law, "that whatever can go wrong does go wrong," but it is possible to reverse this. in all situations. In a matercentric world, the law is that if it can go right it will go right,—but only if we do not consciously interfere.

All of us have been brought up to believe in discord and disharmony as an unalterable fact of life, and the notion that we can live harmoniously is foreign to us. If we can surrender, and accept the possibility that letting go of all our cherished problem-solving strategies might result in greater success, we will inevitably find it is true. This is another reason why women will become the guiding sex in future. Simply because they are used to bearing and nurturing children, they are more accustomed to following their instincts and feelings than men are. During the birth of a child they have no choice but to let go and allow Nature to take over, for example. They tend to make decisions based not on "calm clear logic " but on intuitive and emotional response. This has earned them the contempt of men, who criticize them as hysterical, weak, sentimental and biased by feelings instead of reason. In some ways they are justified. A woman reacting through fear, who is not strongly connected to the Great Mother, may behave as foolishly as a man who solves all difficulties using his intellect. However, those women who can use their intuition to tap into the Great Mother, can and will show us the way forward.

This does not mean that men will have to relinquish logic and reasoning. What it does mean is that they must not attempt to use them to control situations and people. They must offer up their intellectual capabilities to women, who will then use intuition to decide what should happen, and they must begin to develop their intuitive links to the Great Mother. This does not occur at the moment, resulting in an unbalanced society.

Nor do we have to abandon Technology and Science, but we must ask in a given situation whether they might be disharmonious. In a patriarchal society, we tend to go by the maxim "the end justifies the means," but in a matercentric society the means and the ends are the same. All technology will have to be used in a harmless way, and the very idea of utilizing it in a destructive or harmful way to create peace and harmony later on, will be seen as totally stupid. There is nothing intrinsically wrong with Science and Technology, or logic and reason. The fault lies in their misapplication. Women, who are better balanced between reasoning and feelings, will be a more competent judge of how to use technology. At present this is not recognized. Our over evaluation of men's ability to create on a scientific and technological level has blinded us to the fact that women have special and invaluable gifts too. A woman who has a well developed intuition, is more likely to be denigrated as illogical than consulted on important questions by patriarchal man.

This being so, how will we arrive at the position where women guide men? If a matercentric society is one in which there is no coercion or control, it cannot come about by those means. The answer is that women will have to do nothing to achieve leadership, even though many women are under the misapprehension that they have to "fight for their rights." Men on the path of the god will never relinquish control to women. To coerce them only leads to a later backlash. But men on the path of the Goddess will gladly surrender to women because it is the Will of the Great Mother, and they will be in tune with Her Will.

We can see if we look carefully at our present day society, how powerful forces are operating to make it possible for women to gain advantages, despite strong opposition from patriarchal society. There is only one requirement for women in order to achieve a matercentric world. They must accept the Great Mother within themselves, and recognize that they are Her representatives on earth. Once they do this, men will begin worshipping them and accepting their authority without question, for the greater good of all.

IV

THE GODDESS IN PRESENT DAY SOCIETY

Robert Graves made an observation in his book *The White Goddess*, that a poem was a true poem if it gave you a "tickly" feeling when you read it, and that the feeling would come when the poem was related to the White Goddess. It's what the author James Joyce called "the agenbite of inwit," and can be experienced through art, music and dance, as well as through literature and film. The feeling has no accepted label in our society, but can be described as a recognition of truth, which is felt at an emotional or intuitive level. It arises from connection to the Great Mother, who is the whole of truth, and reminds us of Her existence. The words recognition and remind show us that we are remembering something which we have forgotten, since the prefix, re, means "again." The form in which the "aha!" is experienced varies enormously, but in essence it is always a re-connection to the love we experienced when we were fully one with the Great Mother. Often, it can be painful, since it reminds us, however briefly, of the time when we were blissfully happy, in union with Her and with All that is. As a result of the pain of separation from the Great Mother and each other, we may look for Her in outer things; in money, in sexual activity, in drugs; all the things which seem likely to give us a taste of joy. We have forgotten that the capacity for joy comes from within, and we move from one transient pleasure to another, seeking, but always looking in the wrong place.

Some popular music taps into our connections with the Goddess, since it is not only "classical" or "serious" music which has a monopoly on this. John Lennon, for example, in songs like "Woman," or "Imagine," could reach a wide audience with his insights. Even "Heavy Metal" music, often derided as mindless sexist garbage, sometimes contains images and sounds which reach to the part of us crying for help from the Great Mother. Just because a song seems banal to us on an intellectual level, does not mean it is valueless. It may be extremely helpful to those who wish to find a way home to the Great Mother, and absolutely right for them.

Many love stories through the ages have also evoked the Goddess; Shakespeare's *Romeo and Juliet*, for example. Although Romeo and Juliet had a matercentric concept of love for each other, they lived within a patriarchal society; their families were more interested in conflict and control than love.

The secrecy which resulted from this, led eventually to the tragic deaths of the lovers. Obviously, many patriarchal commentators on the play have come to different conclusions, explaining the tragedy as having been caused by the impulsiveness and inexperience of two teenagers, who have unrealistic and probably temporary feelings of love for each other. There have been thousands of love stories which paint a similar picture. In them, lovers desire a world in which they can freely express themselves, yet this is denied by society, which insists on setting love within very firm boundaries, and controlling the way in which it is expressed. Other love stories show another aspect of the Goddess—one in which She works through a mortal woman to act as the inspirational Muse for a writer or artist. The Italian writer Dante exemplifies this. He fell in love with a woman called Beatrice, whom he had only seen from a distance. His immense feelings of love gave him his creative energy, even though there was never a "proper" relationship between them.

Over the years, all great artists have attacked patriarchal society in one way or another, whether by focusing on its narrowness, greed, selfishness and disharmony, or by seeking themselves to live life differently, in a more life affirming way. It is unavoidable that they do this, since the vision and genius which makes them great writers and painters, comes directly from the Great Mother, even if the patriarchal side of them distorts the information they receive from Her. Society has attempted to counteract their vision: by making their art into a religious activity, interpreted and controlled by the rulers, by censorship, or by turning their work into a bland, watered down version of itself, acceptable to patriarchal society and thus no threat to it.

It is not only art which patriarchal society seeks to suppress. Anything which reflects the Goddess is fearful to the rulers, and must be eliminated or controlled. This is particularly true of sexuality. In no other area of life is there so much fear, conditioning, secrecy and hypocrisy. A President of the United States can remain in office despite his secret dealings with the enemies of the state, yet could not survive any sort of sex scandal. Our laws on pornography, to give another example, are riddled with fear, confusion, and very strong emotions.

In a male dominated society, it is easy to see why pornography which reduces woman to a two dimensional image is popular. It allows men solitary sexual stimulation without the tedious business of having to relate to a flesh and blood human being. It also allows fantasies to be explored which cannot be acted out in real life. Prostitution offers the same advantages to men. What is difficult to understand is why some men oppose it, and pass laws to eradicate it. In many ways, pornography can be quite useful, in that it shows us the gap between behavior and fantasy. We may wish to be a certain kind of person, and control our actions to fit in with this, but if we have not suppressed our fantasies, they show us where we're really at on the level of desire.

Bill: I had experience of this some years ago, when I began to realize that some of my sexual fantasies were quite sick. My first reaction was to suppress them. I was not "that sort of person." This worked for a time, then they returned, stronger than before, showing that this was not the way to deal with them. I surrendered to them, and used them for masturbation, whereupon they lost their power to attract me. I found that my "sick" fantasies gave me an awareness of myself which enabled me to grow, and that opportunity would have been lost had I censored them as unacceptable and pushed them from my awareness.

If we look closely at pornography, it reveals not only a great deal of information about ourselves, but about our society and the Great Mother. A common male fantasy, for example, is of using a woman sexually in a selfish and disposable way. This may be acted out by visiting a prostitute, or it may stay firmly in the realm of ideas. What it shows, is that part of the man is still firmly on the path of the god, and whatever his outward behavior, is still desiring to use women rather than serve them.

Another fairly common male fantasy is of seducing a virginal child or inexperienced girl. The scenarios vary. Sometimes force is used, sometimes not. Sometimes the girl responds with delight, thus boosting the man's ego, or she responds with fear, giving him a sense of power in a different way. Other men have heavily sadistic fantasies, of raping or torturing women, or, another favorite, watching two women making love. These are all fairly solidly patriarchal fantasies. The man is not yet ready to see women as anything other than objects for the gratification of his ego. He may of course go even further in his desires, into the realms of the totally socially unacceptable, and be stimulated by the idea of sex with small children or animals, by violence to the point of death, and by things like excreta, urine and fetishistic objects.

Not all pornography paints the same picture. It ranges over all the possible levels of development, and gives us a truer vision of our society than observable sexual behavior does. We can see for example, that when a man turns on to the path of the Goddess, his sexual fantasies change. Many will begin to dream about a dominating woman, who initiates sex, or one who uses him as a sex slave for her own pleasure. In their "ordinary" lives, they may still behave in an entirely patriarchal way, yet have a strong desire for punishment by a woman because of their misuse of her over the millennia, and act this out with a prostitute or through pornographic literature. Others may have taken their development further, and at the fantasy level, adore and worship women. Possibly, in "real" life they cannot find a woman willing to be worshipped, or they wish to test out what it feels like in fantasy, before risking it in actuality.

There is, of course, a similar pattern with women. Patriarchal women commonly have rape fantasies, or ones in which they are irresistibly taken over by a man who skillfully and excitingly makes love to them. If they have been conditioned almost entirely out of sexual desire, this may be transmuted into fantasies of meeting a man who is loving, caring and sensitive, without any sexual element being present. Some imagine making love with a group of men, who may restrain or force them, yet they enjoy the experience. The common thread is the passivity. Sex is something which happens to them, and they do not initiate it, even though in daily life they may be relatively assertive women. In some cases this passivity may be a denial that they want sex, and in others it may be a lingering hope that if they do remain "good" girls, the Prince will come, and they will live in bliss for ever.

When women move on to the path of the Goddess, their fantasies also change, just as men's do, but they move into a more active expression of desire. They may dream of humiliating a man, by having sex with someone else in front of him, or physically punishing him. They may fantasize about choosing a partner from ten willing sex slaves, and having total fulfillment without the need to consider the man's satisfaction all the time. The common factor is that they are now willing to acknowledge their sexual desires, and take steps to satisfy them, rather than waiting meekly for a man to do this.

Fantasy and pornography do not only show us some of our levels of development, they also display clearly some of our internal conflicts. A man who has the extremely common fantasy of wishing to use a woman sexually, without any concern for her consent or pleasure, also wants, although he may not be conscious of it, the unconditional love of a woman. Many women who have been raped can support this contention. They report that the man, after brutally raping them, asked for love and forgiveness. It would be easy to say that this desire is quite easy to fulfill for men. Women seem to adore men who are utterly selfish, and will endure all kinds of mistreatment at their hands without ever wavering in their affections. The problem is, that at the level of the unconscious, the man is completely dependent on the love of the woman, however independent he appears to be at the conscious level. If she withdraws her love, which sustains him in ways he does not recognize or admit to, his security is lost. Out of fear at losing this unconditional love, which is of course coming to him from the Great Mother via the woman, he seeks to control her, while at the same time giving all sorts of reasons other than the true one for his actions. He is unaware of the true reason. Since unconditional love, by its very nature, can't be controlled, he is either unsuccessful, or what is more likely, he ends up receiving only conditional love from the woman, mixed in with a large dollop of fear and guilt. Because her nature is unlimited, the woman would love all men, and this is unacceptable to a patriarchal man, who does not want to share her. He truncates her nature through his jealousy, possessiveness and fear, and the result is that he does not get what he wants—unconditional love, but a severely limited version of it. The woman herself restricts her natural way of being because the man tells her it is correct, and yet she knows intuitively that something is wrong.

We see this phenomenon more widely in patriarchal society, where man wishes to completely control the Goddess in the form of Nature and the earth. Though he knows he is entirely supported by Nature, and can't exist without her, he still distorts that knowledge, and attempts to make her subservient to him. Because Nature has not so far resisted this control has blinded him to the fact that he is trying to make something far greater than him bow to his will. In his arrogance, he rapes and despoils the planet in the same way he rapes and controls women.

So far we have only discussed heterosexual fantasies, but homosexuals also show their level of development by what they dream about. Gay men often see the Great Mother so clearly in women, perhaps due to a dominating mother, that they are terrified. They do not see the unconditional love, because of their fears, and focus on the dark side of the Mother, whom they see as engulfing them. Other men seem much safer than this. They may also be fascinated by strong women at the same time, and have friendships with them in which there is no overt sexual element. There is an attraction/repulsion energy, which shows an internal problem with females, and men do not have to be practicing homosexuals to exhibit it.

Nearly all men have a strong reaction to powerful women, even though there are so few examples in our society to point towards. Margaret Thatcher is an exception. She remained as leader of the Conservative Party for fifteen years and was Prime Minister for eleven. She survived politically despite various periods of unpopularity, and dramatically changed the image of women through this. Almost no one was indifferent to her. She provoked loyalty, loathing and admiration, in equal measure. She is clearly a dominant woman, who enjoyed political power, and was adept at hanging on to it. Her behavior reversed almost all the old stereotypes we have about women, which appalls some people and delights others. Many like to imagine that the men in Cabinet groveled before her, and reams have been written about why this was so, whether the men secretly enjoyed this, and what such actions do to harm democratic procedure. Also, much has been said about her apparent reluctance to include women in her Cabinet, and her habit of encouraging other women to return to their homes, to resume their old roles as wives and mothers. Did she dislike competition from other women, fearing they would not succumb to the same tactics as used on male politicians, or, as one author has suggested, did she actually see herself as a man, with the same attitude towards other women as a totally patriarchal male has?

To many observers, Margaret Thatcher was a traitor to her sex. Though she is female, they say, she has in fact worsened the lot of British women. Because she was the leader of the Conservative Party, which upholds the status quo within patriarchal society, she encouraged and advocated behavior which has led to an even more uncaring and materialistic society. Other commentators focus on her leadership qualities of determination and toughness, and applaud her unwavering resoluteness in the face of opposition. She is seen as having put the "Great" back into "Great Britain," especially after her actions during the Falklands War. What most people seem to have missed is that her behavior, while seeming to endorse all the values and structures of patriarchal society, actually undermines them. They relied on secrecy, lies and repression to achieve control, and Margaret Thatcher exposed them to the light of day. She did not seem at all willing to cover her actions with the all enveloping cloak of hypocrisy which politicians usually use when explaining why a particular action is necessary and inevitable. Because of this, she has unveiled the power games and ruthlessness which support society, in all their nakedness.

The more that women gain control and power within patriarchal structures, the more those structures will deteriorate and die. It does not matter that it is only women who are still highly patriarchal who occupy these positions, and appear to uphold competition and conflict—it would be impossible for a truly matercentric woman, if in fact they exist at all, to be successful within politics or business today. It has already been noticed that when women begin to enter prestigious occupations, the status of that profession diminishes. In the U.S.A., where most doctors and surgeons are male, medicine is a highly regarded profession, with great financial rewards for some. In the U.S.S.R., most doctors are women, and the status of the profession is low. It is not only that an occupation with women in it has less status because women themselves are held in low regard by society; women, by their very nature, change the internal structures of the profession. Patriarchal men are able to behave in a way which allows them to acquire status, power and wealth without internal conflict. It is perfectly easy for them to care about no one but themselves. They build job structures to reflect this. To begin with, when women enter such structures, they have to toe the line. They may in fact agree with the rules, and if they are suppressing unconditional love, be every bit as tough and competitive as men. However, if they have power, it is the power of the Goddess, and sooner or later, their fear will die away, enabling them to both care for others, and have some status and reward within society. Before this, it will have looked to them that it was an either/or situation—either they could love and nourish others, or they could have something for themselves. When they reach this realization, the ethos and therefore the organization of their profession begins to change, attracting more similarly minded women, and the rot sets in as far as patriarchal society is concerned. Once a profession begins to care about the welfare of people, both within and without it, and loses its ruthlessness, patriarchal men lose interest. They begin to choose other occupations, which still allow them to be selfish and competitive. Eventually, there will be no place to run for the patriarchal individual, but that time is a long way off.

If the image of a strong woman like Margaret Thatcher is disturbing to men, it is even more disturbing to women. Women in our society are not accustomed to the idea of being dominant, and if they are, they will often conceal the fact. Actresses who have impersonated Margaret Thatcher on stage or television, have reported feeling surprised at the amount of power they sense in themselves when assuming this persona. It is an unusual sensation for women in our society.

Patriarchal society, over the last few thousand years, has quite successfully undermined the self esteem of women, and the number of strong, confident females is minimal. It is considered acceptable and indeed desirable, for a man to be assertive, but a woman is still largely expected to be "nice" and compliant. This causes problems for women when faced with a real life example of a bossy woman like Margaret Thatcher. Some are likely to reject her completely because she does not fit the patriarchal image of women, who place children and husband before self. If they were to allow that she was right to seek political power, then it makes their life of sacrifice to a man's ambitions look like foolishness. Other women accept that it is O.K. to want power, but criticize the lack of compassion they see in Mrs. Thatcher. They wish to see a woman who is clearly caring and cooperative in a position of authority. In this they are not wrong, but unrealistic about just how successful such a woman could be in the merciless jungle of present day politics. Another group of women are fiercely loyal and devoted to Margaret Thatcher, because they see her as a role model for the emergence of similar females. They endorse all of her patriarchal attitudes, and see the way forward in terms of women becoming like men, i.e. individualistic, competitive and tough. The last group of women also favor Mrs. Thatcher, but in this case only because she is a woman. They are grateful that there is a strong woman around, and do not care what her politics are, even if they disagree with them. To this group of women, she is a ground breaker, and they are happy that she has had the courage to be herself and pursue her ambitions. It will not be clear for some time what effect she has had on society, but for these women, it can only be good. She paves the way for other women, and they applaud her for that.

Attitudes towards a woman who is turning onto the path of the Goddess, despite the way we've depicted it, is never simple. There is always a mixture of emotions, both negative and positive.

Pamela: Both my mother and my ex mother-in-law have shown me this ambivalence in equal measure, and confused me because of my own lack of certainty. When I was a full-time professional "career woman," my mother was both proud and approving. My mother in law was uneasy. She felt I should be bearing and raising children as she had done. She couldn't wait to be presented with grandchildren, and for me to become a "proper" wife. When I finally had a child, however, they united. My priority was my daughter; therefore I should work only a little, if at all, they agreed. Since I was guilty about my desire to resume my career, I was in conflict, and resolved it badly by going into an emotional decline which was only reversed by taking a part-time job. It was the best I could do at the time. When I separated from my husband, both women again changed position. My mother saw it as common sense that if I was going to be a single mother, I should re-enter my profession as quickly as possible, before my skills became rusty and unacceptable. My mother-in-law demanded that I go back to work because otherwise her son would be burdened with substantial maintenance payments. For my part, the very thought of working in a tough profession when I was physically and emotionally bankrupt, was an impossibility. Eventually I had no choice, because my husband, backed up by a judge, paid such a tiny amount towards the maintenance of his child that I was forced to return to work. In the long run, this may have been the best course of action, however unfair it seemed at the time. I was made to become self- sufficient, which was painful and exhausting, yet from it I drew great strength, which only now do I realize came from the Great Mother.

It is difficult for a woman to realize the power she will have over men if she draws on the Great Mother. We are accustomed to the sexual "pull" of a desirable woman, and the way this can be used to manipulate men, but we have not as yet thought of other ways in which power can be manifested or used. This is mainly because women have not dared to think what they might want if somehow their desires could be fulfilled. It will be interesting to see what form the wishes of women will take, once they realize that they can choose for themselves, rather than being told by men what it is they want or are.

One of the ways in which women's power will benefit society is by the proper use of men who are geniuses. We have spoken before of how the man's brain is designed. He can access his intellect or his intuition, but not both, unlike a woman, who is able to balance both sides of the brain and use them at the same time. When a man manifests genius, he uses his intuition, leaving his intellect out in the cold. This often causes instability, and sometimes madness, since the intellect is needed for everyday life in patriarchal society. All patriarchal men are also unstable, of course, even when they do not employ intuition. The exclusive use of the intellect, however, is such a fundamental bed rock of society that they are classed as sane. Many male geniuses have died young, committed suicide, drunk themselves to death, or been incarcerated in institutions for the insane, because they could not cope with the flood of information coming from their right brain. Those who have survived, either switched back and forth between intellect and intuition, or relied on a strong and stable woman to take care of them. While women had no power within society, the insanity of both intuitive geniuses and intellectually oriented men went unchecked. When men made moves towards contacting the Goddess, unless they managed to fit a stereotype of creativity, they would be repressed. Young men who like to gamble or drive cars very fast, for example, are not necessarily being "macho." These activities are ones in which the intellect is of no use after a certain point, and intuition is important, yet they can still be included in the activities "proper" to a full blooded male. When women have more power in society, male geniuses will be able to tap into the Great Mother without fear, because they will always be looked after. At present, there is a huge reservoir of untapped potential in the human race, because the rigidity of our society prevents its development. This will not be the case in a matercentric society, in which men are voluntarily subservient to women, because there will be no fear of uncontrolled men wreaking havoc and destroying the fabric of society. Men will be free to use both intellect and intuition, knowing that neither they nor anyone else will come to any harm.

Another growing manifestation of the Goddess is the increasing number of male mediums. In patriarchal society, most mediums have been women, because it has been easier for women to contact their intuitive side and receive information from the Great Mother. There is no guarantee that the information will not be distorted by the medium of course, and many women have been guilty of this. Now that we are moving into a matercentric era, many men are becoming mediums. They are likely to be much better mediums than women, provided they are stabilized and allowed to feel safe by the control of a strong woman. The reason for their success is that they are able to go more deeply into the intuitive side of their brain without the information being censored by the intellect, as happens in women. The possibilities opened up for mankind by this direct contact with the Great Mother are tremendous. We will be able to travel far, far beyond the limited universe discovered by patriarchal society, into realms of timelessness underrate of until now. Many science fiction writers have explored the possibilities of time travel, parallel universes and faster than light journeys, to name but a few ideas. These will seem ordinary in the light of new knowledge revealed by the deepening contact with the Great Mother. Our future is unlimited, and the only barrier to reaching it is our fear of the unknown, which causes us to live in a closed and tiny world.

The future will not only bring an exploration of our true potential, but an end to suffering and illness on earth. These two things are caused by control and conflict. If you impose your will on another person, and attempt to make him fit a pattern he has not chosen for himself, suffering and disease is the result. The same occurs if you do this to yourself. Illness is not caused by viruses or malfunctioning bodies, but by disharmony. If this lack of harmony between desire and action is not resolved at the spiritual level, it moves to the emotional level, where we have nameless fears and desires. If nothing is healed at this stage, we move on to the mental level. Here we try to understand our fears and desires. But if we fail, or refuse to deal with our disease, then we move on yet again, to the physical level. If it is still not resolved, physical disease and death is the result. In a sense, we allow our conflict to kill us; in a natural state, our bodies would be perfectly healthy. When conflict reaches the physical level, it is followed by symptoms of illness, which is a cry for help from the body. If we listen to its messages, and find time to address the problems which are indicated by illness, we recover. Even rest and relaxation helps here, since we take time off from all our worries in order to get better. If we do not do this, the symptoms will recur, until the point at which the body cannot hold any more disharmony. It then dies. Even death from old age has the same cause. The only difference is that we have accumulated pain and suffering slowly, over a lifetime, and the body is no longer able to hold it.

We have all heard of the concept of Freewill. This was a gift to us from the Great Mother, who created us, and was meant to allow us to create freely in a similar way. Instead of choosing to do what best fits our natures and desires, however, we have given away our freewill to others, or have taken over their wills by propaganda and force. We do what pleases others, or what the law, social expectations and our religious belief says we must do. As a result, we spend most of our lives in a strait-jacket. Even if we follow the form of right behavior, in many cases, because the actions do not spring from our own freewill, they have no love in them. We are too afraid at the moment to do much about this. Those who control society fear that chaos and loss of power for themselves will result if we remove the strait-jacket. People will run amok, being nasty, brutish and selfish, and allow the carefully built up social structures to fall into ruin. Women in particular, with their unfathom-able emotional natures, are seen as likely to cause trouble to the rulers, because one of their demands is for men to become more loving and emo-tionally responsive to them. Even those whose actions are already more loving, and who are trying desperately to save the planet and its life forms, are afraid of Freewill. In their case they are afraid that if they do what they want, they will hurt others. They cling firmly to duty and responsibility for the needs of others, fearing that they would become selfish and dictatorial if they removed the guilt they feel at having any desires at all.

The movement towards the Great Mother in society will force those who are not exercising freewill into doing so, and those who are imposing their will on others into stopping. This will not happen overnight, and there will be much anger, fear and possible violence as the balance is restored. The best that anyone who is evolving can do is to pray to the Great Mother for help, and accept that changes are necessary and inevitable. Those who are selfish must listen to and love others more; those who are unselfish must allow that they have a right to the fulfillment of their desires. Both groups will have tremendous emotional adjustments to make because of this, but the result will be harmony, happiness, and freedom from suffering of all kinds.

As we have said several times, men will come under the domination of women in a matercentric age. This is not the same kind of dominance that we find in patriarchal society, in which a few men impose their will on the majority of people. It is difficult to find a word which expresses clearly what we mean, because we are using language developed by men, who are inter-ested in control and hierarchies. The sovereignty of women, to try another word, will be much like the influence of a loving mother over her son. The mother wishes the son to be happy. The son knows this and accepts both his mother's love and advice, out of an awareness that she is wiser than he. To do this, patriarchal man must go through many changes. From despising and using women, he must turn to revering and obeying her. This requires that he accept her guidance, and relinquish his ego, which is telling him that women are inferior to him, and that his only hope for happiness is to fight others for it. Women, in their turn, must learn that they are the repre-sentatives of the Great Mother, and accept their task of guiding men for everyone's happiness.

The changes already apparent in our society, as it moves onto the path of the Goddess, are incredible. As more souls leave the path of the god, there will be huge leaps in understanding and love. Society is only a reflection of the state of mind of the people within it, so changes will happen automat-ically. The Great Mother does not ask us to be anything more or less than our true selves, warts and all. As we realize this, we will stop trying to be perfect according to some image we have of what she requires.

It seemed to us on the path of the god that we needed to struggle to survive. Independence and individuality had to be fought for. Now, for increasing numbers of people, this has been achieved, and their way forward is into acceptance and harmony. Those on the path of the Goddess will have to show understanding towards those still on the path of the god; it will be part of their learning process to allow them to continue with their suffering, if that is what they choose. This does not mean a kind of hard-hearted shrugging off of the pain of others. If we are in touch with the Great Mother, we can't help but love others and feel their pain. What it means is that we extend ourselves to assist others, if we wish, but without all the patriarchal trimmings, such as feelings of superiority, self denial in their favor, and coercion of people "for their own good." We must respect the choices of other people, yet be ready to help when help is genuinely asked for. It will be difficult to do this, especially for women, who readily empathize with others, and wish to "make it all better." This might not be the right thing to do for a particular person's growth. We must realize that, while on the path of the god, it is impossible for an individual to learn except through suffering. This gives them the necessary growth to realize eventually that suffering is not required. Until they reach that point, any interference will slow their development. Compassion requires us not to intervene when our help, however well meaning, is resisted.

Pamela: To give you a concrete example of what we mean, I will draw on my experiences with women in Refuges, who are in flight from brutal husbands. Those who work in such places will readily tell you that a woman who has been repeatedly abused by a man, sometimes over thirty or forty years, does not change overnight. It might seem sensible to us that she should leave such a man. She may agree with us whole heartedly, on an intellectual level, then return to him for another beating almost as soon as we have all decided that the situation is intolerable. It does no good whatsoever to force the woman to change her behavior. Only when she has genuinely had enough of suffering at the hands of a man will she begin to listen properly to the advice given to her. Even then it may take years to build up enough self-confidence to leave him, or to eradicate the ingrained habits of expecting or indeed welcoming violence from men. To be judgmental about women in this situation does not assist them, nor does it say much for the level of development of the one doing the judging. We all have areas in which we are still patriarchal, and only pain seems to work in bringing us to the point of scrutinizing them. Just as physical pain makes you aware that a part of the body is requiring attention, so emotional or mental pain directs us to distress in the emotional and physical bodies. Once we have learned that we can grow through joy, we abandon pain as a teacher, but until that stage is reached, we crucify ourselves.

It is not only patriarchal people who must be allowed to live how they choose; so must those on the path of the Goddess. Already, groups of like minded people are forming communities which reflect ideas about living that do not fit in with patriarchal society. Some of these will undoubtedly fail, but it will be a learning experience for those involved, if they are at all willing to grow. What we need is a sort of truce between matercentric and patriarchal groups, which says, "I'll live my way, you live yours." It may be that there will be patriarchal and matercentric countries in the future. Perhaps that is also what happened in the past, when the changeover went the other way. We don't really know, since records have been lost or destroyed—if they ever existed. However, there is still a whisper left that there were matercentric societies in the past, and we shall discuss this in the next chapter.

V

CHE MACERCENCRIC SYSTEMS OF CHE PAST

At present, most of the souls on earth are halfway through a soul cycle of spiritual development. The first half, for man, involves movement away from the Great Mother, into independent creativity, followed by a return to Her through unconditional love. The first part of the cycle has resulted in a male dominated society, which stresses the fulfillment of men's individual desire and creativity. It devalues the feminine and unconditional love for all, as a way of focusing on separation and self-consciousness for men. Once this part of the cycle is complete, the second half begins, which necessarily reevaluates the feminine, and restores the sovereignty of women as the representatives of the Creator. During the first part of the cycle, it is men who develop a strong ego, supported and nourished by women. In the second half, women are able to do the same, this time supported by men, who voluntarily place their skills in the service of women, in order to learn about unconditional love.

Before our known history, there was a previous cycle in which a patriarchal society was followed by a matercentric one, and there may have been others even before that. We do not know how far back this pattern goes, because there are few records left to inform us, even if we could interpret them correctly. It is indisputably clear, however, even though evidence has been lost, destroyed or suppressed, that we have not always lived in a patriarchal society, in which women are regarded as inferior beings. Many books have been written recently on these matercentric cultures, which revered a Goddess rather than a god, and paid homage to females as equal to, if not superior to, males. We have difficulties in interpreting information which comes from a vastly different culture, but it seems clear that these societies were characterized by harmony and cooperation. Men were not mistreated, as women are in a patriarchy, which has led many male scholars to say that they could not possibly be matercentric. At best, they see them as ones in which women were allowed a share in all aspects of community life. They cannot imagine a society in which one group of people governs without oppression being present, nor one where women are the governors.

In the previous matercentric age, there were many old souls, ones who had been through all the reincarnations they needed on earth, and they were ready to leave for new experiences in other dimensions. To replace these old souls, a new group of young souls came to earth, and began a new cycle. To begin with, the old souls protected and advised the young and baby souls who were incarnating for the first time. They were probably the princes, religious leaders and government of the time, and the new souls were the common people. It seems likely too that the old souls were women, and that those they nurtured to the point of independence were the males who would take over. This system worked very well until the old souls left, leaving behind them inexperienced and relatively unevolved souls who had to exist without their support. This was a necessary event, even though it led to apparent chaos. Man needed to make his own mistakes, learn from them, and acquire consciousness, if he was to become an independent creator.

There are many people around today who believe that man has previously reached a level of technological ability which matches that of modern society, then lost it. The stories of Atlantis, for example, describe a sophisticated society, able to harness huge amounts of energy through the use of crystals. It is possible that the destruction of Atlantean society, if it existed, was for the same reason that our own society faces a threat to its survival. The level of evolution of those who ruled society was not sufficient to cope with the development of Science. Even if the evolved souls who left the planet warned the young souls of the danger, it is likely that their warnings went unheeded. They may in fact have removed most of what they thought was harmful from the new souls, in much the same way as we lock the bleach in a cupboard out of the way of the baby. Nevertheless, the patriarchal societies could have continued to produce scientific wonders, without the balancing effect of unconditional love. The result was destruction.

When human society changes from a matercentric to a patriarchal system, there is a resultant loss of harmony. What was once happy and peaceful becomes discordant and troubled by conflict. We seem to have stories about this in the Bible, which talks about the Garden of Eden before the Fall, when Adam and Eve lived in Paradise. After their banishment from Eden, they had to work by the sweat of their brow to survive. Eve was cursed with pain in childbirth to punish her for her disobedience of god, and the first murder occurred, when Cain killed his brother, Abel. The story as told in the Bible does not fit our ideas of a matercentric society giving way to a patriarchy, until we look at even earlier Jewish stories. In them, the first woman was not Eve, who was created from a rib of Adam, but Lilith. She was free and independent, not subservient to Adam. She represents the matercentric woman. After a while, she did not suit Adam, and was pushed out of Eden. Eve was her replacement, a woman created by the male god for man's use. She represents patriarchal woman, who is told by god that obedience and submission is her role. As soon as man i.e. Adam ceases to connect totally with the Great Mother and goes his own way , then Paradise comes to an end. Naturally enough, Eve is blamed for the hardship and unhappiness which followed, and which has not yet come to an end. She is seen as the one who tempted Adam to disobey the god, and caused our fall from grace and sinlessness. All we can say is that she was framed!

There are echoes of this same story in the Tarot, about which we'll say more later. But if we briefly look at the card which is called *The Lovers*, we can see the same scenario. A man is choosing between two women. Each artist who has interpreted the Tarot has drawn it in different ways, but the underlying message is always the same. When man chooses the matercentric woman, often symbolized by an older woman, or his mother, he is choosing the path of the Goddess. When he selects the younger, or more passive woman, he is following the path of the god.

Nowadays, it seems normal to us to have a male god. When we look at some Eastern religions which still have goddesses, we dismiss them as pagan or superstitious belief systems. But the further back one looks into history, the more one finds goddesses and not gods. Men tend to dismiss this finding with comments about primitive nature worship, and the supposition that women were revered only because of their childbearing powers. There is a widespread attitude that goddess worship was a part of man's religious "childhood," and that he abandoned it as soon as he became more mature and enlightened. Man does not wish to know that at one time women were leaders of their people, and men, as well as women, prayed to a female deity. A good example of this way of thinking can be shown when we look at Egypt and the Pharaohs. Originally, the Pharaohs were female, and the representatives of the all powerful goddess Isis. They were looked on as divine themselves. Later on, when Egypt became patriarchal, descent was still traced through the female line, because this was the link to Isis. In order for a man to rule, he had to marry either his sister, or in some cases, his mother. Not only did this shock the Victorian men who were exploring the tombs of the Pharaohs, it left them baffled, because they could think of no other reason than moral decadence to explain this behavior. What is even more telling, is that they uncovered the rich tombs of the earlier Pharaohs, who were clearly the supreme rulers, and assumed that they were men. Even when the sarcophagus contained the remains of a woman, they thought that this must be the wife of the Pharaoh, or perhaps his mother. The same has occurred when the graves of female warriors have been opened. Even though the women were buried with their weapons and clearly died in battle, the archaeologists have refused to accept the obvious conclusion. They have twisted themselves in knots with stories of wives who were buried instead of the male warrior because his body was not recovered from the battlefield etc. Sometimes, of course, women have been forced to commit suicide and be interred with their husband's body when he died. Slaves too. But in these cases, the male is clearly identifiable and in a prominent position in the grave.

Britain was also matercentric at one time, though of course, records do not exist of this time, only myth and legend. When we look back only two thousand years or so, to the time when the Romans invaded Britain, there were still female leaders. Boudicca, or Boadicea, was a queen in her own right, and any school child can give you her name. The Romans, who were the incoming patriarchal culture, were aware that descent came through the female line, not the male. It was for this reason that they raped and then murdered her daughters, ensuring that Boudicca's kingdom (sic) would be left without heirs.

The deities in the last matercentric society were not all female, although the Great Mother was seen as the Creator. There was god worship too. Sometimes the Goddess had a consort, or a son, who was always lesser than Her. His role varied. In many societies, he became the sacrificial victim who ensured that the crops grew. This was often enacted literally, and a young man would be killed to safeguard the harvest. His blood was the offering of the people to the Great Mother, in return for which they would receive food to sustain them. His death also reflected the endless cycle of birth, death and renewal which the people saw around them and accepted as part of the Great Mother's nature. The parallels between these beliefs and Christianity have been pointed out by many writers. In both traditions, a young man sacrifices himself for others, and his blood is offered as new life for them. In both traditions he is the son of a virgin, either the Great Mother, or the Virgin Mary. In the matercentric system, however, a virgin is a whole woman, who needs no man to complete her. She is independent and self-sufficient. In a patriarchy, a virgin is a woman who has not had sex with a man, and is valued because of this. She can be bought and possessed by her husband as untouched goods.

Some matercentric gods, like Pan, were half-animal, half-human, because the Great Mother is also Goddess of Nature. Pan was half-goat, half-man, but there were others which combined horses, bulls, stags and dogs with humans. The strength and potency of these animals was emphasized in the god, who would often be depicted with a huge erect phallus. Although we like to talk knowledgeably today about "phallic symbols," like cars, tall buildings etc., what we have to remember is that the penis is itself a phallic symbol. It represents the part of man which belongs to the Great Mother, and can create by reuniting with her. Matercentric society celebrated sexuality, as we have mentioned before. A rampant male god not only emphasized fertility and abundance, but indicated an honest appreciation of the male sex organ. Elsewhere, of course, the breasts and vulva of the woman were depicted as sacred, which is a long way from our society's distaste for them as anything other than secret sex toys for men. Now we have lost our reverence for our Creator, the penis, breasts and vulva are seen from an entirely sexual viewpoint, rather than a reproductive or creative one. Because we do not wish to inquire too closely into the sacredness of these parts of the body, because they are representative of the Great Mother, we have placed taboos on them. They are "naughty".

It may be that in a matercentric age, men were subservient sexually as well as politically, which is the reverse of the case in our society. Christianity emphasizes to us that it is a woman's duty to satisfy her husband's sexual needs, because it is a patriarchal religion.

Pamela: When I first married, out of my sexual ignorance I bought a book which promised me a totally wonderful sex life as a married woman. It told me that my happiness lay in what was called "loving service" to my man.

Even if I felt no desire for sex, I was to submit to my husband's desires, and in that way find fulfillment. Eventually, the book said, emotional gratification at having pleased my husband would give rise to physical pleasure, but if it never happened, I would still be happy because my husband was satisfied.

This attitude towards female sexuality is still prevalent twenty years on, despite reams of articles and books on the "new woman" and her enjoyment of multiple orgasms. Nor is it wrong. The patriarchal woman can gain immense emotional satisfaction from seeing the pleasure of her husband, and desire nothing for herself. Others simply put up with sex as a duty, or positively hate it. In a matercentric society, part of man's service to women may well be to place her sexual pleasure before his own desires, and women may expect as well as want this. More and more women are moving towards this by reconnecting with their full sexual nature, and demanding fulfillment. The fulfillment will come when both sexes move onto the path of the Goddess. Until then, women will still need to give, and men to receive.

In patriarchal pornography, we find fantasies of men subjugating women, and taking the emotional content out of sex. This allows men to use women without giving love to them. In matercentric times, men will have fantasies of worshipping women. Here, the emotional contact is much greater, and there may be no thought at all of sex with the woman. The very idea of this both frightens and repulses a truly patriarchal man, because he always does his best to remove feelings for the woman from any sexual experience. He fears that if he were to begin to care, then his selfish behavior would be compromised, and he would gain less pleasure. Many men today feel forced to take their partner's needs seriously, when in fact they don't care two hoots whether she has an orgasm or not. This produces a confusing situation. The woman does not experience much pleasure, because the man is not giving her love, yet he may be a technically proficient lover. She may conclude that she is at fault, which does nothing for the development of either her ego or her sex life. Or she may have a very loving man as a partner, yet still be unable to enjoy sex fully. There is no way that a woman can become completely responsive on a sexual level while she still has internal conflict, however loving her partner is. She needs to resolve this rather than try complicated sexual maneuvers. The form of her difficulties may vary but the content is always the same—the patriarchal part of the woman is denying her in favor of the man, or the man, whatever his overt behavior, is still locked into the patriarchal attitude that his pleasure is paramount. The answer for all women is to develop their connection to the Great Mother, and learn to love themselves, in whatever way is necessary.

Although we can say definitely that Jehovah, Allah and Jupiter are patriarchal gods, and that Pan is a matercentric god, there are others who fall between the two categories, such as Dionysius, Jesus and Buddha. Dionysius and Jesus were both reputedly sons of a virgin and therefore of the Great Mother. Both died and were reborn. They each talked about freedom and unconditional love, and attacked the unloving rigid patriarchal societies of their day. They were unconventional and life-affirming. The worship of

Dionysius, like the worship of Jesus, soon became corrupted from its original ideals. Like Pan, who ended his days as the Christian Devil, Dionysius was eventually seen as a dissolute and evil character. As for Jesus,—his words were twisted to serve patriarchal society, when in fact many of his values and aspirations for people are totally in line with those of the Goddess worshippers before him. Buddhism, which arose from the words and ideas of Gautama Buddha, was likewise never entirely patriarchal in concept. It is very similar to Taoism, which was probably a matercentric religion, and which slowly became patriarchal as the patriarchal age dawned in China.

Matercentric beliefs never completely died out, despite the strenuous efforts of the rulers and priests. Christianity incorporates many ideas which come from a much older system than Jehovah worship. The idea of "turning the other cheek," for example, did not fit in with Jewish ideas of retribution and revenge by god. Nor did Christ's teachings on god being a god for all peoples, not merely the Jews. Other matercentric ideas were practiced in secret, or changed into a form which could be incorporated into the prevailing patriarchal religion. Festivals and celebrations which had originated to worship the Great Mother, were Christianized and purified of all "pagan" content.

There was no lack of effort when it came to patriarchal society's attempt to eradicate all vestiges of goddess worship. People were not only told that the new male god would punish them for worshipping a female deity, but that such activity was evil and immoral. We have few reliable records of what bloodshed resulted from the wiping out of matercentric religions, but we do have an example much closer to our own era, which has been well documented. The wholesale slaughter of women claimed to be witches, in Medieval times, is a clear manifestation of the fear and hatred of the Great Mother. Some of the women may have practiced the Old religion, Wicca, in which women were valued, but many were entirely innocent and ignorant victims of a mad blood lust focused on females. The male priests claimed the women were in league with the Devil, who was the Horned god, or Pan, of the Old religion. No mention was made that the supreme deity they worshipped was female. Having said the women were evil, the men felt free to practice all sorts of cruelties on them. This process of dehumanizing people so that you can torture and kill them is not confined to the era of witch hunting, of course. We can see it in society today, wherever there is war and hatred of any kind.

There is good reason to believe that the elimination of knowledge about matercentric societies still goes on. It is now too difficult to deny that the old Minoan civilization, centered on Crete, was female oriented, but scholars can still evade or diminish the mounting evidence that Amazonian i.e. warrior women, existed. Patriarchal society is unhappy to acknowledge that women were ever anything other than pawns in a male game. Even when we have a female ruler of a country, the woman is criticized for behavior which would go unremarked on in a male. A good example is Catherine the Great of Russia, whose supposed proclivity for young male lovers is commented on far more than if she had been male. There is also patronizing surprise in historians' voices when a female rules capably, and credit is often given to her male advisers.

One of the difficulties faced by anyone trying to piece together a picture of a matercentric society is the lack of hard evidence. Part of the problem is undoubtedly the destruction of information by patriarchal men, but other factors contribute as well. Patriarchal society enjoys laws, rules, hierarchies and structures, knowledge of which is usually preserved in documents or on tablets of stone. The Ten Commandments is a classic example of this. Matercentric society, being much freer and laissez-faire, would be unlikely to have so many records, except perhaps ones concerning harvests or trade. The art of the culture would be well represented, since it would be highly valued as an expression of the life force, but it is more difficult to interpret clearly than lists of kings, wars and conquests. Also, we may not have evidence from any truly matercentric society, but from ones which were a transitional stage. If we look for example at Wicca, which has managed to survive for many centuries, despite Christianity's attempts to eradicate it, we see a religion which is a mishmash of both patriarchal and matercentric features. It worships the Great Mother, and espouses individual freedom and love, but it has rituals and regulations, and a hierarchical structure of high priests and priestesses. In a truly matercentric society, the woman who becomes the leader does not do so by virtue of passing exams, fighting for supremacy, or having a title conferred on her. She exhibits the wisdom and love of the Great Mother, in great measure, and it is this which gives her power. In such a society, there can be no artificial demarcation lines between religious and secular life. All is one.

In one sense, it could be said that there will never be a matercentric religion or society, and one has never existed in the past. The coming of a matercentric age means the end of organized religion, with its dogma and structures. Each person will be free to worship the Great Mother in any form,—in ways which we may not be able to imagine at the moment. There will be no necessity for books which instruct you in how to live your life, or for buildings which separate worship from everyday existence. Every activity will be harmonious, and therefore an offering to the Great Mother, who merely wishes us to be happy and creative. Naturally, people may still congregate together for all sorts of reasons, but the formalizing of this into a set ritual will no longer exist, because it destroys spontaneity. Priests also cannot be necessary in a society which allows an individual to contact the Creator directly. While the matercentric age is still coming into being, there will be those who are "further along" in their evolution than others, and therefore more in touch with the Great Mother. They can help and advise others who wish it, but in no way will this imply that they are superior or that they must be obeyed. It is patriarchal society which insists on rank and concepts of progress towards the deity or a heaven. Such a thing will not exist in a truly matercentric era, which sees everyone as a unique individual, yet an equal part of an undivided creation.

Some of these ideas are very difficult to assimilate. We are so used to rigid structures in both religion and society in general that we can't envisage doing without them. But men in particular are going to find that a world in which no one gives or receives orders is much happier for them. Very few men get to give orders; most have to follow them, and not usually in the interests of their own good. We can see this very clearly if we look at the events of the First World War. Millions of men went "over the top" to be mowed down by machine gun fire, on the orders of generals safely tucked up at Headquarters. Most obeyed the orders without question. Those who refused, or deserted to avoid their fate, were killed by their own side as traitors. We can't imagine women in the same situation. Not only would it put paid to the reproduction of human beings if this happened, but a large group of women would not walk to their deaths simply because someone has ordered them to. They are quite capable of sacrificing themselves for love of people, but not for an abstract idea like patriotism.

Some people will argue that if society is not organized, then there will be a wasting of resources, and this is one of the reasons why the last matercentric society, if it indeed existed, died out. Discipline, efficiency and structures are necessary to progress. If people are allowed to do whatever they want to do, who will plant the crops and harvest them; who will do the jobs no one wants to do—the shit-work of society, like emptying dustbins and cleaning the streets, digging for coal and caring for the mentally insane? There is an underlying assumption that most of our actions are motivated by necessity, duty or financial need rather than pleasure. Remove those, and everyone will sit around contemplating their navels or getting drunk rather than working. If there is no reward in the shape of money, power and status, the story goes, who will bother to train for years to become an accountant or doctor?

The collision between the matercentric way of looking at life and the patriarchal equivalent is shown by Shakespeare in *Anthony and Cleopatra*. Cleopatra's Egypt was a last bastion of matercentric society, with a Queen who was the divine representative of the Goddess Isis, and a relaxed, pleasure-loving ethos. The Egyptians loved their queen, who was the embodiment of a rounded human being. She was not perfect, but she loved life, and she was capable of deep emotional and physical response to others. The Romans, in contrast, were focused on work, which in this case meant conquest, and the disciplining of large bodies of men into armies. They had a contempt for the common people which enabled them to use them as pawns in a power game. They saw women, emotions and pleasure as unnecessary luxuries, and despised them. Anthony has a foot in both camps. The matercentric side of him adores Cleopatra, but the patriarchal part owes allegiance to Rome and concepts such as honor, loyalty and obedience. Though he chooses Cleopatra, he is still divided within himself, and loses his life as a result. Rome wins, and Caesar adds Egypt to the Empire. Cleopatra's children are murdered, so that there will be no rebellions in the future.

So, to get back to the issue of the whether a matercentric society is wasteful, what exactly would happen within it? Would there be large scale idleness and hedonism, leaving essential work undone, as Caesar obviously thought in *Anthony and Cleopatra*? The answer is both yes and no. Our society makes meaningless work in large quantities. Most bureaucracies and legal or governmental systems generate huge amounts of non-productive paperwork. Large multinational companies do the same. Products are manufactured to have a brief life, so that the consumer will have to replace the item within a short space of time. Efficient and long lasting machines are suppressed by vested interests. We use fossil fuels in large quantities to run internal combustion engines, which are only 20—25% efficient, and run about in them while they are half empty. It is a cliché to say that we have a disposable society, but nevertheless it is true. We cut down trees to make advertising hand outs which reach only as far as the rubbish bin, and package everything in plastic which then has to be thrown away. Our technology has enabled us to lead healthier and more prosperous lives, in some ways, but there is no doubt that it is hugely wasteful of time, energy, resources and human potential. In a matercentric society, since there would be no structures, there would be no waste of people's time in supporting the structures. No taxation or law means no tax inspectors or lawyers. No crime means no policemen or criminals. Health as a result of harmony means fewer doctors or nurses. People will be free to choose an activity which fulfills them, and makes them happy. In a system which has underlying harmony, no direction of people into specific areas, like agriculture or mining will be necessary. It will work organically, without the necessity for regulatory devices and coercion, and no one will be deprived of anything because they choose not to "work." Jesus puts it beautifully in the Bible when he describes his vision of a world which is responding only to love.

"Consider the lilies of the field. They toil not, neither do they spin. Yet Solomon in all his glory was not arrayed like one of these."

All this is a long way off, and we could be accused of naive idealism about the far future, which may never happen. Of course none of this will occur overnight, just as the change over from the last matercentric era did not happen in an instant. What we can do, though, is to trust that the Great Mother has our welfare in mind, and that harmony and happiness is possible. Only our belief that structures and rules are necessary keeps them in existence. We can, if we choose, throw away the crutches, and walk without them, or we can dig in our heels and refuse to move.

It is far easier and more sensible, to mix our metaphors well and truly now, to swim with the current rather than against it. In the last analysis, it makes very little difference if we resist the changes which are happening in our society. They are manifestations of the Will of the Great Mother moving, and both necessary and inevitable. They will produce confusion, upheaval and distress in direct proportion to our resistance to them. If we do not trust that the changes are for the good of all, however they might look, we will fight to retain the world as we have known it. Men in particular may resist the growing power of women with great fear and rage, to the point of being willing to destroy the planet rather than allow the necessary movement towards the feminine. There are many famous predictions that the world will come to an end towards the close of this century. They are right, but it does not have to be through fire, famine, nuclear war or a comet striking the earth, as some of the hypotheses suggest. The end of the world will be the end of patriarchal society. Those souls who refuse to move with the Will of the Great Mother may shift to another reality in which one of these awful scenarios actually occurs. This will not be punishment by the Great Mother, but a result of their own choices. They will prefer to experience this catastrophe rather than respond to the movement towards the Great Mother. Others may not have such an extreme response, but feel that a few concessions here and there are all that is necessary. They may go through the motions of changing their behavior to fit in with new levels of consciousness they do not actually feel, and be confused when their intellect tells them one thing and their emotions another. We all prefer the devil we know to the devil we don't, except that in this case the devil is not evil but the Great Mother, misunderstood and devalued for millennia. She is here to give us all we need. All we have to do is ask. As Jesus said. "Knock and the door will be opened. Seek and you shall find." As soon as we want joy and unlimited creativity, the Great Mother will show us the way to find it.

VI

CHANGING PATHS

FROM THE LIMITED TO THE UNLIMITED UNIVERSE

I f you believe in flying saucers and aliens, pixies and fairies, ghosts and clairvoyance, not to mention parallel universes, time travel and the existence of reincarnation, then you are not a patriarchal scientist. All of these things are outside the model of the universe which such people have built, because whether or not they exist is something which cannot be proved. Patriarchal scientists want a controllable universe, and anything which is outside the reach of empirical proof, which can't be verified, doesn't exist, as far as they are concerned.

Despite the fact that many scientists (the most famous example being Einstein) use intuition to arrive at answers to difficult questions, they refuse to acknowledge its validity as the prime source of their knowledge. They prefer to use the tools of logic and mathematics to prove that what they currently think is true, backed up by actual physical proof if at all possible. Emotion and subjectivity are held to have no place in scientific research. Because of this, we have had a singularly unbalanced view of the universe until recently, when more matercentrically inclined scientists emerged. The universe described by patriarchal scientists seemed to have a finite boundary. It worked something like an amazingly large clock, with rules and regulations which covered its actions, and it possessed no mechanism for interaction with human beings. It satisfied the inherent need for order possessed by patriarchal scientists, yet it was an order that had no soul. It was entirely impersonal and external.

Scientists resisted new ideas and new ways of looking at the world with amazing tenacity, despite their apparent thirst for knowledge. One of the reasons they did this was that the ego, which in itself is not an impediment, blocked their vision. On a simple level, they didn't want to let go of old ideas, because they may have spent long years learning about them, or developing them, and to acknowledge that they needed to revise their ideas would have been devastating. A man who has been given status, honors and respect for his knowledge in a certain area, is often loath to abandon his fixed ideas in favor of new ones. He will obstruct younger men arriving on the scene with fresh views unless the evidence for them is overwhelming, and even then he may still resist. This is all explained quite rationally in terms of "necessary proof," and sensible comments about "insufficient evidence," but behind all this is usually the massive ego of some powerful scientist, or the vested interests of those who are similarly threatened by the new theories.

On a collective level, the ego also prevents the influx of new ideas. It was easy, for example, for white scientists to "prove" the inferiority of other races when there was an investment in this being true. Only when society changed its attitude towards such people, and it began to affect the scientists' views, could we see that most of the "evidence" was irrelevant or spurious. The myth of the patriarchal scientist, that his ideas have been unaffected by emotion or bias, and are hard cold truth, is absolute nonsense. Once the so-called "rational" scientist had escaped the censorship of the medieval church, and was not likely to be burned at the stake for telling us that the Earth circled the sun, he firmly believed that he was dealing with objective facts in his scientific experiments, and nothing else. He chose not to see that the very areas he looked at were determined by his consciousness. He selected avenues of knowledge which could be used in a physical way, for example. He found methods of harnessing and controlling energy , of exploring the mechanics of disease, without any desire to probe into the deeper meanings of these things. In doing so, he improved the lot of mankind in many ways, but without addressing the real malaise at the heart of society, negative use of ego energies and ignorance. His aim was merely to gain knowledge which he could use in a controlling way, and therefore the information had to be "real," i.e. repeatable, physical and exploitable.

People who believe in ghosts, aliens and nature spirits etc., operate from a different premise altogether. Those who have encountered such beings have strikingly similar experiences. There is never any "hard" evidence to support their stories as being true, rendering them inevitably "false" to a conventional patriarchal scientist. At best such people are seen as imaginative, at worst, nuts. The limiting of information to the sphere of the purely physical is what we call Science. Anything else is put in another category, such as "religious experience," "mental illness" or "primitive beliefs." This is not to say that ghosts exist, or that aliens land on this planet, just that the attitude of patriarchal science is one which precludes us finding out. We are brain washed by their methods, into believing that what they say is real, is all there is.

Recent discoveries in science have blurred these hard and fast boundaries between what is "real" i.e. predictable, and what is not real. We have realized that the subjective experience of the universe is as valid as the so-called "objective" one. In other words, we are seeing that we are connected to the universe and not external to it. At the same time, we learn from relativistic theory that we are the center of the universe, but then so is everyone else. We have also realized that the universe does not conform to the limitations we place on it, and like the Great Mother, is beyond the scope of our limited minds and experiments. So we are returning to a more holistic view of the universe, one in which there is room for both interaction and mystery.

When male scientists change onto the path of the Goddess, they encounter the same problems as anyone else. Their certainty about what is real or right becomes less sure. It is no longer so easy to say in any given situation that a particular thing will definitely happen, or, in moral terms, that it should. This may show itself as a lack of confidence. When you have been told for millennia that certain things are "right," so others are "wrong," the ability to suspend judgment because you're not so sure anymore can look like weakness. All around you are people who seem to be decisive about everything. They know and you don't anymore. The capacity to decide on a purely selfish basis also disappears, because you begin to feel that others have a point of view, and your ego no longer feels the need to be right at any cost. The patriarchal view of god being on your side because in some way you are one of the chosen, begins to fade. You can't deceive yourself anymore that your belief systems are Absolute Truth. The Tao Te Ching described the sense of confusion experienced by a man moving onto the path of the Goddess, over two thousand years ago.

> *Sacrifice learning*
> *And you will have no anxieties.*
> *For what difference is there*
> *Between Yes and No?*
> *What difference is there*
> *Between Good and Evil?*
> *What all men fear*
> *Must I also fear?*
> *Their fears are endless.*
> *All men seem happy*
> *As if enjoying a party*
> *Or dancing on the Spring terraces.*
> *I alone am quiet*
> *Not expressing my thoughts*
> *Like a baby who has not learned to smile*
> *Alone, with no place to go.*
> *All men have what they want*
> *I alone seem to have nothing.*
> *I seem to be a fool*
> *Unsure and indecisive.*
> *Other men are clever*
> *I alone am dull.*
> *Other men sparkle*
> *I am just a bore.*
> *I am aimless, like the wind*
> *Drifting through my life.*
> *All men know their position*
> *I alone do not.*
> *For I differ from other men*
> *I seek only to be cared for by the Mother.*

At the point of changing to the path of the Goddess, each person begins to make a stronger connection to the Great Mother, and starts to feel an awareness of Her true nature, although this may be resisted because of fear. Men particularly, who have abused and denied women, may fear terrible punishment from a dark and vengeful Mother Goddess. Their god was interested in retribution, so they cannot imagine "getting away with" all their "sins".

The renewal of the links with the Great Mother is accomplished in an entirely individual way, since everyone is unique, but it can have its difficulties. There is very little literature, for example, to guide someone who is changing paths, and so they may continue to practice a patriarchal religion, but with a different emphasis. Others may feel their way into a new relationship with Her on an entirely intuitive basis, somehow "knowing" without words. This knowledge leads to different behavior, without any consciously formulated reason why.

Since many people do not practice a religion at all, and have no conscious ideas about changing their concept of a deity, sometimes more mundane images are used to tune into the Great Mother. For example, in sexual fantasy there is the image of the dominatrix, or dominant mistress. She usually dresses in black leather and boots, often carries a whip, and may wear a mask. This figure provokes fear, adoration and sexual lust in certain men, because she embodies for them their new consciousness of the Great Mother. In submitting to a dominant female, the man shows humility, in contrast to his normal arrogance, which shows he is changing paths. In the woman, even if she is only acting out a role, it gives a feeling of power, which she may translate quite literally as power over the man, because she too is still in the process of abandoning patriarchal values. Just because this figure is sexual, and mixes in with it all sorts of patriarchal ideas of punishment, hierarchy and submission to a greater power, does not mean it is wrong. It may be just the right image to allow both the man and the woman to evolve.

The dominatrix wears black because this is the color of the Great Mother. For millennia, we in the West have associated white with good and black with evil. Witches, for example, traditionally rode at night and had black cats as familiars. The "black" races on earth have been regarded as inferior to the white races. The feminine side of our nature is seen as evil by Christianity, so it became black by definition. When we have "sinned," our souls are described as being black as a result, and when we die, our mourners wear black, the color of death, to show respect. Light, or day, is seen as good , and night or darkness as bad. All our religious imagery centers around this. We talk about "seeing the light," or "becoming enlightened," for example, and many people who have mystical experiences describe a pure and clear light which transports them into a state of ecstasy. All this is a consequence of our dualistic way of perceiving the universe. We divide it into light and dark, good and bad, male and female, then decide one is better than the other. In our patriarchal world, light, which is consciousness, and is associated with males, becomes good, and darkness, which is everything else, becomes bad.

It is a little like shining a tiny torch beam into a vast space, then saying only those things which can be picked out by the light are valuable. Everything else is worthless.

In the beginning was the Great Mother, who is all there is. It was her will to create, and her child is Light or consciousness. But Light is not separate from her, and in opposition. It is merely the part of Her which is conscious of seeing. A simpler way of thinking about it is to imagine yourself immersed in a warm bath. If you allow your fingers to emerge from the water, they become visible as eight disconnected objects; not only that, but they appear to be able to move independently, strengthening the idea that they are totally separate. Under the water, of course, they are joined to the rest of your body, and their freedom of movement is limited by that fact.

The part of your body under the water can be seen as the unconscious, i.e. it is everything we can't see and be aware of. In this sense the water is darkness, because it contains everything which is not visible to our conscious minds. The light, which is everything we can see, is represented by the air above the water. Because light, or consciousness, illuminates such a tiny part of everything, it can seem that we are separate from each other, just as the fingers seem separate. This has led to disharmony, because we attempt to build our societies on the basis of our feelings of individuality, ignoring the fact that we are connected at a level below our conscious minds. The knowledge of our connectedness is available, and we can make it conscious, just as you can make the completeness of your body clear by stepping out of the bath. Normally, our fingers are "aware" of each other. The fingers can still be moving in a different way from their neighbors, but they work together harmoniously, the result being that the hands perform useful actions. If they attempted to move with no regard for one another at all, the outcome would be chaos. We have chosen to ignore our connectedness to others, and put it in the darkness, along with the Great Mother. We have instead, "lit up" the patriarchal values of the separate ego, and seen everything else as either non-existent or evil.

This metaphor has its limits, but it serves to explain why the color of the Great Mother is black. We came from her darkness, and we will return to it, not as we do now, through death, but through allowing ourselves to be aware of all that we are, and responding with acceptance.

The dominatrix also wears a mask, to represent the mysteriousness of the Great Mother, who is unknown and unknowable. If we look back in history, we find that the goddess Isis was always veiled, because of her unfathomable nature. No mortal man could look on her true being until he had passed all the tests of the soul, which of course meant he had to acknowledge her power.

If we look at the style of clothes the dominatrix wears, we find that they are not in any way conventionally "feminine." Nor is her way of behaving. She is a "doing" type of woman, so in our patriarchal terms, much more "masculine" in orientation than a stereotypical female. She makes things happen, whereas a "feminine" woman is one who has things happen to her. She allows a man to make her decisions for her. In return she devotes herself to him, and forgets any desires she might have that do not promote his welfare. A dominant woman remains free to choose her own path. She is the one in control of her life, but at the same time she is still looking after the man. One does not exclude the other as it does in patriarchal society. In this she reflects the Great Mother, who knows how to help us, if we will allow that help, yet we always have free will. The man who desires a dominatrix wants to surrender to the Great Mother through his submission to a woman, even if his motivation is sexual pleasure.

The whip is another potent and ancient symbol. Pharaohs of Ancient Egypt were depicted holding a crook in one hand, and a whip or flail in the other. The crook was to guide the people, and the whip was to punish or control them. When we look at some of the images associated with Jesus Christ, we see that the "Good Shepherd" is a prominent one. The shepherd leads his flock and gathers in the strays with his crook, but the emphasis is on caring. It is a matercentric symbol. The whip is for the path of the god, because it is an instrument of coercion. It shows us that a man who gains pleasure from being punished, or from the threat of punishment, is still on that path, still changing over from a patriarchal to a matercentric way of thinking.

Many people in our world believe in Karma, though they have different ideas of what it is. The most commonly accepted definition is summed up in the phrase, "As ye sow, so shall you reap." If you have harmed someone, then in turn you will be harmed, perhaps in a future life if you believe in reincarnation. At its most primitive level, karma is seen as a punishment. You may be born blind, for example, because you have blinded someone in a previous life, and the punishment will allow you not only to suffer because of your wrongdoing, but experience blindness as a "lesson". It is part and parcel of the patriarchal ethos of suffering as a teacher. In recent history, this particular idea of karma has been expanded a little to allow for freewill. It now says that you experience retribution for your sins through your own free choice. Before you incarnate, you decide which "bad" karma to pay off, and live your life accordingly, suffering meekly at the hands of those you harmed in other lives. There is "good" karma of course, favors to be paid back to you because of helpful actions you have done, but the emphasis is on retribution.

The idea of karma as a punishment can only exist in a world which worships a wrathful deity. It also ignores the fact that everyone is connected at a deeper level, and emphasizes the separation of victim and aggressor, so it must be a patriarchal idea. There can be no such thing as a victim when we realize that we choose everything that happens to us, and collude with our oppressors at an unconscious level. Even women, who have been abused for thousands of years, consented to this abuse, by giving their power over to men, so that mankind could pursue the path of the god. This does not in any way excuse unloving actions and place the blame for everything with the "victim." Too many patriarchal apologists have done this already, by blaming the poor for their poverty, or the oppressed for their oppression, in an attempt to justify their lack of compassion and involvement in the plight of those who are suffering. It merely shows us that we can choose again, either to reclaim our power from the abuser, or to stop oppressing others. Indeed we must. Our life and destiny are firmly in our hands, and we should realize this. If you can change your consciousness, then external events will also alter, to fit in with your new state of being. Once you realize that all the "bad" things that have happened to you were because of your own confusion and denial of your will, how could you wish to punish anyone? All you will want to do is to seek out and rescue those parts of you which still wish to suffer, in order to comfort them, and teach them about self-love. Having done that, you can then take action to change the world about you.

The man who is adoring and obeying a dominatrix who carries a whip is still in the grip of patriarchal ideas about karma. He firmly believes that punishment is necessary if you have been "bad." He has a dim idea that he has been a naughty boy in the past, by behaving selfishly and callously towards women, so he must be chastised. Though he will feel pain from this punishment at a physical level, at an emotional level it will satisfy him, because in some way he sees the pain as "atonement" for his "sins." The woman herself is also still partly patriarchal. She too still believes in punishment. Men have used her selfishly, and reduced her to the status of a slave, so they deserve to be hurt. She may take great pleasure in inflicting pain on the man, out of a strong desire for revenge.

The scenario we've described, though it still contains many patriarchal elements, may be a great leap forward for the participants. The man has begun to realize that he has caused pain to other people, by denying and controlling them, and he feels remorse, however unconscious this is. Because he is only just beginning to change paths, he does not know that all he has to do is be different from now on, forgive himself, and allow the will of the Great Mother to assist him in responding lovingly to others. Even that will be difficult enough, because his ego is still very strong. It assures him that dreadful things will happen if he stops being so selfish, and he still fears the unknown. He is caught between fear of loss if he changes, and a growing realization that he is changing anyway. To "practice" submission and adoration of a woman in a sexual context may enable him eventually to extend his growth into other areas. The woman, similarly, may find that she does not have the feelings in "normal life" that she experiences as a dominatrix. She too can experience her power in a limited way, in this context, and see what it feels like. To dismiss this activity as debased, trivial or imperfect, is to miss its significance. It is possible to leap from a patriarchal way of being to a matercentric one in an instant of total realization, but most people require slow and steady change, through activities which suit them as individuals.

We are reaching a stage of society where many women are becoming increasingly aware of their oppressed role within patriarchal society, and are slowly changing paths. Many of them are extremely angry, and willing to express this anger in a forcible way. If a man comes along who wishes to be dominated or punished by them, they will happily oblige, whether he has actually harmed them or not. In this way they release the patriarchal side of them, which looks for retribution and revenge, and sees life in terms of a power game. Other women do not feel anger, because they have truly reached the stage of forgiveness and understanding. They merely cease to be in the state of mind which allows them to be oppressed, by recovering their connection to the Great Mother. Still other women are angry, but not yet aware of it, or too afraid to act it out. They may resort to subtle manipulation and cruelty in an effort to "get even" with men, yet still appear "nice" people to themselves and others.

Many feminists leaving the path of the god have decided that they want nothing more to do with men. They view them as so destructive that any contact is anathema. Sometimes such women also become lesbians, and refuse to rear male children. They mix only with women, and interpret everything in their lives in terms of female energies and symbols.

In the old witches' covens, although women predominated, there was an attempt to pair the sexes so as to have a balance of male and female energies. Some of the "New Age" witches have dispensed with this, and only allow women to join. They say that this leaves them free to worship the Great Mother without the negativity of men interfering. Some of these women have also written books reinterpreting history only in terms of women. Just as the patriarchs removed all goddesses and feminine symbols from their religions, and saw women as unworthy and unclean, so these women are doing the same to masculine symbols. They have, for instance, brought out a version of the Tarot which has no men in it. The Magician becomes The Witch, and on the Lovers card there are three women, not two women and a man.

There are many manifestations of different behaviors when a person is changing paths, since each person is on an individual road which eventually leads to reunion. We should not be fooled into making judgments on the basis of the outward form of behavior. Our perceptions are so limited that we really can't tell whether an action is loving or unloving; nor can we see inner motivations. Someone who appears to be caring and responsible may be acting that way in order to earn brownie points from their deity. The action doesn't spring from love, but is part of their self-discipline and control. Perhaps the best thing for us all to do is to get on with our own growth, and interfere with others as little as possible, asking for help from the Great Mother to achieve this.

When people change to the path of the Goddess, they not only experience confusion and uncertainty because they are moving into new areas of expression; they can also encounter the resistance of patriarchal society. This can range from disapproval and derision to violence, imprisonment or death. To a certain extent, this can be avoided by removing internal conflict before acting out new beliefs, but not all of us are so methodical or sure what's going on. The human race is moving into new territory, and no one has yet explained to us what the purpose is.

Twenty years ago, a man who stayed home to look after his children would have been looked on as unmanly. So too would a man who made it clear that he was totally uninterested in his career. We have moved on, yet those now in the forefront of change are just as likely to be laughed at or locked up. We can just about accept that a young man may be eccentric enough to love a woman much older than himself, but we still consider transvestites as abnormal or sick. Yet such a man may only be expressing his inability to cope with the role society has handed him as a male. He may wish to be more "feminine," i.e. more passive and caring, and translates this into dressing in female clothes, or wearing frilly knickers under his more conventional male garments. It is not that he is homosexual. Most transvestites are not. He simply does not wish to "wear the trousers" anymore, in the sense of being in charge within a heterosexual relationship. We may say that he is being a little too literal in the way he has shown us his dissatisfaction, but in the end it's up to him. He may also be following a long tradition of worshipping the Great Mother by wearing female clothes, although he is unlikely to be aware of this. Shamans and other devotees of the healing and magical powers of the Goddess in ancient religions, wore female clothes, to acknowledge the supremacy of the Goddess. To a certain extent, this was also sympathetic magic, as it is with the transvestite. The priests of the Goddess wore long dresses because they hoped to tap into the female power of women, as matercentric cultures became patriarchal. We can see the last vestiges of this in the long robes of male priests today.

Men with "dominating" wives are similarly looked on with contempt by patriarchal society. It is seen as unnatural and unfeminine for a woman to make decisions, whereas a decisive, assertive man is not only a "real" man, but attractive to women as well. Those men who find a strong woman just as sexy as the patriarchal woman finds the strong man, are growing in number, yet they will still encounter opposition from other men, who feel threatened by such women's confidence and lack of passivity.

The whole realm of sexuality is bound to change as we move onto the path of the Goddess. For thousands of years, while men have been separating themselves from the Great Mother, and hating both Her and women, they have been also redefining for us all what sex is and how it should be used. One of the most fundamental distortions has been their over-simplification of sexuality. This comes out in the Christian church as "sex is for reproduction only," something which reduces women to a walking womb for the production of male children. But it also leads to other nonsense. Until recently, our society has divided us neatly at the level of sexuality, as it divides us at every other level, and assigns values to those artificial divisions. We are men who are attracted to women, or we are women who are attracted to men. If we do not fall into either category 100% of the time, then we are evil, sick, or if they are being kind, "confused." Although some patriarchal societies have allowed and encouraged male homosexual behavior, this has largely been an unhealthy way of denigrating women even further, and reinforcing the solidarity of men and male values. If women are seen as loathsome and inferior, then one turns to another male for love and friendship, if this is still a need. Or one turns to another male because he knows the rules; sexual gratification with no strings attached. Although patriarchal society has attempted to tell us that we are sexually either heterosexual or homosexual, it is not true. We are all different, and at different stages of personal development anyway. Some of us may feel attraction towards the opposite sex on a physical level, some of us only for our own sex, and others for both. Nor will this necessarily be fixed for our entire life or lives. Our wish to express love and connection with someone through sexual activity has no limits. A matercentric society will allow us to do that, in a way that suits us but does not imply fear of other modes of expression, as occurs today.

Women's new role for men will involve them in massive changes. They must begin to allow the power and wisdom of the Great Mother to flow through them, so that they can guide and advise men, and fulfill their own creativity. Power is a loaded word, so we have to emphasize that this is not power over, but merely the power which comes from unconditional love. Most women, for centuries, have equated love with service and self-sacrifice; the love of others. They have been "givers," with no reward other than the satisfaction of seeing the people they love thrive and achieve. Any pain or suffering endured by women came from seeing harm come to their loved ones. Later on, they began to develop an ego, and feel their own pain,, but they still saw it as their duty to love others, and put themselves last.

Pamela: I can give an example of this which used to stun me as a child. My mother often told me stories of her childhood, and I would press her for details if anything particularly interesting came up. She was brought up during the years of the Great Depression, when jobs were scarce, and sometimes there was not enough food to feed all the family. At times like this, her mother would cook whatever food she could afford, and the family would eat in strict rotation. First the "master," then the other males, and finally the mother and female children. My mother thought nothing of this, and indeed the point of the story was to show how times have changed. No one in our family goes hungry any more.

Women who are even reasonable representatives of the Great Mother are few and far between. We have no acceptance of the "Wise Woman" in society. The most admired woman on the planet is probably Mother Theresa of Calcutta, simply because she was an example of someone who dedicated her life and energy to helping others. Other women we might admire, such as Mrs. Ghandi, or Margaret Thatcher, are or were politicians, and therefore working within the parameters of patriarchal structures. They show that women can be leaders, but they do not show the blend of compassion, wisdom and strength which a Wise Woman would have. Within religions, it is impossible to find a female spiritual leader, though there have been some, such as Mary Baker Eddy, who founded Christian Science. We do see women priests and ministers, but again, it is impossible for the Great Mother to manifest fully in this situation, because the women are operating within a patriarchal structure, and preaching about a male god. There is too little room for intuitive wisdom, when what you are supposed to do and believe has already been laid down by men.

What is needed are priestesses, some of whom have always existed within witches' communes, and are now appearing in the "New Age" movement. So far they have not reached the consciousness of the general public. A priestess is not the female equivalent of a priest, who relies on an organized religion to validate him. The Church appoints him as a priest because he accepts the dogma he is given, and sends him off to be the representative of the god for the ordinary person. His wisdom and Knowledge may be non-existent. A priestess, in comparison, does not need an organization around her. She is also unlikely to wish to collect followers; she knows that the truth she has may be different from that of others. She will help other people, but not lay down rules to achieve heaven or enlightenment, as men have done. In fact it seems unlikely that we will ever see a "great" female religious leader, in the sense we know it. Perhaps, at the beginning of the matercentric age, while people still have many patriarchal values, there may be such a woman, but after that there will only be women who are priestesses by virtue of their wisdom, and can help those within their immediate vicinity. To function properly, they will have to eliminate from themselves all patriarchal ideas and values, so it is extremely unlikely that many exist at present. Most women are only just beginning to change paths, and have not yet begun to allow the Great Mother to work through them in any significant way.

There are many "priestesses" today who are trying to ride two horses; still attempting to work within a patriarchal structure, yet put forward matercentric ideas. This is because of habit and fear. No one is brave enough at the moment to do away with all rules and operate in total freedom, trusting that everything will still work out fine. It takes courage to remove all props, and step out into the unknown, saying—there are no rules, only love. Some of this same conflict can be seen if we look around at the many communes which exist today. Almost all of them have even tighter structures than the average business or nuclear family. There are rotas for cooking and cleaning, often a leader, and rules about being vegetarian, non-smoking, a Buddhist, etc. We are not saying that these things are wrong, just that they are indicative of a need to maintain organization within a community. When the matercentric age gets underway in a serious fashion, these needs will die away, because the fear behind them will have disappeared. We will still all choose who we wish to live with, but having done that, there will be total freedom. If we decide to leave a community or individual relationship, it will not be because we think the other people are inferior or "bad," but simply because we wish to go; our desire will to be where we are joyful, and that will be the only motive. Since at the moment we are mostly learning through suffering and pain, we often stay in an unhappy situation, either through ignorance of any other way to be, or from loyalty and duty. This means we suffer guilt and inhibition of our essential natures. Once we have realized that we no longer have to do that, and that we can learn through joy, we will no longer experience pain and restriction.

At this point, many people might ask, "But what about children; what about the care of the old and sick?" Are you saying that we can abandon people when we no longer wish to be with them, when they are incapable of looking after themselves? It seems to women in particular, that freedom has meant freedom for the male to sow his seed, then clear off to pursue his own selfish desires, leaving women with the job of rearing children, looking after aged relatives and caring for the sick and needy. Freedom in this situation has a hollow and selfish ring to it. We agree that this has often been the case. In fact,

Pamela: several of my friends and I have a stock phrase which we use, albeit fairly jokingly, when we hear of any man being lauded for heroism, new discoveries, or rising to the top within his chosen sphere. "Bet he isn't looking after three kids under five," we say, trying to envisage a captain of industry achieving his position with such a massive extra responsibility. It seemed to us that freedom meant only freedom for a man to make his dreams actual, and that for women, dreams had to be fitted into the five minutes left over after responsibilities to others had been met.

This has been true throughout the patriarchal era, simply because men, who did not love others, had no compunction about pursuing their own personal desires, whatever the cost in suffering. When men begin to move onto the path of the goddess, this option will no longer be open to them, because they will begin to be aware of others, and care for them more and more. They will find themselves unable to ignore this growing sense of love, even if at first they suppress it. Eventually, they will see that in helping others, they are helping themselves, because there is nothing that is not connected to them, and freedom will come to have a totally different meaning for them. Women, in their turn, will have space to choose freely what it is they wish to do, as they will no longer be solely responsible for the care of others, who will be less dependent anyway within a matercentric society. Harmony and happiness means that far fewer people will require help because they are sick, infirm or needy in some other way. Since women's spiritual development is moving them towards individual creativity, they will feel less and less guilty about taking time for themselves. They will no longer desire to spend their whole lives supporting and encouraging others, as many women still do today. Internal change will push them into acknowledging that they have to expand and grow into the area which they have always felt was the province of men; independent creativity.

THE END OF WAR

From the little that we know of the changeover from the last matercentric society to a patriarchal one, we can undoubtedly say that violence and war was involved. The female-centered societies seem not to have had armies, and their art suggests that they did not celebrate heroism in battle or the conquest of other peoples. It was difficult for such societies to resist the invasion of war-like tribes who worshipped a male sky-god, and who were quite happy to gain what they wanted by force. It may be from this time that we have the legends of female warriors like the Amazons, since the women leaders may have attempted resistance. The male warriors would undoubtedly have had the edge, not only because they were ruthless and intent on expansion, but because it was the will of the Great Mother that they win, however insane this seems to us.

We now have a society which threatens us with extinction. Both Russia and America, despite their recent friendship, have enough nuclear missiles trained on each other to wipe out life on this planet. In its recent past, the US. has been willing to use nuclear bombs to wage war on its enemy, Japan, which could not retaliate. We have people who if ordered to press a button which destroys us all, will undoubtedly follow orders and do so. We are also seeing nuclear weapons in the hands of more and more countries, some of whom are headed by despotic dictators. There is also the possibility of terrorist groups gaining access to weapons of mass destruction, and using them as levers for political ends. It is a clear pointer that the time for change has arrived, and the misuse of the power of the ego, whether it is an individual one or a national one, has to end.

The use of violence to achieve a particular end is not likely to disappear overnight. The tradition of obedience to strong leaders and a rigidly organized chain of command will likewise be around for some time. In the past, the powerful male leader has often been seen as a god, or at least a semi-divine representative of a deity who is not far removed from being an omnipotent warrior-king himself. In many countries, this still prevails, and the people will often endure dreadful suffering in war because the leader has decreed that the cause is righteous in the eyes of god. There are also many people who still believe that if they go to war for any reason, then god is on their side. We can point to many countries for proof of this. Each side in a conflict can be entirely sure, with no apparent hypocrisy, that truth, justice and god is with them. However peaceable many of the inhabitants are, for example, the leadership of many Middle Eastern countries still thinks in terms of believers and infidels, Arabs and "others," and can justify a holy war on that basis. The West tends to be a little more sophisticated, and speaks of fighting for world peace, and the suppression of tyrants, but there is still the idea that one side is right, and the other side must of course be wrong.

In the West, we pay lip service to the idea that to invade another country because it is militarily weaker is immoral. Though we still maintain armies, navies and air forces, we claim that they are merely for defense. To a certain extent this is true, but we are also reluctant to wage war at the drop of a hat because of the cost, in terms of both money and human life. The advantages to be gained from conquering other nations has to be very substantial before we are likely to do so. We are far more likely to take them over by economic and cultural methods. Though we are slowly moving from the path of the whip to the path of the crook, attempting to persuade others rather than always bludgeoning them into submission, as yet we have only just begun.

As mankind moves from the path of the god, there would seem to be a danger that peacefully inclined peoples on the path of the Goddess will be overrun by countries which are still firmly patriarchal, and think in terms of war and force. If matercentric countries disarm entirely, in love and trust, will their bloodthirsty neighbors clap their hands with glee, and make immediate invasion plans? Many people today believe that this would happen, and are reluctant to disarm for that reason. They see a standing army and nuclear weapons as a necessary deterrent to aggressors. Looking around at the world, they see many unenlightened countries where despotic rulers are intent on expansion through aggression, and say "not yet" to disarmament.

It is not sufficient to use "common sense" when looking at this question. We have to take into consideration that the Will of the Great Mother exerts an influence. When we were changing to a patriarchal society, it was inevitable that the violence of the patriarchal societies would win them supremacy. Now, it is inevitable that the more peaceful societies will succeed in the long run. This may not happen in an obvious way, say from military superiority, but through what appears to be luck or chance, which is one of the aspects of the Great Mother. It defies logic, and seems to be bestowed indiscriminately. Gamblers rely on it simply because it has nothing to do with reason, and one of the ways they develop intuition is by tuning into "Lady Luck."

A good example of the apparently chaotic way luck works to fulfill the will of the Great Mother, can be seen in the election of Margaret Thatcher as leader of the Conservative party in Britain. Even a month before the election, she seemed the least likely winner, even to herself. Not only was she relatively inexperienced, she was a woman seeking the leadership of a party which feels women are very good at licking envelopes and supporting male candidates, but not much else. It came as a surprise to all concerned when the Conservatives discovered they now had a female in charge. Whatever we might think of Margaret Thatcher on a personal level, and however Machiavellian we see her as being, there is no doubt that without luck, she would never have achieved her position.

We are saying that the will of the Great Mother ensures the eventual establishment of a peaceful society, for those of us who wish it, however violent the remaining patriarchal people are. But this does not mean that we must throw away all our weapons, disband our armies, and turn our swords into plowshares tomorrow. For one thing, there will be too much left of the patriarchal ethos within most of us for that to work. If we are still afraid of aggressors, or condemning of them, we have to come to terms with those emotions, because they are symptomatic of a patriarchal outlook. To override fear and anger is foolish. They will merely go underground, into our subconscious mind, and wreak havoc there. We will find that others still attack us, still try to force us, because whatever is inside us expresses itself in the outside world. If we are all connected, then the oppressor is part of our larger consciousness, and our fear or condemnation of him is known to him too. He can do no other than home in on our fear and give us what we were expecting anyway, though to those outside us, we look like innocent victims. If we can see him as expressing that part of us all which still has a heavy investment in violence, then we inevitably wish to help him rather than judge him, even if that help seems to take a relatively violent form. If we do not, we will merely put the problem outside ourselves. We will see him as a baddie, and end up either feeling self righteously "peaceful," or waging yet another war in the name of eventual peace and freedom. In forgiving the oppressor, we forgive ourselves collectively for still having violent and selfish urges, and pave the way for the day when there will be no more war, and we can throw away our weapons.

There can be no question of the Great Mother being on "our side" in a war, as a male god is. The Great Mother sees no one as outside her love. If we are to reconnect with Her, we must feel the same way. Not with our intellect, but truly, throughout our whole being. Until we can do this, it is likely that we will need to maintain armies to defend ourselves and others from aggression. But what we must also do, is to pray to the Great Mother for help with the part of us that still sees through such fearful and judgmental eyes. If we do this, we will gain the trust and love which enables us to throw away our defenses. We will realize that our supposed vulnerability to attack only comes from fear, and that love is the answer, in all cases.

THE ENVIRONMENT

Another manifestation of the change to the path of the Goddess is our growing desire to treat our environment more lovingly. It is no accident that we call our planet "Mother Earth," and refer to "Mother Nature." Since the beginning of the current patriarchal age, man has been as much at war with nature in his attempts to control and exploit it, as he has been with women, and anything else he sees as "feminine." They are representative of the Great Mother, the Creator, whom he both hates and fears. In his desire to become independent, and see himself as separate, man has unfortunately seen himself as so separated from all other forms of life that he cannot any longer feel his connection. This has enabled him to plunder the earth of its resources, without recognizing his dependence on it. His god has given him permission to do this, by saying that he has dominion over every living thing. He could have seen this in a responsible way, and exercised his power for the good of all, but this has not happened. Instead, he has used it to ruthlessly exploit people, animals, plants and the earth itself for his own personal gain. As we have said many times, this can only occur because he has lost his feeling of connectedness with his source, the Great Mother, and therefore his links with everything else. In his desire to be individual, he has forgotten that he is also a part of everything else, and interdependent with it. Seeing himself as separate from Nature, separate from his god, and separate from the of women, has allowed him to be selfish, but it has also led to loss. He is alone, and limited to his own individual resources, instead of being able to tap into the inexhaustible collective energy of All That Is. Not only that, but the earth herself can be exhausted if she is abused too much. Just as he cannot torture a person beyond the point of death, so he cannot torture planet earth forever.

At some stage, she will be unable to provide him with what he wants, because he is taking without replenishing, and with no thought for the harm he is causing. Though the Great Mother does not need gratitude for what she freely gives, and there are no limits to her giving, we do not know this. We appear to have a finite number of resources, and, like the Prodigal son, have almost spent them. Those people who are beginning to realign with the Great Mother necessarily begin to feel differently about all of the things which patriarchal society have associated with Her, and one of these is the planet and its various life forms. They begin to care more for some or all aspects of planetary life, and seek to restore balance. Of course this can take as many forms as there are people. Some may join movements which aim to preserve species on the verge of extinction, or protest about acid rain and deforestation. Others may simply feel a diffuse emotional rapport with the earth, and begin to take long walks in the forest. And all points between. All are correct. There is no one right way to reconnect with the earth. We all have our own path and our own truth.

Many people are beginning to panic about the "death" of the earth if we do not take radical and immediate steps to stop our mistreatment of her. They feel that even if we change our patterns of behavior, future generations will still suffer the consequences of what we have done in the past. They point to continuing damage which shows no sign of being stopped, and despair of ever finding a solution, because the problem of environmental abuse is so complex, so harmful and so widespread. If we can stop the torture of people within dictatorships, or the abuse of women and children, they say, then there is no long lasting damage, as there is when huge tracts of Amazonian rain forests are burned, wiping out an environment which may take centuries to restore. We can't bring back species of animals which have become extinct, or wipe out the effects of radioactivity, in the way that we can make rapid changes within human society. Because of this, they believe that we should concentrate on environmental issues alone now, and forget everything else until we are out of danger. What does it matter if women are disadvantaged, or black people disenfranchised, when we may not be able to sustain life at all quite soon. It has priority.

This is simply not true. The damage we have done in every direction is the same, because the consciousness which has created the conditions is the same, the movement away from the Great Mother into feeling totally separate beings from Her and each other. Anyone who in any way begins to reconnect to Her helps the environmental problem, because everything is related to everything else. We have a great deal of healing to do in so many areas, it may seem that we have to have some sort of hierarchy again. This problem is more important than that, so why are you worrying about the lack of facilities for disabled people when the planet is dying? Not only does this allow those who work for environmental protest groups to feel superior to others, and thus perpetuate their patriarchal consciousness in another form, it pushes guilt onto those who have different priorities. They may leave their path to follow another's because of this, yet have no real interest or commitment to it.

Trust is again the answer. If we allow ourselves to go with our feelings, we will be drawn to the very areas in which we can best help on the path of the Goddess. If we listen to the still small voice of the Great Mother inside us, and follow that, then healing will happen, of both ourselves and everything else. The planet can recover, but it will come through genuine love for her rather than because of fear of loss. If we go through the motions of attempting to prevent environmental damage because it is fashionable to do so, and confers status of some kind, because of guilt, or because we are afraid that we are going to die if we don't, then we are still on the path of the god. We have simply swapped what we do, and retained the same consciousness. No real healing will result from such actions. But if we join groups to help the earth through love of her, that love will heal her. There is nothing else that will succeed but love.

Again, Lao Tse realized what our relationship with Nature should be over two thousand years ago. To quote the Tao Te Ching once more,

When men control the world to improve it
They cannot succeed.
For the world is a sacred vessel
Not to be interfered with.
He who improves it, spoils it.
He who tries to control it
Has failed to understand.
When we do not seek to better the world
We do no harm.

HEALING OUR SEPARATIONS

Perhaps the most fundamental, but most difficult thing we will do as we change paths is begin to recognize and solve the paradox of being both separate from and united with each other. Males were created by the Great Mother to be the outsiders. Their function was to enable us to move away from the Great Mother into independent creativity. To do this, they were given a drive which propelled them outwards and away from her, into exploration of being separate. They began to develop an ego which told them that they were unique individuals, with unique desires, and that it was right and proper to fulfill them. This separate sense of "I," eventually became all that they knew, and they forgot their source. Everything seemed outside this ego, which they mistakenly defined as being the whole of themselves; other people, the planet, and the god were external. All of the problems we have had within the patriarchal system have sprung from the misuse of this perception.

Because it was the will of the Great Mother, and therefore our will, for men to develop a sense of being separate, we had to have the path of the god, in which male, separatist values predominate. Women, whether consciously willing or not, followed men, and accepted their leadership. Though they retained a link with the Great Mother, and both loved and cared for others, they could not resist the development of patriarchal society. At the spiritual level, they knew it was necessary. Many writers, commenting on the peaceful and settled Neolithic communities which existed in the last matercentric age, see patriarchy as unequivocally evil. Certainly it has been a bloody, painful and apparently futile era to some people, but in essence it was intended merely as a learning device for the human race. We have explored what being separate is like, largely through the actions and consciousness of males, but it is now time to relearn that we are all connected. Since women already know this more than men do, men must learn it from them, and become more loving of others. Since men have acquired an ego, they can teach women about self-love.

Since patriarchal society emphasizes our separateness from each other, and not our common humanity, it is no accident that the sexes have been so clearly set apart. Western man has defined woman as negative, and himself as positive, in ideological, physical and spiritual terms. Man is described by what he does do, and woman in terms of what she does not do. Man is active, woman is passive, and so on. When the patriarchal era began, man decided that since the sun was important, it was male, so the male sky and sun gods replaced the female deities who represented the totality of creation, not just part of it. Earth and water were assigned to the female sphere, and only the fertility aspects of the Goddess were retained, for a while, as having value in producing food and new, male children. Women were associated solely with the moon, since their menstrual cycle followed the moon's waxing and waning, and they were put in charge of emotions, i.e. caring feelings for the whole of the human race. The Sun, light, and consciousness were seen as male; females then had to be darkness, the unconscious and the moon, since by now we were living in a world which contained opposites. As the holistic world view of the previous matercentric era began to fade, we forgot that this dualism was an artificial invention, and enshrined it as holy writ.

In terms of this dualism, of active=male=creative=yin, opposed to passive=female=receptive=yang, women and men are moving towards the opposite pole, in order to restore balance, both in themselves, and in society. Men will learn how to be passive and receptive, women how to be active and creative. During this process the opposites will disappear, since both sexes will retain what they already know, and build on it. We will all necessarily move towards our center, which is both within us and outside us. However, the movement does not necessarily stop at this ideal; it continues past the center, to produce a reversal of the polarities and a new cycle.

It is for this reason that there will be no similarities between a matercentric world, and our present patriarchal one. Our movement is towards the reconciliation of the opposites, into the restoration of our intrinsic unity. In such a situation, there can be no question of a simple flipping of the coin, replacing male domination through conflict and separation, with a female ruled world operating in exactly the same way. We are bound to become more, not less cooperative with each other, as the matercentric era gets under way. Man will lose the illusion that he is separate from the Great Mother, as he begins to realize he is not alone. Through following the lead of those women who are in touch with the Great Mother, he will learn all that he needs to know, and experience joy as a result.

How long will this take? The prospect of a happy and harmonious world is an attractive one, even if we are suspicious of its being yet another impossible Utopian dream. The answer depends entirely on our desire for peace and cooperation. While we are still interested in suffering, and separation, then we do not want joy. Men, for example, presented with the prospect of a world led by women, may well still choose to be oppressed by other men in the form of patriarchal structures and laws, rather than face the loss of ego in relinquishing their ideas of being the superior sex. While they have such a heavy investment in this, they will not move onto the path of the Goddess. Nor can they be helped by women until women exist who have begun to throw off patriarchal conditioning. A world ruled by women who have absorbed and accepted the path of the god, for example, would not be a happy one. Such female "Patriarchs " exist, and have always done so, but they are merely aping the methods and attitudes of male separatists. It is possible that the numbers of such women will rise as we move onto the path towards the Great Mother. It is one of the ways for women to develop their personal power. Later on, when they realize that men do not have enough will or power to block them, they will relax, and allow the love which they are suppressing to resurface.

Although the past is not necessarily a good guide to the future, we can see from examining it that change may not be swift. It took many hundreds of years, in some cases, for a matercentric society to become male dominated, even though force was being used. For centuries, the worship of the Great Mother lingered on amongst the common people, often secretly. In fact it could not disappear entirely, even when it was renamed and distorted. This would have meant a total breakdown of any sort of society, which depends on cooperation far more than conflict for its continuance. Since men still needed and loved women, the earth, and the Great Mother, and knew this at an unconscious level, they could not entirely break free of them. Seeds remained which are now beginning to grow into a desire to return to harmony. If we wish these small tendrils of change to flower into a wholesale return to bliss, then we must be patient—with ourselves as much as with others—open-minded and trusting. All the information we need will be available to us from the Great Mother, but we can prevent ourselves from hearing it because of our fears. We may need time to adjust to new ideas, but feel that time is not available. This in itself is a product of patriarchal ways, which have speeded up the pace of life to the point that we feel unable to cope. Life sometimes seems like a fast-food meal; speedy but somehow insubstantial and lacking in true nourishment. We may have many diverse and interesting experiences, but lack time in which to digest and assimilate them, because we live life at such break-neck speed.

The reason behind the speed of Western life is the movement away from the Great Mother. For one thing, we have lost touch with the natural rhythms of the earth, and our bodies, because they have been identified with the female side of us. In choosing to ignore natural cycles such as day and night, and by living in environments which are essentially "dead matter," we have lost natural time, and replaced it with an artificial one, regulated by clocks. This does not, however, prevent us from experiencing subjective time, which is an internal process.

In a matercentric world, creation in all its forms proceeds from the feminine, and works according to a different sense of time from the patriarchal world. If we look to our own biology for an illustration, we can see how the male's part in creating new life is fairly rapid. Once he has supplied his sperm, it takes about nine months for a baby to be brought to term by the mother. This allows proper growth of the infant, and a chance to abort the fetus if the situation is not suitable for its birth. In a matercentric world, women choose whether to conceive or not. Their desire to give birth is necessary. In a patriarchal world, no such freedom exists. The woman often has no choice about whether she wishes to become pregnant, and no opportunity to refuse sex because of lack of desire. She may give birth to a child a year in this situation, beginning as a very young woman.

How does this relate to time? In a patriarchal world, the male produces ideas as he produces sperm, prolifically. Man possesses the spark of creative genius. But instead of offering this seed to the woman, or a balanced world, to be gestated for a time before being put into action, he births it himself. He leaves women, (and the earth and all it contains,) out of the creative and decision making process. He deprives himself of their contribution, and also shortens the time which was needed to see whether the idea might have deleterious effects on human society. In forgetting the female part of the equation, man is not just disenfranchising half of the human race, and imposing his will on women. Since he lacks unconditional love, he is leaving love out of the process of creating his world. The result is a very fast moving but unbalanced society, where change is made on the basis of men's priorities and men's needs. The unlimited wisdom and love of the Great Mother is nowhere to be seen.

So the ability to wait patiently for the right time will be a facet of a matercentric world. There will be no need to feel desperate that change is not occurring rapidly enough for us, because we will trust that it will happen when the time is right. Men will bring their creative ideas to women, to be given guidance and to see whether the idea has love in it, until they can do this for themselves. Women will learn once more the ability to generate creative ideas, instead of looking to men for this. Eventually we will all be able to both impregnate ourselves, and bring forth our own fruit, because we will be whole. At this point, balance will be restored within society, because it will have been restored within us. What we do next will probably not involve separate sexes. How could it? The job of learning to be both separate and united will have been learned. We will go on to other experiences in other dimensions because we have at last learned how to be fully human, and found peace and happiness as a result. If we leave the planet it will be because our nature is forever to expand into new ways of creating through love. We will transcend the body and the three-dimensional world when our exploration of them is complete, and our desire is to seek new experiences. Not because of fear and pain, but for joy.

VII

MARRIAGE IN THE MATERCENTRIC ERA

The changeover to a matercentric society will be important to the institution of marriage, in ways we cannot envisage. Although we can look back at previous matercentric societies for guidance, we know that human evolution does not go back on itself in a full circle, but is more like a spiral. So we may not reproduce the patterns of those times. Marriage at present has a patriarchal emphasis, which we have commented on in earlier chapters. It ensures that a man can pass on his property to his biological heirs, by restricting women to sex with only one man, (and theoretically the man to only one woman.) In order to do this, it has to convince women that their sexuality should be restrained, by emphasizing religious codes, or persuading them that sex itself is highly dangerous, and/or solely for the pleasure of men and the reproduction of the species. Patriarchal society designates the roles of the sexes in a specific way, assigning childcare, the running of the home, and emotional support of the family unit to the woman. Work which is at a distance from the home, including going to war, is given to the male.

This is an over-simplistic picture of course, and does not apply to many cultures outside Western society. Nor do we adhere to it except in theory any more. Many mothers are both raising children and working outside the home, albeit often in menial jobs. Almost as many women have affairs outside marriage as men do. Nor do we all have one partner for life, because of the high incidence of divorce. Often, we cohabit with someone, rather than marry them.

There have already been changes. Women's sexuality is now seen as having some validity, rather than being seen as non-existent or sinful and dangerous. Men occasionally change nappies and cook dinner in many families, though, as many women complain, there is a long way to go before men take as much responsibility for the running of the home as women do.

These changes are as yet superficial. If we look back at some matercentric societies of the past, we find that women were not sexually possessed by any man. They were free to choose at all times. Nor was pregnancy dictated by the constant sexual availability of females for the benefit of males. The cycles of menstruation, pregnancy, birth and death were venerated, not avoided, technologized or hated and feared, as they are today. There was no insistence that women follow the cycles of men. No woman who responds emotionally or physically to her menstrual period, can succeed in a workplace situation, which is geared entirely to the male. Nor is she allowed to both care for her children, and pursue an occupation which interests her. Although some women in the Western world have skills which are in demand, and can avoid the loss of promotion which comes with a motherhood-time-out from climbing the career ladder, for most women, there is only an either/or; motherhood or a satisfying career. Those who attempt to do both, often referred to as Superwomen, find that they are plagued by guilt, exhaustion, and a nagging sense of emptiness. They have been asked to behave like a substitute male, and succeed on male ground, on male terms, in a society defined by male values and structures. The cost is very great at a psychic level, because they are inevitably still strongly in tune with the god, and not the Goddess; with competitiveness, striving and achieving patriarchal goals.

All of this has been said many times by feminists. They see the "equal" marriage as a solution, a relationship in which both men and women share child care, housework and work outside the home. So far, this hasn't come about. Until children arrive, many couples can have a stab at trying the "equal marriage" route. Although the man is likely to have a better paid job, and more chances of promotion, at least the work in the home can be shared. So it goes in theory, but in practice, most men avoid the sharing of household chores, and merely "help," which forces responsibility onto the woman. As soon as children are born, the situation frequently deteriorates for the woman. Either she leaves her job, in which case she is economically dependent on her husband, or she returns to work, part-time or full-time. If she is working part-time, she will find that she is not taken seriously any more, and moreover, seems to have lost all of her employment rights and career prospects in one fell swoop. If she returns to work full time, she will find that it is still her responsibility to rear her children while pursuing a demanding job. She is usually the one who has to find child care, stay off work when the kids are sick, and ferry them about to and from school. Her husband, as with housework, "helps," which may range from token things like taking the kids to the park while the woman catches up with the ironing, to genuine participation. The latter is rare, since many men undergo an astonishing transformation when their wives have children. They revert to age-old attitudes and ways of behaving which betray their confusion. A childless wife may be a partner, but a woman with children is a mother, and completely different. He may become sexually uninterested in her, stubbornly undo all the strides he has made in terms of their equal marriage, and begin to have affairs. The change has been well documented by bewildered and angry women, who thought they knew the man they married extremely well. It has been explained by many commentators as a result of the extra work and responsibilities of parenthood, the lack of sexual desire in mothers, the Catholic madonna/whore split, the jealousy of the man when faced with competition from his children for his wife's attention, and so on. Behind all these explanations, which may well have validity at one level, is the root change. The woman is now in a new world, one he can't enter, because he cannot give birth. He can love and look after his children, or out of fear, he can revert to selfish patriarchal attitudes. But at bottom, the change in him is caused by his reaction to the inescapable fact that women create life, and men do not. His god allows him to forget this, as does the patriarchal world he has constructed, which shunts childbirth into a corner. So it is all the more shocking to him when his wife turns out to be "the other," instead of more or less like him, give or take a few anatomical details. If he is changing paths, he will be awed and responsive to this new change in her. If he is still on the path of the god, he is likely to react by reinforcing his patriarchal attitudes, which have lurked below the surface of his relatively "enlightened" behavior.

The "equal" marriage is an impossibility in a patriarchal world. It attempts to ignore the fundamental loading of the dice against women in our society, and creates an illusion of parity. At any moment, the power of the man can be reasserted, backed up by all the force of patriarchal law and custom. It is as if the king is pretending to be a slave, to humor a favorite concubine, but if he tires of the game, or the concubine displeases him, he reverts instantly to his former status. A man can count on the fact that if he fails to keep up his side of the bargain, women will still ensure that children are cared for, and the home maintained, partly because they have been conditioned into seeing this as their responsibility, and partly because they genuinely love their husbands and children, and wish to care for them. Safe in that knowledge, a man can play at equality for a while, then abandon it if he sees fit, leaving the woman impotent to do anything about it. We have only to look at the behavior of divorced fathers to see how little we have achieved. Many men, after divorce, neither maintain their children financially, nor take much interest in them. It is assumed by both men and women that the mother will take over the role of both parents after a divorce, while being disadvantaged by that choice in almost every way.

Pamela: Speaking as a divorced mother myself I have found that despite the poverty and lack of personal space, bringing up children alone has developed my strength immensely, in an entirely positive way. So maybe it is one of the many routes which women have chosen to break free of some patriarchal values, even if it is a relatively tough one.

What then is the answer to this failure of the "equal" marriage? Many women writers, scrutinizing the customs of the previous matercentric era, see communal living as the answer. Looking at the nuclear marriage, of wife, husband and 2.2 children, they see a recipe for the isolation and repression of women, within a world which has abandoned "communities" of human beings, and replaced them with a soulless economic unit of three or four people. The modern house defines the limits of a woman's life, especially if she is at home with small children, and renders her likely to suffer depression from such an unnatural lifestyle. If she were to live in a way which allowed her easier access to other people, particularly other women, this would not happen. She could share her children, thus reducing the relentless task of full time mothering, which might not be at all what she wants to do. In addition, these writers point out, there would be no need to reproduce identical machinery in every house. There could be communal washing machines, vacuum cleaners and perhaps cars, thus using the earth's resources more efficiently. Some women, those who chose to, would look after children, all children, while others might work outside the community or on other tasks within it. Nor would that have to be at all inflexible. There would be enough people involved for changes to happen, either long or short term, in what an individual woman actually did with her time. The emotional support from others would be invaluable, especially in a situation which had no or few rules.

The drawback of communal systems in a patriarchal world is that pressure is placed on individuals to conform to group norms. In fact, many people have seen communal living as so stifling of the individual that they can see no attraction in it. This would not be the case within a matercentric society, which allows and encourages individual desires to be expressed. As we have said before, only fear forces us to force others. When we know that all action is prompted by love, then there can be no need to fear that "different" is harmful to us. We can allow others to be as "individual" as they choose to be, yet not feel that the community is threatened. At present, any community which exists does so by having written or unwritten rules, in order to ensure "fairness" or to keep the limits of behavior clear. We will not need to do this when love is the root of all action, since no one could harm or subjugate another human being. This can only happen in a woman-centered world, which allows us to be both a unique individual yet totally connected to everyone else. In a patriarchal world, there seems to be a choice; either you can fulfill your individual desires, or you can compromise them to ensure the stability of the community. What this adds up to, usually, is that dominant men within a community make sure they get what they want, and apply regulations and laws to everyone else to ensure that this continues without interruption. There is little love in a society built on such foundations.

Although both men and women could live communally, each contributing according to particular desires and talents, most writers agree that this is a difficult proposition at the moment. Men still think in dominance/submission patterns, and have little idea how to cooperate instead of compete. Since we still live in a patriarchal world, they would have the advantage of still feeling superior to women, who struggle to achieve even a small measure of self-confidence. It would be very easy for them to subtly dominate any community in which they were involved, and indeed there is a great deal of evidence from studies of communes, that this happens even when the men make strenuous efforts to avoid it. Perhaps, some people say, we may have a situation in which all female communities are necessary for particular women, until they are more in touch with the Great Mother. After that, it will simply be a matter of choice as to who they live with, rather than an action dictated by their need for self development.

If we begin to live communally in future, sharing and cooperating more, it is likely that another change within modern marriage will be accelerated. Fatherhood as a potent patriarchal force is in decline, and it is inevitable that it will become totally changed in meaning within a matercentric society. In a totally male-dominated world, with a father god, the father of a family naturally has all the power. His behavior, and the perceived behavior of the god, are identical, since the deity was created to reflect male, separatist values in isolation from female, connecting ones. The father god is stern, judgmental but just, punitive , lacking in all human emotions save anger if disobeyed, contemptuous of females, sex , and bodies (because he is male and spirit only), a law-giver, and most importantly, separate from us rather than interdependent with us. The last fact is important because it is so fundamentally tied in with the path of the god. If you are developing a sense of being separate from other people, then of course your deity will be separate from you, and outside you, as you are from him and from all other human beings. What a lonely position to be in, for both the god and the man!

Since many people within society are changing to the path of the Goddess, matercentric values are "contaminating" this picture of both fathers and the father god. As men become more loving, and less authoritarian, so their god becomes a little more loving and less intent on sending us to hell for our sins against his authority. In fact, Christianity is now beginning to make a few attempts to incorporate some teachings of Christ into its behavior and attitudes, though the Catholics still firmly draw the line at acknowledging that women exist to do anything other than bear children and serve men. Fathers today, in Western society, are less frightening figures than they were even a generation ago, and this trend will continue. Men will begin to care more for their children, instead of seeing them as economic resources, nuisances, or heirs, if they are male. Where we see difficulties arising from this is when a more patriarchal culture is imported into our own. Girls from Asian families, for example, whose mothers accept the total control of husbands over the whole family, often rebel against the traditional arranged marriage. It is not that one person is right and another is wrong in this situation, merely that you have instant change when swapping countries, instead of a more gradual one. The result is that the two generations have a chasm between them which spans centuries of change instead of decades.

Since a woman's relationship with her father fundamentally affects her attitude to men within a patriarchal society, we will see changes accelerating in the next generation of females, who have not all been fathered by dictatorial and distant males. In the future, when the nuclear family begins to give way to much more experimental ways of living together, the influence of the biological father will be less intense. We can already see this in the aftermath of the explosion in divorces. Many men are fathering children who are not "theirs" in a biological sense, and many children have several "fathers," by which we mean men who take an interest in their welfare and development. Again, change produces its difficulties. We have already mentioned the phenomenon of the father who loses interest in his children after divorce. He may find it is too painful to be reminded of the mother when he sees them, so he stops, or he may never have cared for his children at all. They were something "everyone" had, and he provided for them financially perhaps, but otherwise ignored them. After divorce, he can leave them behind with the ease of total lack of love. Still other men simply do not know how to relate to children, however much they might love them. They are used to a woman being around to look after the children, and without her, they panic. They avoid seeing their children out of an inability to parent them, rather than a lack of affection, yet do not love them enough to try to overcome this.

Another problem arises when a patriarchal man is involved in caring for a child who is biologically not his "own." He is likely to be deeply outraged at an unconscious level, because the child does not carry his genes, and attempt to rid himself of the responsibility. With very little provocation, he may use violence against the child, to the point of brutal murder. Many men throughout the patriarchal era have physically and sexually abused their children, as well as their wives. This is nothing new. But a man who places a premium on a child being "his" is still firmly on the path of the god, whereas on the path of the Goddess, we are all connected, so in a wider sense, all children are "ours." When such a man is fathering another man's child, he is far more likely to be mentally, physically and emotionally cruel than if he is the biological father. We can see this phenomenon in some other species; a male taking over a female or group of females, will kill the existing young, because they do not carry his genes.

Another problem linked with both step-parenting and the growing love of men for children, is sexual abuse. This is not the sexual exploitation indulged in by men who see all other people as objects for their use. Such men are still on the path of the god. As we have said before, a particular action cannot be judged by its form alone. The consciousness which has produced the behavior is all that is real. So a man may have a sexual relationship with a child, not to harm the child, but because he knows no other way of expressing love. He may also be changing paths, and therefore at odds with himself. One part of him loves the child, and wishes to show this, while the patriarchal part is still interested in its own selfish gratification. So the energy is twisted into a form which is unacceptable in our society, and can cause severe trauma all round. Because our codes of behavior prohibit sexual contact between children and adults, especially within a family, the whole issue is clouded by secrecy, guilt, horror and condemnation. It is judged, for example, that a child who has been in some sort of sexual contact with an adult will be irreparably damaged by this, as it is also said that women who have been raped will "never get over it." Discussing this subject is like walking into a minefield. Sexual abuse of children is perhaps the one crime which arouses universal outrage in our society. Even men who say that a woman who is raped was "asking for it," draw the line at implying that the child might be doing the same.

Part of our problem is that in a patriarchal society, children are at the bottom of a hypothetical pecking order, headed by dominant males. The abuse of that power, to force sexual contact on a child, contravenes freewill, just as it does when a woman is raped. If we wish to eliminate child sex abuse, we must not indulge in punishment of abusers, without addressing the real problem; a society which allows a man to think that he is free to coerce, cajole or trick a child into participating in sexual activity. We give this message to the child as well as the adult, even if we then throw up our hands in horror when it happens. We still tell men that their sexual desires are so strong that sometimes force is unavoidable, and correct. We still tell females of all ages that to fulfill men's sexual needs is their duty, and that anyway, they are to blame because they stimulate men's desires. We say that if they do not, loss of love will follow, and until very recently, that meant loss of everything for a woman or child, because they could not exist without the economic support of a male. A child is in a no win position. The adult is loved, and/or in a position of power . All of our conditioning tells the child to succumb. The fact that there seems to be complicity between the child and adult in some cases should not cloud the issue, which is the inherent selfishness of men, given assent to by all of the structures and morals of our society.

In a matercentric society, without power ranking, and with men able to both love and respect others, this problem will not occur. No one will consent to anything they do not wish to do because of fear or guilt. There will be no rape anymore, whether it's rape of children, women, or the planet. Those who live together will do so because of love, and this means that there will be diversity. To begin with, as we change paths, there will be many experiments, some attempting to combine patriarchal ideas with matercentric ones. Undoubtedly, we will be told that one particular form of marriage or relationship is now the "right" one, and all the others are wrong, because people will still believe that what is truth for them is truth for all. There may be those who wish to continue living in traditional marriages for quite some time. Others may decide that a series of exclusive "marriages" is what they like. "Open" marriage, in which the two people have sexual relationships outside the primary one, is currently fashionable, and right for those who wish to do it, though it does seem a contradiction in terms. We see many homosexual relationships in which the partners are learning about themselves in ways which they feel could not happen within a heterosexual relationship. People will still use relationships either to grow or to hide from growth, as they have always done. They may cling to others who harm them because of need and fear that there are no alternatives, but in the last analysis, no one can resist change.

It is impossible to predict what form communities will take, simply because we are all unique individuals. This knowledge has been denied by patriarchal society, and we have been forced into a paralysingly narrow range of ways in which we are allowed to interact with other human beings. Marriage in particular, has been a source of immense restriction, especially for women, and it seems unlikely that it can survive for long in its present form. We will change slowly, and make mistakes along the way; but eventually, we will find that our trust in the Great Mother will allow us to relinquish relationships which are not based on total and unconditional love, and find joy.

CHE QUABALAH

The Quabalah[2], or Tree of Life, is a map of the spirit, mind or emotions, and can be used by people at any level of consciousness. Its origin is in an oral Jewish tradition which was first written down in its present form in the Middle Ages. In many circles it is regarded as dangerous or heretical because it gives equal value to the masculine and the feminine, although it does assign negative qualities to the feminine pillar and positive ones to the masculine pillar. Before the Quabalah was written down, it was probably changed and censored to make it acceptable to patriarchal religions. We can see the distortions quite clearly, because when we look at the meaning of some of the Sephiroth, they are quite clearly on the wrong pillar.

The first two Sephiroth, at the top of the masculine and feminine pillars, could be in their right places. We can perhaps accept Binah, understanding, as feminine, and Chokmah, wisdom, as masculine, though we could also argue that they should be the other way round. But when we move down to Geburah on the feminine pillar, we find it is associated with severity, punishment, and fear, and with Mars, who is the traditionally accepted male god of war. None of these things can be linked with the feminine, since it is men who indulge in war, fear, punishment and severity, even though it may be said that women are often the victims of these things.

Likewise, Chesed, which is on the masculine pillar, is associated with love, grace, mercy and compassion, traditionally female qualities which have little to do with the typical behavior of patriarchal man. Moving down the feminine pillar, we reach Hod, which means splendor and glory. Again, these are very masculine sounding ideas, unless we are discussing women in a matercentric society. At the base of the masculine pillar is Netzach, which is associated with triumph and victory. This at least seems to be in the correct position until we discover that Netzach is also linked with Venus, the goddess of love and beauty. She seems an incongruous figure to have on the masculine side.

All this merely allows us to realize that the Quabalah we have today is probably very different in form from the original. It had to be radically changed to conform with patriarchal values, just as many other mythologies and belief systems were when the last matercentric age came to an end. Of course no one knows its origin, but there are many theories, including one which suggests it came as a gift from the Angels. This is not as ludicrous as

---

2. You may find this, and the following, chapters easier to follow if you refer to the illustration of the Quabalah on page 169.

it sounds. In the Old Testament, all the Angels are male, but even now, we still associate the word " Angel" with a kind, saintly or stunningly beautiful woman, not a man.

We already know that originally, deities were goddesses and that the first "spiritual" people were priestesses. Later, these were replaced by gods and male priests. In much the same way, the gender of angels was changed from female to male in religious texts, though it was never modified in normal speech. People continued to assume that Angels were female, as they always had been. This leads us to believe that the Quabalah came from the priestesses of the old matercentric age, and contains valuable information which can help us in our understanding of our spiritual path.

THE OUTER PATHS

We have already established that the paths of men and women in their personal evolution are very different. Women have, by and large, learned about unconditional love, and have sacrificed the development of their ego in favor of serving men and their children. Men have moved away from the Great Mother into independent creativity, and have developed strong personal egos. From now on, the paths of men and women will involve completing their growth, by developing whatever the missing qualities are. Women will now reclaim their power, and develop a conscious ego, while men will learn to serve through unconditional love. All this can be related to the outer paths between the Sephiroth on the Quabalah, and give us fundamental insights.

The path of development for an ordinary man begins at Kether. From there, he moves down the masculine pillar to Malkuth, returning in a full loop via the feminine pillar to his original position. The path of an ordinary woman is the reverse of this. She too begins at Kether, travels down the feminine or left-hand pillar to Malkuth, then returns to Kether by way of the masculine pillar.

The first movement for a man on his spiritual journey is from Kether to Chokmah, and for a woman, from Kether to Binah. We can assume for the purposes of our story that Kether is the vagina of the Great Mother, and Ain Soph, above Kether, is the Great Mother Herself.

Both men and women commence their journey from Kether on equal terms. They have both been safe in the embrace of the Great Mother and totally looked after. Then man moves towards the masculine pillar, which is associated with self-love and awareness, while women move towards the feminine pillar which is one of unconditional love and universal awareness. When women reach Binah they are still controlled by instinct, the voice of the Great Mother. They have no self awareness and are merely observers of the three dimensional world. They always know the correct action in any situation, with no awareness of how they know, because their actions are prompted by intuition, not thought.

When man reaches Chokmah he begins to become self aware and starts to create an ego. Since many thought systems use the word ego, we will define it clearly at this point. In terms of the paths of the god and Goddess, the ego is the sense of being separate from the rest of the universe, and is necessary for independent creation. The ego gradually cuts man off from the Great Mother because it feeds him with independent thoughts, different from those coming from the Great Mother. This brings about the beginnings of the intellect or limited mind. The man starts to see himself as being different from the world he lives in, allowing the emergence of conflict and fear. Although the sense of being separate from others gives him the freedom to create independently of them, it also leads to feelings of aloneness in the universe. Suddenly the rest of creation is external to him, and becomes the unknown: something to be feared.

The first "civilizations" were created by women, with all the unlimited wisdom of the Great Mother to draw on. They were the old souls we referred to in a previous chapter, who guided the baby souls incarnating for the first time. As time moved on, the proportion of old souls diminished, until, by the time society reached Hod and Netzach, all had left. The baby souls by this time had enough experience to assist the incoming new souls.

With no concept of separateness to produce conflict, it was easy for women to work together in complete harmony. Man's ego, however, began to be a burden to him since it made it difficult for him to cooperate with others, and interfered with his ability to survive. He found he had to compromise his own growing individual desires in order to gain what he wanted from the rest of society. So at Binah, woman adopted the role of mother and mothered all men no matter what age they were. We can still see this in some societies today. In some North African countries like the Sudan, all work is done by the women, leaving the men with virtually no role in society. The West has not always recognized this. When famine threatened the Sudan, Aid was given to the men because of the patriarchal beliefs of the Aid agencies, who assumed the men controlled society. The men, having no sense of responsibility, bought exciting toys like machine guns and tanks to play with, causing more suffering to the people.

In many ways, the first societies were similar to those of bees, with the women behaving like worker bees and men like drones. Women, having no sense of self, in no way resented the dependency of men, and accepted unconditionally the behavior of all people. They enabled men to survive within human society and find their feet as independent creatures, by themselves remaining linked to the Great Mother. If both sexes had attempted to leave the Great Mother simultaneously, and develop an ego, no viable societies could possibly have existed. We would have had a collection of independent human beings, all wishing to have their new-found individual desires met, without the linking mechanism of unconditional love which allows harmonious and cooperative behavior.

As man moved from Chokmah to Chesed, and woman moved from Binah to Geburah, man's ego continued to grow, until some individual men began to question the status quo. They began to realize that instead of sharing food, shelter and belongings under the supervision of women, they could take these things for themselves alone. The use of violence and intimidation allowed them to achieve this, and for the first time, men were able to "get the better of" women. The successful use of force destroyed men's illusion that in all situations, women had more power than they had. Only their growing ego, with its attendant selfishness, allowed them to see themselves as separate enough to do this. Their own desires, weighed against the needs of others, were stronger. They had also begun to lose their innate trust that they would be provided for, as they moved further away from the Great Mother, and felt they had to sustain themselves in a world which did not have enough of everything to go round. They saw things which they wanted, and did not have, because the loss of connection with the Great Mother was experienced as "something missing." The void was filled with possessions and power.

Through his limited intellect, man noticed that not only was he different from the world, but that everything in it was also separate from everything else. In his attempt to understand all this through his mind, he began to use value judgments. To begin with, because women played the mothering role, he judged them as superior to him; but when he found that women could be intimidated through violence, he began to question his assumptions. At this stage, which continues today, it was no longer possible for him to consider two things as being distinct from each other yet of equal value. He was led to the inescapable conclusion that if women were no longer to be considered superior to him, then they must be inferior. Although this now gave him the freedom to mistreat women, it meant he no longer had a powerful mother, able to care for him in a totally knowledgeable way. For a period of time, man was in conflict with himself. On the one hand he was becoming more egoistic and confident in his ability to look after himself and get what wanted, yet he yearned to be comforted and looked after by women in the role of mother. Even when the ego in man eventually won, he still felt the loss of an all-nurturing, all-knowing mother, though he often hid this from himself, on the grounds that it showed weakness and emotional need. His ego did not allow any blame to be attached to him for this deficiency, so women became the scapegoat, and were attacked for being weak in allowing men to take control.

Man also had other reasons for being angry. As he began to enslave women, he found himself enslaved by men even stronger and more selfish than himself. He moved from a harmonious, balanced society, to one of conflict that could only be sustained by fear. It was obvious that he was worse off than before, but again, his ego wouldn't allow him to attach any blame to himself. More and more, his anger focused on women. Not only were they enslaved, but punished for allowing him to get himself into such an unhappy mess. We can still see this anger in some Muslim countries today. Women are mutilated sexually by clitoridectomies or the sewing up of the vagina before marriage, and a constant propaganda war is waged by the patriarchal religion to prove how inferior and evil women are, in order to justify their complete subjugation by men. They are said to have no souls, making them fit only to be beasts of burden or the carriers of men's children.

When man first conceived that he could be superior to women, he also began to question and reject the Great Mother. How could he, logically, feel superior to females yet worship a female deity? This inevitably led to the invention of a father god in man's own image. For a time, society worshipped both gods and goddesses until the supremacy of male deities was generally established. Meanwhile, most women accepted all of these changes without much resistance; only the Amazons fought back. Women had learned to love men, despite the fact that they contributed little to society. Now they had to love them even though they were abusing and despising women, thus extending their capacity for unconditional love even more. In becoming part of this divisive society, characterized by separation, fear and hatred, women moved further away from the Great Mother. The inevitable question arises. Why did they allow it? The main reason was their defenselessness. In a society which needs no laws because no one wishes to harm others, women operated instinctively, not by rules of behavior. They had no conscious ego with which to feel injustice towards themselves, and therefore felt no pain at their mistreatment. Men had the advantage over women, of being able to take what they wanted without reflecting on what that might imply for others' happiness. Women were also told that they were inferior, by patriarchal society. Since they had moved away from the Great Mother in order to look after men, the voice of man's propaganda was stronger than intuition. They slowly became convinced that it was true, to the extent of seeing themselves as the property of their husbands. A woman who was brutally raped could feel shame and guilt rather than pain on her own account, because she had dishonored her husband.

As man moved from Chesed to Netzach, and woman moved from Geburah to Hod, man found the universe to be an increasingly fearful place to inhabit without the protection of the Great Mother. Although his ego was growing, it was still fairly small, so he felt unsure and uncertain of himself. The Kings, Princes and Priests who ruled him were those with the largest egos, and therefore more evolved towards independence of the Great Mother, the use of force, and self-will. They had far more confidence in themselves than the average man, and greater personal authority with which to reassure or coerce the common people. But even these people were not able to bring harmony to society. Devils and evil spirits had to be created to blame for the results of the leaders' inadequacies. Because the ordinary man was still so dependent and unsure of himself, he was easily ruled, but as the egos of the general population grew, increasing numbers of men questioned the status quo. The Priests and Kings found they had to justify their position of power, or have it taken away from them. Force was not enough. The result was such concepts as the Divine Right of Kings, and the idea that all men are sinners who can only be redeemed through strict obedience to the rules of patriarchal religion. These tactics were successful for hundreds of years, but eventually, the common man, still growing in confidence, began to question why the rules always gave power and privilege to a select few. His ego had grown, and he began to see himself as just as important as his rulers. There was the beginning of rebellions against tyrannical rulers, and the patriarchal authorities became increasingly defensive and oppressive as their grip on power was threatened. Under pressure, they would allow some rights to the common man in order to retain power, but this was always given grudgingly and when there was no other alternative. At the same time, we see the rise of Scientific man, who no longer believes the propaganda about the male deity fed to him by his rulers. He has the audacity to question the very existence of the father god. Among the common people, there was an urge to have more say in the running of their lives, which brought about the French, American, and later on, the Russian Revolutions.

Meanwhile, women moved from Geburah to Hod. They were less reliant on the Great Mother than before, and therefore less intuitive. Those still using instinct and intuition in a major way, or who defied patriarchal rules, were likely to be ostracized or even killed by those who found their behavior frightening or unacceptable. Increasingly, women began to rely on the authority of men, who told them that god had decreed this, and they adopted patriarchal values—even the ones which diminished them. For the first time, women became aware of suffering, but it was the pain of her husband and children which aroused her empathy, not her own. Only when they move yet further from the Great Mother and begin to develop ego and the intellect can women have enough self-awareness to suffer on their own account. Before that point, unconditional love prompts a woman to try to care for others, but she does not even know that she is suffering herself. She is still too connected to the Great Mother to see herself as a separate being with needs and desires of her own. She can only feel the pain of everyone in her environment, which includes her, but makes her no more important than anyone else.

As man moves from Netzach to Malkuth, women move from Hod to Malkuth. At this point in the general consciousness, there is a revolution in the way man sees himself. He is at the central pillar, and feeling the first stirrings of love for others. At first, all his "caring" would be done on a selfish basis. You care for me now, because I cared for you yesterday etc. He is also likely to use his unselfish actions as a further device to boost his ego, simply out of habit, and pride himself on what a wonderfully caring chap he is. Women, also at the central pillar, will now have an ego, albeit a small one, and will be beginning to use patriarchal tactics to boost it.

Science begins to triumph over patriarchal religion in the Western World, and the prevailing ethos changes. The scientific view is that we were not created by a father god, but accidentally. Scientific man no longer sees any entity as greater than himself, and in effect takes over the position of god for himself. At the same time, there is a growing desire within society for freedom and equality, although patriarchal needs for control and hierarchy prevent their achievement. As many men approach Malkuth, their egos have grown as large as is possible. They see themselves as gods, with nothing more to aim for. In successive lives they have achieved wealth, status, fame and power, so they have nothing else to desire, and they no longer have total belief in patriarchal religion and philosophy. No matter where they look, there seems to be no meaning to life, a perspective often leading them into cynicism or despair.

They also have another problem. The intellect of these men has expanded to such an extent, they are forced to realize that the interest and well being of their fellow men and women affects their own. Up to this point, their intelligence has been directed into achieving dominance over others, and gaining whatever it is that they desire. Now, they begin to identify themselves with other people, and experience their joy and suffering within themselves. In masculine worldly terms, they are "going soft," and caring for other people, even if they do not act on it, becomes their Achilles heel.

The Greek hero, Achilles, was, symbolically speaking, a man with such a strong ego that he was impregnable. His sense of self was so well developed, that any conflict between his own needs and those of others was impossible. He came first and that was the end of it; possibly it never occurred to him that other people might count in any way at all. His downfall was a poisoned arrow, shot by a priestess, and guided to its target, his unprotected ankle, by a Goddess. His one area of weakness, his ankle, was also caused by a woman, his mother, who held him there while dipping him into water which would leave him invulnerable. The poison Achilles received from the arrow was unconditional love. He could no longer avoid caring for others, and this ended his life as a hero. This mythical story encapsulates the rise and subsequent fall of patriarchal man. When he reaches the furthest limits of his ego growth, and knows he is separate from the rest of the universe, he finds himself in a dilemma. He realizes how limited he is as an individual. If he wishes to evolve more, he must surrender his ego and become one with All That Is. His task now is consciously to use all of his capabilities as an independent being, in the service of others.

In present Western society, there are enough men at this point of evolution to be noticed. They have become disenchanted with material success, and have little regard for authority where it is merely self-serving. Most can see the limitations of patriarchal society, yet have nothing fundamentally different with which to replace it. Because of this, they can often become drug addicts, drifters, or men who seem to feel no happiness whatever they achieve.

Among other men there are many similar attitudes. They do not hold politicians and rich businessmen in such high regard anymore. They are beginning to be impatient with the irresponsible way many countries or corporations squander the earth's resources, or despoil her for profit. As yet, like the others, they can offer no comprehensive alternative to our present way of life, but they are at least conscious of their dissatisfaction. Social experiments such as Communism and Socialism have been tried by men like this, and have failed. It matters very little what system is used; if those controlling society, from the overall leader to the petty bureaucrat, are selfish and uncaring, then no progress is made. The obvious solution, that it should be loving people, particularly women, who should lead, has not yet been attempted. Instead, we seem to believe that if we set up a social system with high ideals, and rules designed to promote justice, somehow that is enough.

Meanwhile, women are moving from Hod to Malkuth, and beginning to take on board the burden of an ego. They must now become fully conscious themselves, while at the same time retaining and strengthening their connection to the Great Mother. This involves a great change in their relationships with men. In a truly patriarchal society, men and women related quite simply. Women loved their husbands, children and the wider society around them, and men loved themselves. Now that a change in consciousness has taken place, and many people have changed paths, there is increasing difficulty within relationships, leading to a high divorce rate, and the necessity for many counselors and marriage therapists.

When a substantial number of women, as opposed to a handful, began to make demands for greater self-satisfaction in marriage, it came from an awareness of their oppression. They began to realize that the satisfaction of serving and loving others was no longer enough to make them happy. Naturally, patriarchal men resisted all moves on the part of women to achieve any changes, and used the usual tools to force them back into line, of coercion, propaganda and fear. Such women were told they were unnatural, ungodly and selfish. If this did not work, law and force were used. Patriarchal man had no intention whatsoever of relinquishing his power over women, and the battle of the sexes ensued. Contrary to popular belief, this war has not always existed. Although individual men and women have always deviated from the "normal" rules of society, in general, the status quo of dominant male, subservient female, has in the past been accepted so widely that relationships were relatively trouble free. Just as each person knew his or her place within a rigidly hierarchical society, and did not really question it, so women and men knew their roles within marriage, and by and large kept to them. Only when a substantial number of people began to evolve and change paths did the real fighting begin.

At first, man won with ease. He had more power, and both law and patriarchal morality were on his side. Since he was not motivated by unconditional love, he had no difficulty in deciding that his own interests were more important than those of women. He had also reached the point where he believed his own propaganda so thoroughly, that he genuinely thought women were inferior, and that his god had decreed them subservient to him. The irony of a male god, male priests, male rulers, male judges and male heads of families deciding quite "impartially" that women were inferior, was lost on him. In much the same way, men have judged all other forms of life on the planet as inferior to them, so they can be exploited for personal gain.

Although at this stage women were beginning to love themselves a little, they were still mostly motivated by love for their husbands and children, and could easily be convinced that they should continue to obey patriarchal rules. If they did not, they were told, their families would suffer. Even today, patriarchal society can restrain women's development by invoking guilt about "neglected" children and reminding women that they are there to support their husbands, not vice-versa. Even if a woman persisted in wanting things for herself, she could only resort to subtle manipulation, since most of the laws and structures of society debarred her from being anything other than a wife and mother.

As women's egos grew, they turned to nagging as a weapon, and for the first time had the temerity to argue with their husbands. It needs a certain level of self-esteem to do even this, and many women were afraid to embark on it. Some were afraid of physical violence, as many still are today, and others felt it made them appear unloving. Since the stereotype of a good wife was of someone docile and pleasant, they kept their desires secret, out of fear that society would judge them a "shrew."

Although all the cards were still held by the husband in terms of power and ruthlessness, women had one advantage. No matter how many times they were defeated in argument, hit or intimidated and made to feel "unwomanly," because of their small egos they were not crushed. The man, because of his large ego, was hurt badly by any defeat. Although he might act even more repressively as a result of having to give ground to a woman, for the first time he was on the defensive. If his government decreed that women could vote, for example, he could still abuse his wife without fear, but overall he was on a losing ticket. No matter how he tried, he could not reverse the progress of women overall.

Women were unable to press home their advantage to any significant degree. While they still loved their husbands unconditionally, what hurt him hurt them. Often they would fight to gain some new freedom, yet relinquish it as soon as it was clear that men were suffering pain as a result. This led to accusations that women were not serious about the acquisition of new freedoms, because they appeared to be, and were, ambivalent about exercising them.

Some women overcame this difficulty by learning to hate men. They suppressed unconditional love in order to progress more quickly, without the anguish of choosing between what would hurt them and what would hurt others. British soldiers in the Afghan War of the last century became victims of this hatred. Afghan women tortured to death any British soldier they found wounded on the battlefield. They were probably doing to these soldiers what they would like to have done to their husbands, but couldn't, not only because of the fear of punishment, but also because they genuinely loved their husbands. Torturing a man to death gave them a power kick, albeit in a fairly gruesome manner, which fed their weak egos without any resulting conflict of loyalties, since the soldiers were strangers.

Western women, meanwhile, were beginning to realize the intolerable burden children placed on them in a patriarchal society. They were almost entirely responsible for the upbringing of children, yet had no control over their own bodies. Men denied them contraception via church dogma, insisted that they had sexual obligations to their husbands, and left them to die of exhaustion or worse, after a lifetime of constant child-bearing. It has been well documented how male doctors also took over the roles of female midwives. In earlier centuries, such men managed to wipe out large numbers of mothers through their ignorance of the way in which disease is transmitted, and this only ceased when sterilization of instruments and hands was understood as a preventative device. Even if they did not kill a woman while attending her, doctors managed to make her feel even less in control of her own destiny and body than ever before.

Women responded to their new realizations by openly choosing not to have children, or bearing far fewer than they had before. Patriarchal society naturally resisted the development and distribution of contraception, because it freed women to do something other than have children, and reduced the overall numbers of people. Fewer children meant fewer soldiers to be used in aggressive or defensive wars, and a smaller pool of expendable slave labor. The fact that over population engenders poverty and short life expectancy was seen as irrelevant to the needs of the leaders. It is still illegal to prevent conception in many countries, notably Roman Catholic or Muslim ones, and the Roman Catholic Church has not so far given its approval to "unnatural" methods of limiting the size of families. This leaves Catholics who respect the rules of their church with only the "rhythm" method, whereby sex is abstained from at fertile points in a woman's menstrual cycle.

If, as was often the case, women were forced to bear children they did not want, because of the manifold pressures of society, they learned to hate them, or at least feel ambivalent about them. Women knew that while they were the sex responsible for the rearing and nurturing of children, there would be no chance for them to develop and grow in any other direction. At that time there was no way to combine motherhood with a career. Working class women often took menial jobs in addition to raising children, where society permitted it, but this was expected to be in addition to their duties as a wife and mother. It led, as it still does today, to total exhaustion. Other women stayed home and looked after their children, but their resentment caused them to abuse their offspring in direct or subtle ways. They gave them conditional love, in the way men did, because they saw their children as the barrier between themselves and their personal growth.

Some men became willing participants in the sex war when they began to find the new demanding woman more exciting than a passive one. At the beginning of the patriarchal era, such men had received satisfaction from mastering a powerful woman, and this had boosted their growing ego. The sort of situation they enjoyed is portrayed in Shakespeare's *Taming of the Shrew*. A woman also gained pleasure from this game, even if this was not apparent, because she loved the man more than herself. She enjoyed the sense of satisfaction the man felt at her defeat, and her smaller ego was not very wounded at having to submit. In time, some women came to rely on mistreatment by men for a sense of self, and gained masochistic pleasure from it. This probably explains why some prostitutes, who earn vast amounts of money, still insist on handing their profits to a pimp, whom they love, yet who mistreats them. Their self-esteem is so low that any personal attention, even if it is abusive, is welcomed.

For a long period, after women became subservient to men, society consisted largely of passive women and selfish, dominating men, with the occasional powerful woman in evidence, who was usually a courtesan. Women were now so easy to control, that there was no boost to a man's ego anymore in ordering her about and using her selfishly. Some turned to rape or sadism to recreate the former excitement, or took pleasure in cuckolding other men for kicks. Once women began to develop an ego, patriarchal man found the idea of dominating her once again a thrilling challenge, and yet another way to extend his ego. This time however, because we are moving into a matercentric, not a patriarchal age, men will be unable to succeed in the long run. Their task this time is to fail, and come under the sovereignty of women. Many men who have enjoyed abusing women sexually in the past, have already encountered failure. Even if society has not introduced stiff penalties for rape, they find that they can no longer act out their desires at the material level. A strange new awareness of the woman as a person prevents them, and they may become disgusted with themselves at having sadistic fantasies. Since dominance and submission is still an ingrained pattern of their lives, they may switch roles, and seek to become the abused slave of a cruel woman.

Some women began to care for themselves so much that they refused to have a relationship with a man at all. They knew that in society as it stood, their only chance for evolution was to avoid marriage, even if they felt strong attraction towards it. We can see this phenomenon in the spinster school mistress, who developed her ego by bossing schoolchildren around, or in such fields as Art, where marriage and creativity was still an impossible combination for a woman.

Many women today find relationships with men exceedingly difficult, because of conflicts within themselves. Although they may desire to be loved and have their needs met, they are still in the situation of loving a man more than themselves. The fact that most men still naturally assume that their needs are paramount compounds the problem. The only way out for these women is to develop and concentrate on their love of self, without denying their love for others. This is problematical in a society which still expects women to be self-sacrificial. When such women become aware that they wish to put their needs before those of a man, they are likely to feel extremely guilty at their "selfishness." It is as difficult for the woman at this point to be "selfish" for the first time as it is for the male at the same level of evolution to be "unselfish." Women's love, whatever form it takes, is always a mothering love, which cares for and nurtures someone or something else. Man, during his quest for an ego, has needed this supportive type of love from women. He has always required reassurance and unconditional love to allow his ego to grow. When he reaches the stage of maximum ego growth, he no longer needs acceptance and reassurance. He is "full of himself," and out of his fullness he needs to give to women what he once received—unconditional love,—in order to support their development. A woman who meets a man ready to give unconditional love, finds there is nothing she can do for him. If she decides to have a relationship with him, she will discover that he gives her love and support without expecting anything in return. Surprisingly, she may not shout "hurrah," but be extremely uncomfortable.

Love has meant giving for so long for women, that she may not understand that it is no longer a requirement. It is her responsibility at this stage to love herself, and open up to receive his love and service.

The type of relationship in which the man gives love and the woman receives it, is barely acknowledged as existing in our society. Those who behave like this often keep the nature of the relationship a secret, in order to avoid criticism or derision. Only when it becomes more acceptable for men to love and serve women will we find to what extent this is already happening.

The rise of Feminism has created a new ideal model for relationships, one where both partners are equal. It would be true to say that many marriages in the Western World appear to achieve this ideal, but it is usually at the cost of enormous amounts of conflict. No one appears willing to acknowledge the unconscious power struggles going on, and instead describe these relationships as "fair" or "reasonable." Usually, the woman gains the upper hand in the power struggle and the man reluctantly gives ground. Quite often, as we see from divorce statistics, these so-called "equal" relationships break down. In some, the woman demands more than the man is willing to give. He may leave to live with a more passive woman, become impotent as a way of punishing her, or because he cannot cope with her demands, or turn to violence as a last resort to prevent further erosion of his ego. The woman may leave because she cannot achieve what she wants, or it is too much of a struggle to get it, and look for a more cooperative man. She may also drive a man away with her neediness, which he is not willing to acknowledge or fulfill, then search for a man who wishes to satisfy her needs.

When a man is prepared to give more than a woman is willing to receive, the same problems occur, and the two people may end up fighting one another to give love rather than receive it. The woman finds it difficult to accept loving support from the man. She simply has no idea what to do with her life if she is not sacrificing herself and supporting a husband and children with unconditional love. If these types of marriage come before a marriage counselor, they can be helped to understand and overcome the difficulties, but only if the counselor is perceptive and unbiased. A marriage in which the man is clearly holding most power is relatively easy to cope with for the therapists. They can attempt to make the man see the error of his ways, or suggest to the woman that it is acceptable for her to gain more from the relationship, if that has been the problem. However, when the marriage is unequal in the woman's favor, she is seen as selfish and unreasonable. She will receive very little support for her way of thinking, and all the sympathy and help will go to the man. She may, as a result, attempt to go backwards in her growth, and relinquish the power she has acquired, out of a misguided sense of "fairness."

When a woman begins to win the "battle of the sexes" she usually encounters a particular quandary. She will feel contempt for the man who has allowed her to dominate him, and be ashamed of his lack of "masculinity," as defined by patriarchal society. She will not want to be seen having a relationship with a "wimp". Part of her is still patriarchally oriented, and feels a man should be strong, sure, and in command at all times. Because the man she is involved with is confident enough to relinquish his ego, and no longer needs any support from a woman to maintain it, the woman feels that he does not need her; she has nothing to give him. A woman can only overcome this problem if she is willing to reverse the polarity, allowing both self-love and love from the man. This takes courage—because society will not approve of her apparent domination of the man—and open-mindedness, since she will have to reverse her own expectations of male-female roles. Some women, who initially find the matercentric man boring, may unconsciously "go backwards" for a time, and enter a relationship with a selfish patriarchal man. This reminds them that although life might be more "exciting" with such a man, it is also painful and frustrating. The experience confirms her desire to move onto the path of the Goddess.

As woman approaches Malkuth, she is as far away as it is possible to get from the Great Mother. The voice of her instinct is at its weakest, and she is reliant on her intellect. The rule of intellect has made it possible for doctors to take control of childbirth from women, to have them laid flat on their backs and to forcibly extract babies from the womb. Women rearing children have been told not to rely on instinct and feeling, but on the guidance of books written by men. They go along with this, partly because they have lost touch with intuition, and partly because men, having larger egos, and authority over women, have undermined their confidence in their natural abilities.

All this changes when a woman passes the central pillar at Malkuth, and begins the journey home to the Great Mother. She begins to tune into her intuition far more, and ignore the advice of patriarchal society. We now see an interest in "natural" childbirth, in which women have a say in how their child is delivered. There is a growing emphasis on participation by the husband or partner, who is often present at the birth. This helps the man to become bonded to the child, and take an active interest in its welfare and upbringing.

Near the central pillar, it is possible for men and women to believe that the two sexes are essentially the same, the only difference being that women give birth to children and men don't. People at this stage often advocate equal treatment and opportunity for both sexes, and envisage a "fairer" world, in which women are equal to men. Logically, this is an entirely reasonable position, but it rests on totally erroneous assumptions, not the least of which is that women will want no revenge for the millennia of oppression by men. In Christian ethics, forgiveness is a noble virtue, and since women are, by and large, much "nicer" than men, the idea is that they will instantly forgive men their sins, and settle for equality. Some women may do so—those who have the link to the all forgiving Great Mother for example. But by far the greatest number, because they are so far away from the Great Mother when they change paths, will not have the capacity to be so instantly saintly. They have to experience and integrate many lives' worth of pain and suffering into their conscious awareness, over a period of time. It would be surprising if they could do this without any desire to exact revenge on, and make them suffer in the way women have suffered. We see this happening when dictators are overthrown, and men who have been savagely oppressed indulge in an orgy of violent retribution directed against those they see as having hurt them.

In fact, they can't really make men suffer pain in the way women have, for two reasons. Firstly, most women, unless they suppress unconditional love very thoroughly, will feel the pain they inflict, thus placing limits on their cruelty; secondly, men are only just beginning to learn how to feel emotional pain, because they have been too busy enlarging and growing their ego. This may not deter some women from attempting to hurt and humiliate men, but it does place limits on what can actually be achieved.

Although many feminists strongly criticize patriarchal society, they do not often think in terms of replacing it with a matercentric society. Any suggestion of a female dominated society is strongly resisted, because in their eyes, it would make women seem no better than men have been. They are still caught up in patriarchal ideas of women being the fairer sex,—in this case, "fair" in the sense of being more reasonable, forgiving and equitable. If we were to have a society in which men and women were equal, they would see it as proof that women are indeed morally superior to men, because they have made no attempt to "take advantage" by dominating men. There is also an underlying assumption that a matercentric society would resemble a patriarchal one, with the only difference being that women would be in control, and would ignore the nature and needs of men in favor of female ones. As there is a fundamental difference between men and women in the way they think, feel and develop spiritually, this would not be true.

In the forthcoming matercentric society, women will only dominate with the complete cooperation of men, just as men controlled society only because women allowed it. Most feminists have trouble envisaging men voluntarily subjugating themselves to women. They look at the present behavior of males, and see no sign of this being possible. While they insist on equality, this will be true. Men will have very little interest in an equal society, because it does not give those who have changed paths the right opportunities for growth. We see a certain amount of stagnation within the equal rights movement as a result. Various reasons have been given for this. Many men who are still patriarchal, insist that women have achieved equality, and that there is no more room for change. Others point to a male backlash of renewed aggression towards women, and either see it as proof that women should go back to the home where they belong, or that change is happening too rapidly for the stability of society. Still others feel that the new area of interest for forward thinkers is the environment, and that we have more pressing concerns than whether women have or should achieve equality.

The real reason for the stagnation is that equality is a logical concept, and people are not driven by logic, but by emotions, most of which are unconscious. The emotional fuel for a man's growth up to now has been his internal archetype of himself as Hero. However little he counts for anything in the wider world, a man carries within him a picture of himself as much greater,—a Hercules or Zeus figure, who wishes to rule the world and achieve all of his desires. In modern terms, he sees himself as James Bond, John F. Kennedy, Rambo or Scott of the Antarctic. Until this archetype is replaced by the figure of the Great Mother, we will not make much progress. Men will then move on from being heroes to being servants of the Great Mother, and begin the second half of their growth cycle, subservient to women as the representatives of the Great Mother on earth.

There are certain problems facing men as they change paths. It was easy for women to love men in a patriarchal era. They had no internal conflict because they had no ego, or self-awareness, to contend with. When man begins to learn to love and serve women, however, he will find that his ego resists, seeing no good reason why he should relinquish his advantages over women, and his long ingrained habits of competitiveness and selfishness. The only way to change will be by seeing women as higher than himself in his internal pecking order, as Goddesses. This process has already begun for many men, though it has not yet reached the awareness of the general public. Any strong woman who has some degree of self-love is already finding that certain men wish to worship her, even though they may not use that term. The woman, consciously or unconsciously, is evoking the archetype of the Great Mother, and those men who are ready to worship a woman are drawn towards her. She comes in three disguises. The first is the "femme fatale," who is able to use men as she pleases, because once they succumb to her sexual magnetism, they are unable to resist her. She behaves and dresses in an aggressively sexual way, and unlike the "pretty maiden" of the patriarchal era, can be described as glamorous. In a matercentric age, she is not necessarily a very young woman. The second is "the mother," who has always been with us, nurturing and supporting both children and the wider society. The interference with her function by patriarchal men, who have excluded her from any real power, has led to a neurotic society. She has been free to sacrifice herself for husband and children, but not free to use her instinctual wisdom to guide them. Instead, she has been told to follow the rules of patriarchal men. Today, this archetype would be more likely to fit the older woman, who though she still controls men, is able to show more kindness and understanding than the "femme fatale." She is likely to be found in an "older woman/toyboy" scenario, or nurturing people in a way which allows her to express the whole of herself. The third is the Matriarch or wise woman. In the patriarchal era, she was a strong and forceful woman, who upheld male values, yet still managed to rule her family and society by using men as puppets. She was as interested in power as a man, and equally ruthless. Her matercentric equivalent has not yet appeared in any numbers within our society, which still believes that women over a certain age are completely valueless, sexually or otherwise. This archetype will only manifest in large numbers when the authority of women becomes greater than that of men. Females who invoke her will be the source of great guidance, wisdom and love within society. They will give advice which uses a blend of unconditional love and intellect. If it is followed, harmony will be the result, because their counsel springs from their own internal harmony.

The Hero archetype, which provides the motivating energy for patriarchal society, can be divided in a similar way. The first type, "the warrior, " is the "macho" man of all kinds, only interested in conquest, whether of women, other men, himself, or a problem he has set himself. The second is "the king," who could be a successful business man today, or a well respected professional in a field which requires "masculine" skills. The third is "the wise man," who at one time would have been the high priest or shaman, but today is the knowledgeable scientist, working at the very edges of current knowledge about our universe. We can see the prevalence of these heroic figures within popular consciousness wherever we look in society, reflecting the strong hold that patriarchy still has on our value systems. The mistake made by many people is to assume that this reverence for heroes will always continue, and that men will always aspire to being one, and women to marrying or loving one. It is not true. The Hero will disappear, to be replaced by a new archetype. The "Green Man" is a possibility,—a man who sees himself as part of Nature and everything else, so cannot oppose or split himself off from the totality. Desire for a challenge will give way to desire for reunion.

Those women who attempt to increase their egos and gain things for themselves without invoking one of the archetypes of the Great Mother, are the ones who suppress unconditional love, and learn to hate men. Such women are certainly strong and selfish, and do achieve some of their desires, but they do so in a way which is patriarchal. They are often aggressive and strident, taking pleasure in "being bad," because they believe that if they do not act like patriarchal men, they will not gain anything. The only alternative they can see is to go back into being submissive "good girls." They copy the way that men behave, and lack trust in the Great Mother to help them achieve what they want without fighting for it. At the root of this is of course, fear. Women who are successfully allowing the Great Mother to flow through them and help them, however, do not behave in this way. They have innate power which allows them to draw towards themselves all the experiences they need to develop their egos and self-confidence, without the need to either fight or emulate men.

So far, it has been relatively easy to talk about the paths on the Quabalah, since we have largely been interpreting known history. But as man moves from Malkuth to Netzach, we are moving into the future, and peering into its possibilities to see what shape it might take. Somewhere along these paths, the patriarchal era will come to an end. It was an age full of conflict because only women, who were not in control of society, were able to love unconditionally. In the new matercentric age, it will be different. Women will be in charge, who have the ability to both love and guide others, and men will be on the path of learning to give service to all, and increasing their capacity for unconditional love.

Until now, man has concentrated on the development of his left brain, his intellect. He has walked around with his head in the clouds, ignoring intuition and most of his emotions. Having done this, he can now concentrate on his right brain, and work with his intuition, which will allow him to see that the forest is as important as the individual trees in it. He will become increasingly passive, and gradually hand over intellectual activity to females. This will be quite safe, since women will never find themselves able to ignore the voice of the Great Mother. They can't make the same mistakes as men, because they are unable to separate themselves completely from others in the name of individual self-realization. Men will tap into their intuitive genius, and allow women to work out what should be done with the results.

Women have not gone to the same extremes as men. Their ego development has been small, and they have retained a link with the Creator through intuition and feeling. In order to come into balance, they will focus on removing the inhibitions placed on their individual creativity by patriarchal society. This means expressing the whole of themselves, not just their capacity to nurture and sustain others. Men can assist them, if they choose to, by encouragement, responsiveness, and a willingness to teach women what they themselves have learned. This necessitates humility, and love for women, which has been missing for millennia. They must give ground to women, instead of occupying so much space. As the confidence of women slowly grows, men must be ready to serve them as they were once served, and learn how to give unconditional love.

As man moves from Hod to Geburah, and women move from Netzach to Chesed, we will see the matercentric era in full flower. At Netzach, women will be Goddesses in much the same way as men were gods at the same Sephiroth. Their dominance will be entirely taken for granted. As this happens, the need to be seen as divine will lessen, and they will be perceived as Queens. Man at Hod will have realized that he made a mess of the earth while he controlled society. This new awareness of his fallibility will bring remorse and humility, and he will attempt to make amends. Though he may expect or even demand punishment for his "sins," the main result will be a willingness to abandon his position of power in society, since he can now see all his mistakes. He will be held in firm bondage by women, but as his new position becomes firmly established, and he learns to love unconditionally, the bondage will slowly be eased. As man moves from Geburah to Binah, and women move from Chesed to Chokmah, the process will continue, until the two sexes are able to work together in an entirely harmonious way which they have never been able to achieve before. Both will begin to resolve the paradox of simultaneously loving both themselves and all that is. At Binah and Chokmah, men and women will become equal in terms of what they have learned, allowing them to move back to Kether, where they can once again be truly in a state of union.

ΤΗΕ ΙΝΝΕΡ ΡΑΤΗS

The inner paths of the Quabalah can be thought of as short cuts, taken by people who are practicing a helpful spiritual discipline, or who are living a life outside of the mainstream of human society. This allows them to return to Kether faster than if they only use the outside pillars, but it does not imply superiority; it is merely their desire, and suitable for their own growth. Nor does it necessarily make life easier for them. In many ways they are out of synch with others, and in the forefront of change, which can be an uncomfortable position.

It's entirely possible for a person to be on more than one path. A tyrant like Hitler or Stalin, for example, could be moving from Netzach to Malkuth, yet be inspired by the path from Chokmah to Tiphereth. The Netzach-Hod and Netzach-Yesod route would be used for originating propaganda. Hitler, being mystically inclined, would also use the paths Chesed-Geburah and Chesed-Tiphereth. We are complex entities, and all of the paths of the Quabalah are open to us, but which ones we use, and the degree to which we explore them, depends upon our interests and spiritual evolution.

The first short cut is between Chokmah and Binah. Generally, this choice took place shortly after human society began to develop some idea of separation from the Great Mother. A man on this path would reach the pillar of self-love at Chokmah. At this point, he makes an enormous leap in understanding. Realizing the suffering that the ego has created for him, he wants to return to the Great Mother, to prevent further pain. He knows he is an individual, and does not need to explore separation further. The remnants of his intuition tell him that the way back is through women, who still have a clear channel to the Great Mother, so he seeks guidance from them. Most women have not moved very far from Kether, so he is able to find help with relative ease. The woman who assists him, is herself at Binah. By acting as a medium for the man, and learning from her own teachings, she moves towards the central pillar, where she now has enough conscious awareness to ask her own questions. The man is now reconnecting with his own intuition once more, because of the teachings given to him by the woman, so he too moves towards the central pillar. Now the couple have a choice; they can attempt to continue their quest alone, and move up the central pillar to Kether, where they reunite; they can decide to share their understanding and wisdom with society, and move down the central pillar to Malkuth; or they can exchange roles. In this case, the man becomes the medium of communication with the Great Mother, because otherwise he will find himself limited by his intellect in what questions he asks, and the woman will find her mind interfering with the answers she receives from the Great Mother, distorting them, or perceiving them as unacceptable in some way. When it is the woman who asks the questions, she is able to combine her growing intellect with her intuition, to ask deeper and more meaningful questions. The man, in playing the passive role, allows himself to switch off his intellect, thus developing a stronger and clearer link to the Great Mother through his intuition.

This path is only possible in societies which do not distinguish between the sexes very much. In many Muslim countries, men and women lead almost wholly separate lives, so they cannot learn from each other. Several Polynesian societies, and the Indians described in Jean Beloff's book *The*

Continuum Concept, do not assign radically different roles and values to men and women. In such a culture, one of relative equality, each sex is in a position to learn from relationships with the other. Both can accept that there is something to gain from seeing the opposite sex as teachers.

The next path across the Quabalah for the man runs from Chokmah, through Tiphereth, up to Binah. The woman's path is the reverse of this. As on the outer paths, we find a man at Chokmah who realizes that he does not have to wait for what women will give him. He can take it by force. Naturally, his behavior will make him unpopular, but he doesn't understand why. Society has not yet developed any formalized moral codes which say that stealing and violence are "wrong." It hasn't experienced anything other than cooperation before, and the voluntary sharing of resources.

The man may become angry because he is being criticized, though it is of course only his growing ego which feels this emotion. He may begin to use more violence, either to get his own way, or to defend himself from others who have the same ideas. If he is not killed, he is likely to find himself an outcast, forced out of society because he has lost the ability to consider others as well as himself. In this situation, without the care and protection of the matercentric society, he has no option but to fall back on his instincts and intuition to survive. He will probably continue to steal from the communities around him, and the planning of these raids will develop his intellect. Any success will lead to further growth of his ego, and a widening gap between himself and the bulk of other men. He will come to despise them because of their "weakness" in submitting to women, whom he now sees as the enemy.

In time, he will be joined by other men like himself, and they will form bandit groups, the first purely patriarchal societies. These bands will have almost nothing in common with matercentric communities. The leader will be the strongest, most violent or most cunning man, and he will lead initially through inculcating fear. Cooperation will only exist because it is a way of gaining something for the individual, or because it has been forced on him through intimidation, so it will always be unstable. Women will have no say in decision making, since the memory of powerful females is still too close for comfort. In fact, most females will be those who have been kidnapped by the men in raids on settled communities, and are used for sex alone.

Eventually, such groups will become so strong that they can wipe out whole villages. However, they will find it is not in their interests to do so, since that will leave no one to grow crops, make pottery and clothes etc., which can be stolen. They have two options; they can become nomadic, and pillage from a wide area which is constantly replenished, or they can introduce the first protection racket. Pay us and we'll leave you alone—maybe. In that way, they survive by using only the threat of violence against the matrifocal societies. The first group, the nomads, grow in number until they are in a position to invade and destroy peaceful agricultural settlements on a large scale. By this time, they have developed ideas of a vengeful male sky god, and impose these on the worshippers of the Great Mother, along with the other attributes of patriarchal culture: violence, conflict, and the abuse of women. The second group, who exact tribute from the matercentric cultures, tend to remain in the same area. In time, the male leader comes to believe that he owns the villages where his protection racket is in force. He will have to fight the leaders of similar bandit groups for the richer spoils. As his success grows, he becomes a primitive "king," and can delegate some of his authority and power to those who have helped him. These become the forerunners of an aristocracy.

The hallmarks of the strong patriarchal leader are his cunning use of power, and his ruthlessness. He learns how to rule, and how to protect his position from others who are equally driven by the desire for power. Although there may be cooperation of a sort within his society, it is based entirely on self-interest or fear. He can never relax, because he sees other men as being exactly like himself; untrustworthy and selfish. So he not only develops his intellect, in learning how to be a king, but his intuition as well. He needs to be able to out guess all those who would take away his power and possessions. For that, he needs both a sixth sense about who is plotting against him, and a keen grasp of what practical maneuvers are necessary for the retention of his power. In learning all these things, he develops far faster than the average man, and quickly reaches Tiphereth.

When, in time, a particular man chooses this path, is variable. Many chose it thousands of years ago, but some are choosing it today. We can look around the world now and see examples of this particular path within many countries. We can decide to look down on such cultures as "primitive" or "uncivilized," but what we have to remember is that all of the people involved have chosen their experiences, and are learning through them. We happen to be doing something different, and if we are on the path of the Goddess, we cannot force our views and morals on others, simply because we "know better." Simply thinking that we are more evolved shows that we are still living in the limited world of the path of the god.

The reverse path for a woman takes her from Binah to Tiphereth. She will develop a relationship with the male bandits which is similar to that between policemen and criminals. When they begin to raid her village, she will defend it as a lioness protects her cubs, through instinctual love of all the people. At first she will be successful, because the raiders are looking for easy loot, rather than a protracted fight. However, as the bandits become more organized and efficient, she too will have to become both violent and cunning, although her motivation is different. She has to become consciously aware of the needs of the people, plan for the times when invasion occurs, and be capable of quick response to any new ploy on the part of the raiders. Eventually, she will have to assume control of all aspects of community life, rather than allowing it to flow in an intuitive way. Though she is doing this in order to protect her people, the end result is much the same as for the men. She becomes an Amazon Queen, physically and mentally able to fight invaders and organize a corps of defenders for her community. The difference lies in her inner being. She is making conscious her unconscious love for others, and developing her intellect for that reason. The man, however, is developing his abilities in order to gain things for himself alone.

When the Amazons and the Kings meet at Tiphereth, they become allies. How and why they do this is seen very clearly in the stories of King Arthur and the Knights of the Round Table. Many people assume that stories of Amazons and Grail seeking knights are merely myths; interesting and thought provoking about the deeper reaches of our psyche maybe, but nevertheless untrue in a factual sense. We know also that the stories we have accumulated about them have far older sources than the ones which have come down to us. So there must have been factual distortion, even if the tales had a grain of truth in them originally. As a result, we treat them as "fairy" tales, not to be trusted as history.

Recently, Russian archaeologists have uncovered the graves of female warriors North of the Black Sea, in exactly the area Greek and Roman writers reported that the Amazons lived. So at least one strand of the myth seems to have some validity. We mostly know of the King Arthur stories through the writings of Geoffrey of Monmouth, an early medieval writer, who turned the fabled king into a full blown hero. Later writers added their own embellishments to the stories, leaving us with a highly romanticized and Christianized monarch. This does not mean that King Arthur did not live, but it does require patience to see through the later glosses to the original stories, which were handed down by the last matercentric societies.

The clues that point to King Arthur's origin as matercentric are numerous. The round table itself is one piece of evidence. Not only is it matercentrically rounded, instead of patriarchally linear, it ensures that everyone seated at it has equal status, which is a matercentric idea. The long, rectangular tables of medieval halls, in contrast, were ideal to designate status. Those of higher rank occupied one end, usually raised, and the lesser mortals sat "below the salt," probably at the end furthest from the fire and entertainment.

Traditionally, the Knights of the Round Table went on a Quest for the Holy Grail, which is variously described as a chalice, a stone, a cup, and a dish into which blood drips from a bleeding lance. One Christianized version claims that the Holy Grail is a cup in which the blood of Christ was caught as he bled on the cross. It was brought from the Holy Land to Glastonbury by Joseph of Arimathea, then disappeared.

The Quests undertaken by the Knights involve them in tests and trials which cleanse them of moral impurity. Only then can they behold the Grail. In this sense, the Grail stories can be seen as the quest of Everyman, for the pure inner Self which he has covered over with the mistakes of the ego. There are parallels with alchemy, especially when the Grail is seen as a stone, since the alchemists also pursued an elusive "philosopher's stone," which conferred power and was representative of one's true being. The stories of the Quests are a metaphor of the Knights' return to the Great Mother, because they must surrender their ego in order to reach Her. In the stories, this is externalized as brave and noble deeds, but it is interesting that the deeds are always done for the benefit of others. Although the Knight possesses all the skills of a warrior, he gains nothing for himself, except, of course, the reward of seeing the Grail. It is also emphasized that the Knight requires humility.

This is exactly the quality most needed when a man changes from the path of the god to the path of the Goddess.

It is clear from the Grail stories that these are tales of men who have developed their egos in the direction of fighting and conquest, probably under the leadership of a ruthless king, and are now ready to move back to the Great Mother. Having reached Tiphereth by the "fast" route, they can relinquish everything to be in the service of the Great Mother. They have no more desire to learn about the acquisition of power, or the use of force. So they turn back towards the Great Mother and return to Kether via Binah. Since they know on an intuitive level that it is the "feminine" side of them which must be redeemed, they behave nobly towards women, and place all their skills in the service of a woman, obeying her every wish.

In most of the stories, the knights are not of noble birth, and have not been reared as princes. Arthur himself follows this tradition. He becomes king only after a series of magical events, the most well known of which is his feat in being the only person able to remove a sword from a block of stone. Later stories explain this by saying that the knights were abducted as children, or deprived of their rights by some sort of wicked relative; but if we leave aside these patriarchal rationalizations, it is clear that the knights came from a matercentric society. In such a culture, either there was no direct inheritance of anything for males, because females were the heirs, or there was no idea of "noble" birth at all. Arthur himself may only have become "King" as a result of his marriage to Guinevere. He was her consort.

Another feature of the tales is the way in which Queen Guinevere takes other lovers, notably Sir Launcelot. In some Christianized versions, she is depicted as virtuous, i.e. faithful to one man, and the test for Arthur is in learning to trust the devotion of his knights to the Queen, instead of being plagued by unnecessary jealousy. Only a patriarchal man would have to go through this ordeal. In such a system, no child of the King could inherit the kingdom unless his parentage was assured. In a matercentric society, where descent came down through the female line, and women were not restricted to one relationship, it wouldn't matter so much who the father was.

In some of the very early Celtic stories, which were used as sources for the Arthurian tales, mention is made of a group of brothers who meet an old hag. She says to them, "If you lie with me, you will become King."

This must indicate that she is Queen. Most of the stories describe the brothers as being repelled by the hag, with the exception of one, who is willing to lie with her, and therefore becomes King. The writer usually ends the story by recounting how the hag is transformed into a beautiful woman when she is kissed. This is to satisfy the patriarchal reader that the brother does not have to suffer marriage to an "old woman" in order to gain the kingdom.

If we remove the magical elements from this story, and apply it to our modern world, we can see that it has become relatively commonplace for men to marry women much older than themselves i.e. hags. It is not so surprising to us that one brother was willing to marry the hag as it was to a purely patriarchal reader. What it meant, in terms of the Quabalah, is that the brother who marries the Queen has passed the central pillar. In his eyes, an older and more authoritative woman would be far more attractive than the younger, passive girl likely to be chosen by his brothers. Even the fact that the hag is bold enough to approach the men with her suggestions indicates clearly that she is matercentric.

The Arthurian story of Sir Gawain and Regnell illustrates beautifully that we are dealing with tales about men who have reached Tiphereth, and are now returning to Kether. In this story, King Arthur has to answer the riddle. "What is it that women most desire?" A hag named Regnell says that she will answer the riddle correctly, providing she can marry Sir Gawain. The knight agrees to this, whereupon she gives the answer.

"Our desire is to have sovereignty over the most manly of men." As in the previous story, when Sir Gawain kisses her, she turns into a beautiful woman, but this time tells him that she can be beautiful by day or by night, but not both. He must choose which it is to be. If she is beautiful by day, he can show her off to other men, who will be envious. If she is beautiful by night, he himself will benefit, but faces the shame of apparently being married to an old woman. Sir Gawain, completely stumped, allows the hag to choose, as a result of which, she becomes beautiful all the time. She explains why this is possible.

"I would not have been transformed, until the best man in England married me, and gave me sovereignty over his body and his goods."

The statement could not be clearer. The true beauty of women cannot be seen unless men are completely subservient to them. Until that point, they see only what patriarchal society has taught them to look for, and judge women accordingly.

King Arthur's knights were once the bandits and warriors who destroyed the previous matercentric age. However, their accelerated development caused them to reach Tiphereth, where their polarity changed. They became defenders of the last remnants of the matercentric society, at a time when most men were only just beginning to develop a strong ego. In many stories, we encounter a woman who has been robbed of her land by an Earl, i.e. a new patriarchally oriented man. She comes to King Arthur's court for help, and he appoints a champion to fight on her behalf. No hardship or danger is ever too much for these knights in the service of their ladies. Nor do they expect sexual favors in return. Later stories and traditions distorted this non-demanding service, implying that the knight would only be rewarded with grace if he abstained from sex. In this way, the knight could be seen as some sort of "soldier of Christ," righting wrongs on behalf of the male asexual god, instead of serving the Great Mother through devotion to a mortal woman. In an era when woman's sexuality was seen as fundamentally dangerous and evil, only a "pure" love for her was safe, and guaranteed entrance to heaven.

Celtic myths contain references to another relevant theme—the land of women. Usually, the hero of the story comes to such a land either because he is lost in some way, or by magical means. He stays there for some years, then wishes to return home. When he does so, he finds that people of his own age are now very old, or have died. Again, we assume that the land of women is a fabrication, for the purposes of spinning a tale, but if we remove the magical element, the story shows us a profound truth. The lands of women were obviously the last remnants of matercentric societies, surviving because they existed in remote areas, or on off shore islands; they were not easy to invade, or unattractive propositions for patriarchal men. Those who lived there would still be on the path of the Goddess.

On the path of the god, we live a life of continuous conflict. Though it is normal to us, it ages us rapidly. For the hero visiting the land of women, there is only harmony. Life must have seemed easy, and time passed in a different way. When he returned to patriarchal society, to disease and disharmony, his contemporaries had aged because of their stressful way of life. Chronologically there was no difference.

When the last matercentric societies finally died out, there would have been very little opportunity for the Amazons to go past the central pillar. A different type of woman now began to emerge, moving down the path between Binah and Tiphereth; the whore. She would set off from Binah when the society she lived in had become completely patriarchal, but she herself did not accept the rules, especially the need to be faithful to one man, or a virgin until marriage. The only way such a woman could survive was as a prostitute. Because of society's attitude to her, she could only associate with criminals, unless she was an exceptionally talented courtesan, in which case she mixed with princes, who could afford her services. They themselves were progressing between Chokmah and Tiphereth. The whore would generally lead a dangerous or at the least, unusual life, on the fringes of society. Like the Amazon, she would have to use her intellect to survive, thereby becoming conscious more rapidly than her more conventional sisters, who were sticking to the rules of patriarchal society.

Today, the Amazon is beginning to return, not as the matercentric warrior, or the woman assisted by knights, and not as a whore, but as a fighter for women's rights. Usually, she is very angry about men's attitudes and behavior towards women, and her anger gives her the fighting stance which is her characteristic. So far, there has been little physical violence towards patriarchal people from the Amazon, but it is possible that it may be a facet of her behavior in the future, especially if men try to reverse the progress towards a more equal society. Her mistake is often in assuming that all women should feel as she does. Many patriarchal women are neither ready nor willing to change paths, but the Amazon is often as critical of such women as she is of men.

The next shortcut is the one between Geburah and Chesed. In many ways, this is a similar path to the one running from Binah to Chokmah, except that its background is a patriarchal society. Both men and women have traveled further away from the Great Mother, so a man cannot simply use a woman as a medium to return. He does not see her as having anything to contribute to his spiritual growth. On this path we find many of the Eastern religions, like Buddhism and Hinduism. The latter is a very ancient religion, and has its roots in old pagan beliefs. It originated when man began to learn from the priestesses, and became priests themselves. For a time, both sexes learned from each other. We can see a few remnants of this cooperation in Hindu Tantra and early Taoism, and it may still exist in Voodoo. Probably it also occurred when Egypt and Greece were changing over to a patriarchal system. Then the priests decided they wanted supremacy. The priestesses were eliminated, but the priest did not forget what he had been taught, and the religion retained the knowledge. Spiritual disciplines such as yoga and meditation were passed on, but without the necessary female energy, the priests could not pass the central pillar.

So a man's journey from Chesed to Geburah would be the path of the yogin in its various forms. Learning to control his mind/body, and developing his spiritual energy, would take him as far as the middle pillar. From then on, he would have to learn Tantra, for which a priestess is necessary, since he needs to reintegrate the female energy he has previously eliminated, in order to continue his journey. Not all men do this. Many stay on the "spiritual" path, which involves the elimination of all body/ emotional energy, and denies the need for a priestess. Buddha and his followers are an example of this. Having rejected priestesses, and the feminine side of the Creator, they had no other choice but to move up the central pillar to Daath, which in Buddhist terms is "Nirvana." Buddhism is called "The Middle Way" because it avoids extremes, but on the Quabalah, we have another reason for calling it that.

This path is also the path of Taoism. Lao Tse, its founder, was reputed to have had women teachers, which would have allowed him to move past the central pillar to Geburah, then up to Binah. Almost the whole of the Taoist book, the Tao Te Ching, is about the path of the Goddess for a man. Since only men tended to become acolytes of the discipline, this was fine, but when women's interest began to stir, we can see some confusion. The sections of society which had always loved, and surrendered what little ego they had in order to serve others, were being told to continue doing this by Eastern religions. This is not correct for women on the path of the Goddess, and shows us very strongly that we must not look on any faith as being the right one for all people. Not only are we unique, but at different times we need different beliefs to fit in with our level of development. Any map or model of reality is a false one, since we are not likely to be able to perceive the whole of truth with our limited minds. Each of us therefore needs a belief system which fits whatever we are presently learning. Even our own paradigm, of the paths of the god and Goddess, is only a model, and certainly not the whole truth.

Taoist modern masters have followed the same path as Lao Tse. J. Krishnamurti is a good example. In his early life, his teacher was Annie Besant, and this allowed him to progress to Geburah. Because of his charisma and insight, he was expected by his followers to become the new Messiah, but he had moved too far towards the pillar of unconditional love to want this kind of reward. He surrendered his ego, renounced all messianic claims, and attempted to help people through his writings and conversations. He did not attempt to found a movement, or "spread the word" beyond those who sought him out.

The second master, Baghwan Shree Rajneesh, also reached the central pillar. From the wise women around him, he absorbed many of the concepts of the path of the Goddess. Unfortunately, because of his strong ego, he allowed his followers to call him "The Enlightened One," and later on to worship him as a god. Although this fulfilled a need in both Baghwan and his followers, it did have the effect of returning him to the path of the god. In this situation, he was only able to go down the central pillar to Malkuth, where he became interested in money and power. He lost his connection to the Great Mother, which had guided him and given him wisdom. The fact that his followers saw him as an infallible god, shows that they too were on the path of the god.

When the priestesses of the old matercentric age died out, it became difficult for women to move along the path between Geburah and Chesed. In the Western world, women could only choose this path in secret, because the Christian church was likely to kill them otherwise. Nor did the mass of women have any idea that powerful priestesses were a possibility. They had been conditioned by patriarchal religion, into believing in a male god, a male Savior, and male priests. Women's role was to listen, worship and serve and obey men.

Throughout this time, some women continued to practice the worship of the Great Mother in secret, and in places like Africa, priestesses remained important among certain tribes. However, it was not until the nineteenth century that we saw the rise of women in the West who acted as channels for the Great Mother, and relied on intuitively gathered information, without the risk of being burned at the stake. These mediums reached the central pillar from Binah by instructing men, but being further from the Great Mother than the old priestesses, they had to go into a trance to achieve this. Unfortunately, since they still lived in a patriarchal system, they were unable to move past the central pillar. They were looked on as being weird, except by their followers, and their knowledge could only reach a few people. Also, since they were often partly patriarchal themselves, they sometimes delivered distorted or highly superficial material which fitted in with society's values.

At the central pillar, we meet many famous mediums, such as Madame Bavlatsky, Alice Bailey, and Jane Roberts. Those who have managed to move past the central pillar tend to be women who interrogate a male medium, rather than being channels themselves. This is the only way they can progress. For one thing, the channel does not hear the information being received, and cannot question the source of it. It is a very passive occupation. So women who are mediums cannot ask questions, and develop their intellects. They can only receive. When they use a male medium, they can ask questions, and based on a combination of intellect and intuition, formulate further questions. Thus they grow in a way which is not possible for a normal female medium.

The next path lies between Chesed, Tiphereth and Geburah. For a man, the path is similar to the previous one in many ways. However, since we are now even further away from the Great Mother, there are also significant differences. One of its characteristics is the combination of politics and religion. This is something which is not found within the Eastern religions of the previous path. In Hinduism and Buddhism, politics and religion are largely kept apart. Obviously there is some cross referencing, since life cannot be neatly compartmentalized, but on the whole, religious leaders within Eastern religions left temporal affairs to the Emperors and princes. In Christianity, Judaism and Mohammedanism, however, the two areas were closely linked. Although a priest of these religions would give spiritual instruction, he would also be concerned with indoctrinating people in such a way that the political power of the Church was maintained. If we look for example at the Catholic Church, we see a ruthless use of politics to retain and increase the power of the church. Dissent, altruistic or otherwise, was suppressed violently, with total disregard for the rights of the common people, or for the spirit of Christ's teachings. Only when revolution threatened were concessions given, and sometimes the Church miscalculated the depth of feeling of its detractors, leading to break away movements. Some, like Henry VIII's, arose out of self-interest, but other movements, such as the one leading to the founding of the Protestant churches, contained many elements of devout belief and a desire to eliminate corruption. Martin Luther, a German priest, was appalled at the sale of indulgences by the papacy, which raked in a formidable amount of money for all those involved. Luther protested, on Scriptural grounds, that buying forgiveness for sins was wrong. Every means was employed to shut him up, forcing him to go into hiding. There was no way the Church would relinquish such a lucrative scam. Many people joined in with Luther's ideas, some for selfish reasons of their own, of course, but the time was opportune to reform the Church. It was quite incredibly wealthy, and mind-bogglingly corrupt, but since it had the reins of both temporal and spiritual power in its hands, it seemed unassailable. For those who were devout, there was the threat of excommunication to keep them in line. For those who couldn't care less about such things, there was the threat of death or confiscation of their property on the grounds of heresy. Since the Church itself defined what was heretical, it seemed to have all the cards. Kings were very careful not to upset the Catholic church, since it had so much power, in so many areas, and tended to form alliances with it almost as if it were a separate state. But in the time of Luther, enough people were disenchanted with the Church to be willing to defy it, and a separate Church was established, which was less ostentatious, and attempted to incorporate the reforms demanded by the people.

So a priest of the religions which combined politics with spirituality, would necessarily move down towards Malkuth while attempting to reach the central pillar, because he is concerned with worldly power. At Tiphereth, he would have many paths open to him. The most common choice would be to become a monk, which is similar to that of Buddha's followers. The decision not to become involved with the Great Mother and females means he cannot cross the central pillar. Alternatively, if he was disillusioned with his calling, he could become more interested in power and status, thus moving down the central pillar to Malkuth. Or he could follow the path from Tiphereth to Binah, though this would be impractical in our society, because powerful sorceresses are thin on the ground. This may have been the path of Merlin, who allowed himself to be held in bondage by Nimui.

The next possible path is from Tiphereth to Geburah, which may have been that of Jesus Christ. The New Testament, as we have already mentioned, is full of teachings reflecting the path of the Goddess. We are told to love our enemies, to forgive, and to "turn the other cheek" when it seems that someone is harming us. God is described as a god of love, who loves all of his creation. Jesus also predicted that the meek would inherit the Earth. The meek, in Jesus' time would have been women, and the few men who were already on the path of the Goddess

Towards the end of Jesus' life, people began to proclaim him as a new King or Messiah. His disciples, and others, began to look to him as the one who would exert his influence against the Romans who ruled Judaea. Jesus did not accept this. He had moved too far towards the pillar of unconditional love to want political power. Since his message of love was becoming misunderstood, he arranged with Judas to be betrayed, delivered into the hands of his enemies, and crucified. Many people have interpreted the death of Christ for themselves and for others. It has been largely seen by the Christian Church as a voluntary sacrifice, which redeems our sins. Others, aware of the various sacrificial rites practiced by previous societies, have seen it as an example of a death and renewal ritual, not much different from the ones used by Goddess worshippers to ensure that the crops grow, and that life goes on. We see the whole crucifixion drama as symbolic of man's need to sacrifice his ego in order to pass the central pillar. Jesus did this in a highly literal way. Faced with a conflict between his matercentric feelings of love and gentleness, and his patriarchal desire to use violence against oppressors, Jesus chose to die. He killed his ego, consciously and willingly, and rose again after its death, renewed.

Although Christian priests profess to follow the teachings of Jesus, it would be very difficult for them to choose the path he did. For a start, the teachings which have come down to us are incomplete because of censorship. We know very little, for example, about Mary Magdalene, who was Jesus' Priestess and teacher, because Christianity has minimized the role of all the women around him. Nor could a Christian priest have a relationship with a priestess, since his Church has banned them. In order to cross the central pillar, he would have to find a female mentor, and serve her, which would undoubtedly result in his leaving the priesthood.

A woman's path between Geburah and Tiphereth would be that of a nun who enters a convent to escape patriarchal society, or who is sent by her family because she is unmanageable. When lunatic asylums were founded, such a woman would be incarcerated in one because she refused to conform to society's expectations. Until very recently, this still happened, and mental homes were packed with women whose only crime was to have given birth to an illegitimate child, or defied their father's wishes in some way. The removal from the mainstream of patriarchal life left a void which could be used as an opportunity for contemplation, and allowed the woman to become aware of herself if she chose to.

The next inner path which a man could choose runs from Tiphereth to Hod, and is probably the one followed by many modern priests, whose sect allows marriage. Here we see the humanistic priest, willing to devote his life to the care of others, and so learning unconditional love. It is not an easy road. He will be hampered by patriarchal dogma, and his status in the eyes of his parishioners makes it difficult to relinquish his ego. Once he sees himself as the servant of his flock, and not their superior, he will be able to move past the central pillar to Hod. The diminishing status of priests within society makes it easier for him to do this today.

For a woman, the reverse path, from Hod to Tiphereth, is symbolized by the nun within a secluded order. A nun is generally regarded as merely the female equivalent of a monk, leading a life of devotion in order to become more saint-like. In actual fact, she is, or has been, a saint already. She has devoted many lifetimes to the welfare of others, and has loved them unconditionally. Now, a life away from marriage, husbands and children gives her the opportunity to cross the central pillar, and move onto the path towards the Great Mother. Since a woman who chooses this path often does so unconsciously, there can be problems. She may be someone who is still consciously looking to give love rather than receive it, and cannot find a recipient. The other nuns, like her, are in no way ready to receive her love, and attempt to give it back. One way out of this quandary is to pour out all her love into a relationship with the god, or with her image of Jesus Christ. Many orders refer to the nuns as "Brides of Christ," and encourage this kind of behavior. It enables the woman to exercise her loving nature, yet still move away from her previous life style. In some ways, we can see her as having been unable to break free of patriarchal conditioning in any other way, because the pull of devotion to a human male or children has been too strong.

Another nun may find that in learning the patriarchal dogmas of her religion, she awakens or increases her ego. An order which tells her that she is likely to go to heaven because she is not "worldly," for example, can help her in this way. So too can the belief that somehow she is purer and more "godly" because she is a virgin. She may begin to look down on, or even to hate those who are not so "pure," or so devoted to the god. It may seem to us to be a retrograde step, but for the woman, it is a necessary part of her development.

When the nun manages to reach Tiphereth, she too has a variety of paths open to her. The most common choice is to remain as a nun, engaged entirely in contemplation and prayer. If the woman opts for this, she moves up the central pillar towards Kether, and slowly reconnects with the Great Mother. It is unlikely that she will have enough of an ego to desire power and material wealth, which would have pushed her down to Malkuth. She could, like Morgan-le-Fay, or Queen Guinevere, move up to Chokmah, but this option is rare in a society which is still mainly patriarchal. So too is the route from Tiphereth to Chesed, which would call for her to be a matercentric priestess. Fear, or ignorance that such a possibility exists, would militate against her making that choice. If she does not become a contemplative nun, she is most likely to become a Mother Superior, and enjoy having power over other nuns. This would take her towards Netzach. Although she is developing her ego, she is still likely to be submissive towards those she sees as more powerful, such as high ranking male priests, and in this way retains part of her patriarchal thinking. Eventually, she may leave religious life, and live alone. As the archetypal eccentric maiden aunt, she may travel round the world on the back of a donkey, knowing full well that her freedom to do so lies in not being tied to a husband and children.

The next inner path runs from Netzach, through Tiphereth to Hod. For a man, this is the way of the priest with a calling. He has heard the "still small voice" of the Great Mother within him, though it will seem to him that it is Christ, God or perhaps the Virgin Mary who speaks. Acting on his inner promptings, the priest moves towards the Great Mother, and arrives at Tiphereth, where he has the same choices faced by others who have arrived at this particular Sephiroth. If he is able to eliminate his patriarchal ideas, he will move upwards, towards Geburah, Binah or Kether, but if he is not ready, he moves down, to Hod.

The woman, tracing the opposite route, may become the female equivalent of the man, and also follow a priestly calling. Though she lives in a patriarchal society, it is still possible to do this, guided and inspired by the Great Mother. She will gain enough confidence from her spiritual information to oppose or infiltrate patriarchal religion, and bring about change in herself and others. At Tiphereth, she too has the same choices as others; to lead a life of contemplation, to found a matercentric sect, or to seek power within her own church.

The next shortcut crosses the Quabalah between Netzach and Hod. At this level, near Malkuth, we are reaching into the more material world, far away from the Great Mother. The man at Netzach has left religious life behind. He believes there is no god, and supposes himself the Lord of the Universe. His main concern is his own status and power within society. He may be an astute businessman, or a political agitator. His desire to improve his status takes him into many areas, and he develops both his intellect and intuition through "positive action." Should he achieve his ultimate ambition, whatever that happens to be, his arrogance will increase. He will believe that he has both the right and the power to change the whole of his world to fit his own beliefs. Taken to extremes, this path produces men like Hitler, Stalin, and more recently, Saddam Hussein of Iraq. The label "psychopath" has been given to such men, who seem to have no conscience at all, but this is not the case. They view themselves, consciously or otherwise, as god, and have no qualms about exercising godlike powers. Many of the apparently cruel behavior patterns are justified to themselves as "good." Any inner promptings which cast doubt on their actions are ruthlessly suppressed, as is any criticism from other people. They "know" that they are right, and moreover, they know because they are god. A man may have voices speaking to him which confirm this, and be seen by others as completely mad. Whether he is locked up or venerated depends on the society he lives in. It also rests on how capable he is of balancing his behavior to take advantage of his inner drives without being imprisoned, killed or certified insane

When the man reaches the central pillar, he will inevitably change. He will no longer use his energies to fight for power for himself, but to assist others. Men like Ghandi or Martin Luther King are examples of this. They both made strenuous efforts to help oppressed people, but increased their status at the same time, which gave them ego satisfaction. Their patriarchal certainty of right and wrong gave them the arrogance to force reforms on society, but there is a big change. Violence is not to be used. If the man gains political power as a result of his efforts to end oppression, he faces a new dilemma. In his past, power has been used for himself alone. Now it has to be employed in a way which benefits others. The temptation to fall back into old patterns of behavior, and behave selfishly or violently again, may be very strong.

Men who have passed the central pillar, and who are moving towards Hod, begin to work anonymously for the good of all. They no longer need to feed their egos, because they have surrendered to the Great Mother. They may work within an area which is not fashionable, or in ways which are undetectable to others, and without looking for reward of any kind. Their methods are more gentle than those of the patriarchal reformers, since they no longer feel that conflict is necessary to produce radical change.

The woman moving from Hod to Netzach begins by fighting for others. She is aware that suffering exists, and pours out her energies into changing this. She may enter politics, or found groups designed to right wrongs all over the world. She may have the support of her husband, and other males, which is helpful in further boosting her confidence. When such a woman reaches the central pillar, she begins to realize the limitations placed on her by society. Although she still continues to care for others, she begins to want more for herself, and becomes tired of being an unsung heroine. Her energies are more and more directed into satisfying her own desires. She realizes that in helping herself, she is still helping others, without any sacrifice of her need to give love.

We can see that the Hod-Netzach path is concerned with power in the political or worldly sense. It is here that the tyrant or petty official uses his position to control, limit or hurt people in the interests of his personal ego. Along this path also lies the power struggle between men and women which is becoming evident today. At the Binah-Chokmah level, men and women are relatively equal, and have only moved a small distance from the Great Mother. When we reach Geburah-Chesed, the sexes alternate between active and passive, and are largely concerned with spiritual matters. However, at Hod-Netzach, the whole issue of dominance/submission is on the agenda. Man is at the bottom of the masculine pillar, and at the height of his arrogance. He has lost all knowledge of voluntary cooperation between equals, and sees everyone in terms of their power and status within the hierarchies he has built himself. If he is relatively high up in terms of power, he wishes to remain in this position, and if he is relatively low down, he wishes to be higher. He is willing to use violence and be selfish in order to achieve greater status. Those groups who compete with him, who wish to change their status relative to him, are very threatening, and he will respond with as many patriarchal weapons as he can find to remove the threat.

Women at Hod are at the height of humility. They are fully trained as men's servants, love them unconditionally, and offer no threat to their status. Men can afford to be relatively kind to such women, since they know their place within the pecking order and keep to it. They are not "uppity." Then both sexes begin to move towards the central pillar. A woman still wishes to care for a man, but becomes aware of his dependence on her to supply his emotional and practical needs. This gives her a feeling of power, which she enjoys, and which boosts her self-esteem. The man, in his turn, begins to appreciate that he is reliant on the woman's love. He shows gratitude for her efforts, rather than taking them for granted, and begins to love her and others just a little more.

If there are no internal conflicts within the man and woman, the situation progresses smoothly. The woman begins to desire things for herself, and moves out into new areas of achievement. The man, recognizing that this is necessary, encourages her, and his growing love for her allows him to want only her happiness. When they cross the central pillar, he becomes interested in serving her and the wider community, and she moves into a phase of independent creativity. He becomes more passive and intuitive, and she becomes more active and intellectually oriented. They move towards the Great Mother in a cooperative union.

We hardly need to point out that this scenario is rarely enacted. Though the man may have been grateful for his wife's loving care, he may become resentful when she attempts to change the status quo, which has been entirely in his favor up to now. If he has to take time to wash his own socks and take care of his own children, because she is learning Sociology at evening classes, his ego may resist. He may make attempts to sabotage her, up to and including leaving the relationship. The woman may perceive the marriage in patriarchal terms, and make a bid for dominance using male strategies. She will employ coercion, attempt to belittle his ego by earning more than him, and refuse to do "feminine" things like cooking and cleaning. One way or another, a power struggle begins, in which the man strains to retain his position, and the woman fights to improve hers.

In such a situation, the only result can be a winner and a loser, just as there are only winners and losers in all patriarchal competitions. Since the woman still loves the man, her victory will give her pain if she is the winner, and she may see-saw between fighting and submission for some considerable time. Even when her desire to love and care for others is suppressed, so she feels no apparent pain, she will not be happy, because her position depends on aggression and defenses. She is in exactly the same lonely and uncomfortable position as a patriarchal man. If the man "loses," his ego will seek ways to retaliate, and if he can't punish his wife, he may go off to find a woman he can humiliate, to restore his self-esteem. He may bully his secretary, take to the streets as a rapist, or join a group dedicated to legislating against abortion.

This power struggle between the sexes is a reality for many people today. A Western patriarchal man can look around and see that as well as other men, he now has to contend with women fighting him for status and power. Not only that, but black people are becoming a threat. It takes more and more of his energy keeping them in their place, since they seem to have forgotten that he is their god. For their part, many women and other disadvantaged groups see no other way than conflict to achieve their ends. The result is a bloody battle of patriarchal egos, both male and female. In the long run, men and patriarchal values cannot win, but there may be a vast amount of unnecessary pain before each side sees that this is the case. Eventually, men will lay down their arms and surrender to women and the Great Mother. Women will see that there is no necessity to fight anymore, and a cooperative world will arise out of the ashes of the old.

The last of the inner paths on the Quabalah runs between Netzach, Yesod and Hod, and can be summarized as the path of dreams. Here you will find the artist or the architect, who can create in the mind before turning the vision into reality. It is also the path of the writer or film maker, who dreams up characters and plots for the enjoyment and edification of others, or describes how they would like reality to be. A man traveling from Netzach to Yesod differs from the one who descends to Malkuth, in that he evolves by using his imagination. He does not need to experience the reality of his ideas in order to learn from them.

In some books on the Quabalah, Yesod is called the Sephiroth of sex, but it would be more accurate to describe it as the Sephiroth of sexually related fantasy. A male writer or film maker, moving towards Yesod, would invent stories of "macho" men and submissive heroines. His heroes would be James Bond, John Wayne, Clint Eastwood, Mel Gibson or Rambo type figures; resourceful, brave, aloof, and if you're lucky, intelligent. In his fantasies he sees himself as a strong man, dominating and using women, and triumphing over other men. The fact that his stories are read by others, allows them to share in the collective dream, without any of them having to go out and kill crocodiles or save the universe from the Clingons.

After the writer passes the central pillar, his fantasies change. He no longer wishes to be the hero who fights for himself. At first he remains triumphant, strong and clever, but with the difference being that his skills are employed to right wrongs on behalf of others, as in the Grail stories. His characters may shun fame and recognition for their efforts, like the self-effacing alter ego of Superman, Clark Kent. Slowly, he becomes more and more fascinated by strong women, and portrays them as both interesting and sexually attractive. Before this, he would only have been concerned to show his hero dominating them, or depicting them as unnatural "bitches." Now, a film maker can have an actress like Sigourney Weaver playing a female character who is resourceful, brave, intelligent and caring. And she doesn't take any crap from stupid or evil men.

Since society as a whole has not moved past the central pillar, the really strong, wise and sexual woman has yet to be portrayed sympathetically in mainstream films and novels. She still tends to be separated out into her component parts, because no one can see that women are perfectly capable of being all of those things. So we may see a "wise woman,"—but she's not sexy; or a successful woman—but her downfall occurs because she's too ruthless or still attracted to men who treat her badly; or a strong woman, but her strength is only in adversity; she is not an initiator.

Women who move from Hod to Yesod also create fantasies for themselves and others, but they are designed to feed patriarchal females like themselves. They will concentrate, to begin with, on romantic novels. In them, the Knight arrives on his shining white charger, sweeps the girl off her feet, and carries her to his castle. There they will live happily ever after. Since this is a patriarchal fantasy, sex is not mentioned, but children are. If the plot contains any complications, it is usually to do with the hero being temporarily distracted from his true love, either by a scheming "bad" woman who uses sexual allure in a bold way, or by other "baddies." Naturally, the baddies are foiled.

In time, the woman tires of this. She wants the man to love her madly, as well as look after her. If he has a hard time winning her, so much the better. Some of Jane Austen's novels show this stage very clearly. In both *Emma* and *Pride and Prejudice*, the heroine initially rejects the hero, and he has to patiently wait to win her. In *Emma*, the hero is even called Mr. Knightley.

Eventually, the woman writer passes the central pillar. Her fantasies change direction. Her heroines become stronger, more independent, and far more adventurous. They still need a man, but they are quite happy to go out and find him for themselves. Nor does he have to look after them in such a "macho" way as before. He is required to be more caring and sensitive than Rambo, but without being a wimp. Some of the heroines can use men unashamedly, without being seen as entirely bad people. It is a way for the writer and her readers to enjoy revenge on men without acting it out in the real world. A good example is Fay Weldon's *Life and Loves of a She-Devil*. In this novel, the heroine is abandoned by her husband in favor of a prettier and richer woman. Up to this point, she has been a conventional loving wife. She is expected to look after her children, and accept her husband's departure with no complaint. She refuses. First she dumps her children on their father, something which a patriarchal woman would not dream of, then spends years planning and scheming to get her revenge on both her husband and his mistress. She succeeds.

What direction the woman writer will take as she moves towards Netzach is unclear, since we are dealing with those who are in the forefront of change. Undoubtedly, the roles of men and women will alter in her stories, allowing the rest of us to experience possibilities and directions we would otherwise not envisage. In this way, writers of both sexes allow us to experiment and grow without leaving the comfort of our own homes.

CROSSING THE CENTRAL PILLAR

Carl Gustav Jung devised a model of the human psyche which postulates that within each man is a feminine component, the Anima, and within each woman is a masculine component, the Animus. These figures, he said, have to be integrated into the personality by each person if they are to achieve wholeness and balance. The impulse to do this comes from what Jung describes as the "Self," which seems to be a larger entity than just the conscious self, or ego.

In terms of the path of the god and Goddess, the Animus currently represents women's need to develop conscious awareness, or a strong ego, and the Anima symbolizes man's need to learn unconditional love and relatedness, all of which happens on the path of the Goddess. In the patriarchal era, man has tended to see woman as separate from him. He has associated her qualities, whether "positive" or "negative" in his terms, as not his own. Woman has done the same with men. Jung saw this as leading to projection; instead of developing these inner figures, and accepting their nature as part of you, patriarchal people have been encouraged to see them as outside themselves, in the other sex. A man, for example, places his capacity for nurturing and compassion with a woman, usually his mother or his wife, and fails to develop them himself, when he is on the path of the god. He can then receive love from these women, rather than give it, because he believes that women are "naturally" caring, and that it is their "job" to ensure he is looked after on an emotional and practical level. Women, in their turn, look to men for assertive self-determination, and fail to develop it themselves. Other, more negative qualities are also projected onto the opposite sex, because of the same denial that those attributes might be part of your own self-hood. Men on the path of the god, for example, often see women as irrational, because they pride themselves on being "reasonable," and women perceive men as selfish and emotionally immature because they feel they themselves are unselfish and responsive to others at an emotional level. These negative projections also serve to keep each sex in the same place.

This separating out of men and women into fixed natures makes crossing the Central pillar the most difficult task a man or woman can do. On the path of the Goddess, a man has to accept that he too can be caring, nurturing, intuitive and passive. A woman has to acknowledge that she can be an assertive individual, with the capacity for initiation, leadership and creativity. If this drive to wholeness is resisted, the inner figures of the Anima and Animus may begin to dominate the personality. The person is ready to change paths, but fear will not allow them to make the necessary moves. We then see a woman who is aggressive, selfish, quarrelsome and bossy, because the inner promptings for growth are being distorted. She becomes a substitute "macho" male, and is regarded as totally unfeminine by patriarchal people, because her Animus has taken over by the use of force. In the case of a man, he becomes a substitute female, and tends to bitchiness, moodiness and hysterical manipulativeness. The fact that these traits are so unattractive points to the negative views held of the opposite sex by the individual concerned. Both the man and the woman in these cases have been unwilling to accept their inner transsexual nature, because the qualities associated with the other sex are so appalling.

We must all cross the central pillar at some time. Men must move from the "masculine" pillar of self-love to the "feminine" pillar of unconditional love for all. The Anima in men must therefore be assimilated, and accepted as an integral part of themselves, not projected onto women. Women have the reverse task. They must realize that the capacity for self-love is not the prerogative of men, but part of the totality of their whole Self.

There are as many ways to cross the central pillar and change paths as there are people. We are all unique. The multiplicity of forms in which the crossover takes place is also complicated by the fact that we are multi-leveled beings. The various Sephiroth represent different elements; Earth, Air, Fire, Water and Ether, which we also contain. Malkuth is Earth, Yesod is Water, Hod/Netzach is Fire, Tiphereth is Air and Geburah/Chesed is Ether. We have to cross the central pillar with all of our Self, but we may do it in stages. We may, for instance, have changed paths at the level of Malkuth, and behave outwardly as if we are becoming matercentric, yet at the dreaming or emotional level, Yesod, still be completely patriarchal. In this case, our dreams and fantasies will show us where we are still on the path of the god. Another person may only have crossed the central pillar at the inspirational level, at Tiphereth. Especially if they are practicing Yoga or Tantra, or are a medium, some may move across between Geburah and Chesed, the level of spiritual energy. Between Hod and Netzach, at the desire level, is another possible crossover point for many.

Being able to cross the central pillar on so many levels can create various problems. The man who pays a dominatrix to beat and humiliate him, for instance, has crossed at the level of Yesod, but elsewhere he may still be on the masculine pillar. In visiting a prostitute he satisfies his sexual fantasy of surrender to a woman, but in his "normal" life he remains a selfish man, with no desire whatsoever to relinquish his ego.

Another man may have crossed the central pillar on the inspirational or desire level. As a teenager he may look for a woman who is a goddess, hoping to surrender to her. Unfortunately, he is living in a world which is still largely patriarchal, and he may not be able to find a woman who will accept the adoration and worship he yearns to give. Nor can he worship a female deity, since society tells him that the god is all male. In his disillusionment, he may withdraw from contact with women, become a homosexual, and even come to hate females because they do not live up to his expectations.

A Woman coming from the opposite direction may have similar problems. She could cross at the level of Malkuth, and be a strong independent female, with a well developed career. However, at the level of fantasy, she could still have desires which are purely patriarchal. She may long for a "strong" man, but if she happens to find one, resent the fact that he expects her to put his career first, or look after their children as well as earn money. Although she may only be able to respond sexually if she is with an assertive man, rather than a "wimp," she also finds that she is restricted by the burdens placed on her by his ego. She may fight him to gain "equality," when the real reason the relationship is in difficulty is that she is moving towards matercentric values, and he is still well rooted in patriarchal ones.

Another woman, having passed the central pillar at the desire and fantasy level, will look for a gentle and passive man, possibly one who is much younger than her. Having found one, she then attempts to nurture him by encouraging him in his career, or pushes him into supporting her financially. She may want him to be more ambitious, or more assertive in social situations. This is impossible, because he has surrendered his ego, and no longer cares about such things.

On another level, we may find a woman who has passed the central pillar on an inspirational level. Though she lives her outward life as a "normal" patriarchal wife and mother, she finds no fulfillment in this. She is resentful of the narrowness and restrictions of her life, but feels that she has no other options. Unconsciously, she may set out to punish her husband and children for her "wasted" life. This can take many forms, from constantly belittling them, to acting in a martyr-like fashion, which drives a wedge between her and her family. The "love" she gives is heavily conditional, based on duty and responsibility, and she looks for rewards from it. When the essential bitterness of her personality causes those around her to move away, she feels alone and unappreciated, not seeing that she has caused her own problems.

The different combinations available when crossing the central pillar are endless, because of our individual paths, which are unique to us. However, the process can be made easier if men and women can come together on the same level to help each other cross over. This requires us to look at relationships from a totally different viewpoint. If we see that their purpose is to allow us to grow in a way which gives us joy, then we can venture into the unknown with more confidence, because we are no longer alone. We have help. However, this doesn't often happen. We can point to many cases of couples who have come together for the purpose of crossing the central pillar, and who have failed, even though this failure is only a postponement of the inevitable. One or other of them may hold back through fear of the unknown, thus destroying the potential within the relationship. The one who is willing to grow becomes disenchanted or confused, yet may not leave the relationship, often because of a sense of duty to the other. We have taught people to believe that an unsuccessful relationship is one in which the people separate, or are not "blissfully" happy, yet we have no idea what the purpose of the relationship was in the first place. It may be, for instance, that a woman has a marriage with an alcoholic, in order to learn that she is no longer responsible for a man's happiness, direction or problems. If he chooses to continue as an alcoholic, she is still free to put her own realizations into practice and leave him, without any sense of "failure." She may still love him deeply, but for the first time be willing to look after herself rather than him. Her lesson has been learned, and she has no further need of the relationship.

A man who is ready to become passive may join with a woman who is developing her assertiveness. This may work well, but it may also encounter difficulties. The woman is quite happy to accept the devotion and obedience of her partner in private, but feels ashamed of him in "normal" society, because he is so clearly "unmasculine." Other women may criticize her, and because she is only just beginning to change paths, she may feel insecure. Or the man may admire his strong, assertive wife immensely, yet find the demands on him to completely surrender his ego too difficult to comply with. He still feels there are areas in which he should be "boss," or be looked up to. Without these, he can't believe he is a real man. There may also be problems because aspects of the relationship are unconscious. The woman's desire for the man to surrender may be denied, because she would then have to see herself as "selfish," an unacceptable female trait in patriarchal society. Yet she still pushes him to relinquish his ego.

We can look at a famous example of the difficulties inherent in crossing the central pillar with a partner. Albert Einstein, possibly the most well known scientist of this century, was at one time married to a woman called Mileva Miric. She was an unusually talented physicist, at a time when it was rare for women to attend University, let alone study "masculine" subjects like Math and Physics. This argues a strength of character necessary to overcome the obstacles placed in her way by patriarchal men.

Albert Einstein was apparently a passive and intuitive man, the perfect partner for Mileva. They worked together on the first papers which led to the theory of Relativity. It is very likely that she acted as the interrogator for Einstein, using her intellect to ask profound questions which were answered through Einstein's intuition. After the acceptance of Einstein's theories on Special and General Relativity, the marriage broke up, and those early theories proved to be the high point of Einstein's work. He worked with male scientists on other projects, but they were unable to give him the blend of intellect and intuition that Mileva supplied. Nor could he become completely passive when working with another man. As a result, the research in his later years bore comparatively little fruit.

Some strong women are able to use passive men to their own and the man's benefit. Annie Besant, for example, was associated with such famous men as George Bernard Shaw, J. Krishnamurti and Ghandi. The men were passive enough, in certain areas, to be willing to learn from or be questioned by a woman. All gained knowledge from this which enabled them to cross the central pillar. Men who feel that women have nothing to contribute except humble service, cannot progress in this way.

The people who cross the central pillar while society is still largely patriarchal are pioneers. Large numbers of them will have to do this in order to change the attitudes and beliefs of society, and allow an easier passage for other people. Being in the arrowhead of change can be an uncomfortable position, however. Women who were seen as unnatural in the past because they dominated their husbands, may have been perfectly happy with their passive man, yet were made to feel that they were going against what was right and good. Those who deviated from patriarchal norms in a significant way, could find themselves on the wrong side of a bonfire. Both men and women had every incentive to keep their unusual ideas secret, yet many did not, and although they suffered for this, at least their ideas reached a wider audience.

It has been difficult for both men and women to change even slightly the stereotyped roles which society assigns them. But as more people cross the central pillar, it will become easier. Once the acknowledgment of the Great Mother as our Source gains wider acceptance, women will be able to resume their role as Her representatives. Their wisdom and strength will return, and they will have the confidence to develop self-love. Men will feel able to love others without fear of loss to the ego, and will contact the Great Mother through the development of their intuition.

The central pillar is the place where we find many homosexuals and celibates. There is no one reason for this, except that such people have chosen their sexual orientation either to learn or to attempt to avoid growth. A homosexual man may have become inspired by the archetype of the Great Mother, and projected her onto his human mother. He remains faithful to her for the rest of his life, which makes it impossible for him to have a normal heterosexual relationship. He has surrendered to the Great Mother, and is generally a passive and intuitive individual, but he sees mortal women as inadequate or frightening. Another man may feel that only men are capable of true love, because women are inferior creatures, not quite human. Or they may seem to him to be so powerful that a relationship with one would swallow him. Some of this may be conscious, or it may be entirely unconscious. He may feel physical attraction only for men, and accept this as right for him. Some of his friends may be women, but they are more than likely to be strong individuals, who manifest the Goddess. He is not yet ready to surrender to such women, but he does feel attracted to them in a nonphysical way. Still other men have succumbed entirely to their Anima, and become substitute females. They may behave in an exaggeratedly "female" way, and long for a tall handsome man to sweep them off their feet. When comedians parody gay men, it is this group they choose to imitate, which infuriates those male homosexuals who are not in the least bit "camp."

When males have a sexual relationship, there can be difficulties which have nothing to do with society's disapproval. If neither have crossed the central pillar, they will both be "takers," who look for short term sexual gratification. There may be a succession of "affairs" on both sides, because they are both still patriarchal. It is still true today, even though many gay men have long term stable relationships, that homosexual males have far more sexual partners than heterosexual men. Because they are still on the path of the god, they can separate love and sex, and indulge in a series of "one night stands" without internal conflict or emotional interaction. This has been given as a reason for the initial rapid spread of Aids within the gay community, though there are certainly other factors which contribute to this.

When a homosexual man crosses the central pillar, he becomes a "giver." He may form a relationship with a gay patriarchal man, and give unconditional love to him, as a patriarchal female might. In doing this, he learns to surrender his ego, and may form a stable relationship for some time. Problems arise when his partner crosses the central pillar as well, because each will attempt to give love to the other, and will wish to be passive. It is possible that such men will turn their energies outward towards society, and become the shamans of the new matercentric era. They will give love to others in general, or become intuitive mediums, as their way of connecting to the Great Mother.

Lesbian females at the central pillar experience some of the same problems as gay men. Many of them are strong, creative women who no longer wish to play second fiddle to a man's ego, or be hurt by them. Having seen how selfish and uncaring most men are, often through painful experiences, they don't want a relationship with one. It may be that they feel any interaction with men is dangerous, and avoid them entirely. If they are not interested in the passive man as a sexual partner, they turn towards other women. If both are patriarchal, they will wish to give love to each other, and neither will know how to receive. In learning how to accept love, each is enabled to cross the central pillar, but without the enormous difficulties faced by men in a similar position. They will be able to both give and receive in a balanced way, because of their connection to the Great Mother. Once they have developed confidence, they can lose their fear and hatred of men, because they now have the power to resist the patriarchal man on both an inner and outer level.

People who are "forced" into homosexual behavior because of circumstances over which they have little control, such as prisoners, sailors, monks, nuns etc., have the same opportunities for growth as those who appear to have had a freer choice. It may be more painful for them, since they feel that they are basically heterosexual, but they are still in a learning situation. It is ironic that the Christian Church, which has been such a potent enemy of sex, has inadvertently hastened the evolution of so many individuals by forcing them into homosexual relationships within the walls of monasteries and convents.

Just before he reaches the central pillar, a man is at the height of his ego growth. A Yogin at this position on the Geburah-Chesed path, for instance, may find himself considered a god by his devoted followers. A priest at Tiphereth may be seen as a saint by his congregation, or hold high office within the Church. If he is a warrior, he could be a successful King. On the Hod-Netzach level, he could be a famous and influential politician, revolutionary or dictator. At the Yesod level, he might be a world famous artist, writer or musician, while at Malkuth, we would encounter the successful businessman, scientist or professional man, although scientists can also be found at other levels.

The problem for all these men is that having achieved ultimate success, as defined by patriarchal society, they have no goals. Some may move up and down the central pillar, postponing the inevitable, and attempt to find new worlds to conquer. A famous musician may try to become a spiritual leader, for example, or a Hollywood actor may seek to become President of the United States. All this may take some time, but eventually the men will realize the futility of power, status and acclaim. For a Yogin this may not be so difficult. There are many spiritual teachings about the "surrender of the ego," which he will be aware of. The only mistake he is likely to make is to be proud of his "humility," which he sees as a great achievement considering he is such an important and evolved soul.

For the priest it will be a similar story. Again, his Church tells him that he must be humble to find god. He has never before followed this advice, being more concerned with the development of his ego, but when he is ready to cross the central pillar, he knows what he is supposed to do. Initially, he may be secretly competitive about his humility, as the Yogin is, and see himself as more or less humble than others, but outwardly he will appear to have surrendered.

At the Hod-Netzach level, the man has a problem because he has no spiritual teachings to guide him. Often he has to learn through bitter experience that the things which once attracted him are no longer satisfying. He may move up the central pillar towards religion, hoping to find a solution there. All he encounters is the god and his priests, who offer him spiritual power if he follows the rules of their religion, and Heaven when he dies. Since he is genuinely looking for a way to cross, he will find those parts of such religions which encourage him to help others. This gives him such satisfaction that he is able to cross the central pillar into unconditional love for all, even though he may initially pride himself on how charitable and self-sacrificing he is.

At Yesod, the man may find that his fantasy of being the all-conquering hero, with a woman under each boot, no longer has the allure and glamour it once possessed. He will look for new ideas, and his fantasies will slowly evolve. From being someone who identified with strong and violent males, who selfishly pursue their desires, he will turn to ideas of men who right wrongs, defend women and children, and use their warrior skills for good. Eventually, women who are strong and capable will appear in his fantasies, and he will both admire and desire them, thus allowing him to cross the central pillar. Once he begins to dream of being rescued by a woman, he's home and dry.

At Malkuth, we see many men who have become disenchanted with the pursuit of wealth. They see that the unequal possession and use of resources by various individuals and nations is killing the planet, and producing an unfair society. In their flight from materialism, they may look for ways of serving "the larger good," and thus cross the central pillar, or they may stay on the path of the god in order to preach the value of their own new perspective on the world. They may despise those who still wish to gain wealth or possessions, and deliberately live in a state of poverty, seeing it as more virtuous than affluence. In this case, their ego is continuing to motivate them, because they are still seeing themselves as superior to others and taking pride in their lack of greed.

For a woman, attempting to pass the central pillar in a patriarchal society is a lonely business. She will find that her guidance tends to come from her own intuition, if she allows it, since there will be very few women around her who have enough wisdom to help. As more women cross the central pillar, and strengthen their contact with the Great Mother, this situation will ease. Those who have developed a relationship with the Great Mother will spread information about their experiences, which can be used to assist others. As it becomes increasingly acceptable to worship a female deity, and be a woman on the path of the Goddess, the transition will be less confusing for those who come after the trail blazers.

At the Geburah-Chesed level, we might find a medium who has become disenchanted with her passive role, and wishes to ask her own questions. She can do this if she finds a male medium who has passed the central pillar, and is not seeking to become a "guru" because of his intuitive abilities. She will use both her intellect and intuition to ask deeper and deeper questions, then use the information to enlarge her own awareness even further.

At Tiphereth, there is no acceptable way for a woman to cross over except by becoming a priestess or witch, and mediating the Great Mother. Often this will have to be done in secret, since society still sees these women as deviant and even evil. The connection between Wicca and things like "Devil worship" or "Black Magic," are still firmly believed in by many patriarchal people. There is greater acceptance of the occult within society, but as yet, very few organizations which train and guide priestesses of the Goddess exist. This means that there are very small numbers of women within society who have crossed the central pillar at this point. Nor have all women who call themselves priestesses actually crossed over. Large earrings, Indian skirts and a command of "New Age" jargon are not the only requirements. We will experience profound inner changes, and we may be surprised at the direction our lives take, if we sincerely call on the Great Mother for help and guidance to manifest Her. Those who wish to cross the central pillar at this point will take the risk.

On the Hod-Netzach level, are many women who have been inspired by the ideas of the Feminist Movement, and are pushing for greater equality for women. Their ethos often lacks a spiritual dimension, which makes it difficult for them to contact the Great Mother, though they may indirectly reach Her through cooperative ventures with groups of women, which produce a high level of matercentric energy. However, since most of their aspirations and methods are patriarchal, and involve conflict, they are not going to move across the central pillar. Once they have enough confidence from the gains they have made to relax into a relationship with the Goddess, then they will cross over. The need to "fight" patriarchal society on an outer level will give way to an understanding and acceptance that the way forward is for both men and women to tune into the Great Mother. All positive changes will flow from this. Once women on this path acknowledge that they want to "rule the world," and are capable of doing it lovingly, they reach Netzach, and can move up the masculine pillar into the harmonious and cooperative society they have envisaged.

The Hod-Netzach level is where many women have already begun to cross. Its advantage is that it is a path which is straight across the Quabalah, and doesn't involve them in moving closer to the Great Mother. In a society which has not begun to manifest the archetype of the Great Mother with any strength, and has no images of Her to use for guidance, this has great advantages. All upward paths, such as Malkuth-Netzach or Tiphereth-Chesed, need a clear image of the Great Mother to provide direction, and as yet, we lack this.

The other "straight across" paths, Geburah-Chesed and Binah-Chokmah, have the same advantage as Hod-Netzach in that there is no Sephiroth at the central pillar. A Sephiroth is a goal we aim for on a particular path, and one we don't see beyond until we have reached it. As far as we are concerned, the Sephiroth we are aimed at is "heaven," true enlightenment or complete happiness. Once we have reached it, we may hang around for several lifetimes enjoying ourselves, until it dawns on us that there are other paths and other goals. Even then, we may take a long time deciding which new goal to aim for out of the choices available.

So it is easier for us if we choose a path which crosses the central pillar without an intervening Sephiroth, which might delay us or send us off in a completely different direction when we reach it. A man at Netzach, for example, might look across at Hod and see responsible use of power as his goal. Until now, he has had power, but used it selfishly. He wants to stop. As a result, he becomes interested in political or social systems which promote responsibility, and while he is still on the path of the god, becomes a benevolent dictator, laying down rules and regulations which compel everyone to be "responsible." When he reaches the central pillar, Hod calls him to abandon the use of coercion to achieve his aims, and emphasizes cooperation. It tells him that he must surrender all external power and develop his connection with the Great Mother. If he responds, he begins to lose his patriarchal power to those who are still willing to use force to gain what they want. He then attempts to actualize his goal of responsibility by selflessly setting an example, and seeking no rewards for this. In terms of the patriarchal system, he has lost the capacity to achieve his goal by the use of personal power, and his ego may not like this. It fears that he will end up at the bottom of the pecking order, unable to achieve any goals at all because he has no "clout" any more. Instead of crossing to Hod, he may move up to Tiphereth and exercise power within a religion, go down to Yesod, where he indulges himself in the pleasure of dreams, or move to Malkuth, where he will have material wealth and power. At each stage, he will be given the opportunity to relinquish patriarchal power, and surrender his ego, though he may not choose to do so.

A woman at Hod will have the same issue of power and responsibility to resolve if she chooses Netzach as her goal. To begin with, she will be a responsible and caring person who has no power, exactly the opposite of the man at Netzach. She will work for the good of others in a selfless way, but as she nears the central pillar she will begin to desire power for herself. Since she is still patriarchal, the only concept of power she possesses is one which involves having money, beauty, political, social and religious status, or well developed muscles. It is an external power, and dependent on hierarchies in which some people get to tell others what to do. The specter of being a tyrant will loom before her, and may cause her to avoid seeking power any further. When she looks around, she sees that those with power use it selfishly, and this causes her to hesitate, feeling that she too would do this. Or she may seek patriarchal power, and behave in exactly the same way as a patriarchal dictator. Only when she knows that the inner power of her contact with the Great Mother is what is real power, and that it is something which cannot be misused, will she cross the central pillar, and assume a position of leadership within a matercentric society.

At the Yesod, or dreaming level, women are finding it difficult to move to the pillar of self-love because of their continuing attachment to the assertive and dynamic patriarchal male. They are seeking, as increasingly "strong" women, to forge a relationship with a male who is a mirror image of themselves at this point of their cycle i.e. caring, emotionally open, yet still powerful and active. With such a man, they believe, they will have the "ideal" marriage. The search for this man can take up a disproportionate amount of their time and energy.

What they are seeking prevents them from crossing the central pillar. Men who have completed the path of the god naturally move towards being more caring individuals, and become less interested in activities which extend their ego. They become emotionally more responsive; to women, to children, and to the wider community. Eventually, they become totally uninterested in "making things happen" or in any achievements for themselves alone. They seek only to serve others, and quietly use all of their abilities in the service of society, without any need for power, status and recognition. However, many women at the central pillar are seeking to halt the cycle of development for men, because they are not aware of the necessity to continue the cycle of change, or because they fear it. A passive, intuitive man, who is completely guided by a woman, or by a matercentric ethos, seems to them unattractive or unmanly. What they are looking for, in seeking a man who is half-patriarchal and half-matercentric, is a cessation of movement for both sexes. They want the man to retain part of his ego, and remain at the central pillar, which of course keeps them there too. There is nothing intrinsically "wrong" with this, because they obviously need time to lose their fear of what lies beyond the pillar of unconditional love, but it can become a hindrance if they decide for other people that this is what everyone "should be" aspiring to. The idea of an "equal" relationship has become very powerful in recent years, as many men and women gather at the central pillar, preparing to cross. It is an attractive proposition, because it saves us from the massive changes which are necessary on the path of the Goddess. However, relationships which are entered into for the purposes of stifling growth, which seek to keep each person in a fixed state, can only be temporary. Eventually, women at Yesod will realize that the image they have of a male who is both loving and "masculine" represents a longing for reunion with the Great Mother at Kether, where it is indeed possible to fulfill this dream, and will move on to complete their evolution to reach it. Even this will change as they become less patriarchal, because they will see that "ideal" anythings, whether marriages, societies or deities, are ever changing, as our consciousness evolves, and might as well be abandoned now as absolutes. The Great Mother is ever mysterious. If we place barriers between us and Her love because of our preconceived ideas, we slow our growth. All of us do this; our book is no exception. The ideas in it will undoubtedly be superseded by new ones. What we can do, though, is to look at the concepts offered to us by individuals or groups and ask whether they are helpful to us. If they are, then we are free to embrace them. If they are not, then we are equally free to look for and to find the "truth" which better assists us.

Most people will cross the central pillar at Malkuth, at the level of Earth. Here we will find men who have lost their ambition for status and money, but have no idea what to do next, since they have no spiritual or inspirational dimension to their lives. Here also are women who have begun to succeed at the material level. They may be completely uninterested in Feminist ideas, religion or the rejection of the ethics of patriarchal society. Their satisfaction comes from owning property, building a career, or competing with men and winning. In order to acquire a confident ego, they may need to feel superior to truly patriarchal women and matercentric men and may scorn cooperation. They may believe that the only way to beat men is to play them at their own game, and fully espouse the "masculine" values of patriarchal society. In order to cross the central pillar, they will need to unburden themselves of their fear that if they do not remain tough and competitive, men will once more "walk all over them." This is a widespread attitude. Many women assume that if they relax their guard for an instant, men will remove all the gains of recent years in an anti-women backlash. The fact that this has happened in many countries does nothing to assuage their anxiety. They do not trust men, and they have as yet, very little connection to the Great Mother.

This will not change overnight. Men who have been forced to allow rights to women by their governments, and resent this because they are still patriarchal, will seek to restore the old balance of power. In some cases they will undoubtedly be successful, and this will cause many women to say "I told you so. You can't trust men." There will be a yo-yoing pattern of change, back and forth between matercentric and patriarchal, for some time to come. It is not easy to undo the habits and fears produced by millennia of male rule. Nor did the last changeover, from the matercentric society to the patriarchal one, happen in a smooth and homogeneous way.

As more people cross the central pillar, the inevitability of the matercentric era will gather momentum. Those who wish to retain patriarchal values will begin to find themselves in a minority, and will be unable to reverse the changes which have occurred. It may seem like "Three steps forward, two steps back," but there is no avoiding it. Eventually, there may be some sort of separation. Those who wish to continue on the path of the god will live together, and those who are now on the path of the Goddess will form matercentric communities. There may be matercentric and patriarchal countries; indeed it can be interpreted that way now. Many Western nations are moving towards the Great Mother, however erratic that movement appears, while other nations appear to be firmly on the path of the god. In the West, we may lose our desire to consume and to control the world, while other nations begin to want such things. Since the future is the unknown, what happens depends on the choices we make as we approach it, and the consciousness which forms it.

Women who cross the central pillar at Malkuth will slowly begin to develop their connection to the Great Mother, as they move up the pillar of self-love towards Kether. This will give them enough trust in Her love to relinquish their patriarchal values. Eventually, they will come close enough to feel Her presence within them, and allow themselves to lose their fear that men will ever again dominate them, or that they will be so will-less as to permit it.

CHE CAROC

T he Tarot is a familiar esoteric device, known to millions of people in the West. Its origin is unclear, but as a tool to contact intuitive knowledge, it has become famous, and it is the basis for the normal pack of playing cards which we all use. As with many devices, it has changed over the years, but if we look at a medieval pack, we can usefully relate the images which we find to the evolution of human beings on the path of the god and the Goddess.

The Tarot pack has two parts; the Major Arcana, of twenty two cards, and the Minor, which contains fifty six cards. The Minor Arcana consists of four suits; Wands (Clubs), Cups (Hearts), Swords (Spades) and Pentacles (Diamonds). In addition to the ten numbered cards in each suit, there is a Page, Knight, Queen and King, so it differs slightly from the standard pack of playing cards.

The Major Arcana's twenty two cards are numbered; each is different, but together they form a unit. They trace the path of spiritual development followed by human beings seeking to learn and grow. What is interesting is that they form a circle. The path begins and ends with "The Fool" card, showing us that our evolution does not progress in a straight line, as we are taught by patriarchal society. This cycle of growth and change can not only be related to the paths of the god and Goddess, but to almost everything else. Time, for example, is seen by our society as having the dimension of a straight line. If we look behind us we see the past, which is unchangeable, and further along the line is the future. At their intersection is now, the present moment.

If we can free ourselves of our fixed ideas about time, we can help ourselves enormously. Imagine, for example, that instead of being a creature which travels along a road between birth and death, that you do not move at all. You are still, and the events of your life come towards you. It's a bit like the video arcade games in which you have to steer an imaginary car along a road which rushes towards you, complete with any number of obstacles, bends and other vehicles. There seems to be movement, but in actual fact it is an illusion. All that happens is that the images on the screen change. Now, add to this picture a further idea. You are steering. Which bit of road you encounter depends on you, and the direction you have decided on. Possibly, the apparent choices are determined at a very deep level by the nature of what you have to learn, but you can still steer away or towards the images on the screen. So far , so good, but this metaphor does not depart too much from standard reality. The only difference is that instead of you moving through time, time moves through you, and allows you freewill. Now we have to add the circular nature of it all. Let's go back to the video arcade game. After standing in front of the screen for a few minutes, you notice that the road begins to look familiar. You've seen that red car before, and that palm tree; and wasn't it over there that you crashed into a brick wall three games ago? It all comes round again. Another opportunity to undo mistakes, and learn from them. Perhaps the form has changed, and the obstacle looks so unfamiliar that you don't immediately recognize it, but the chance to avoid the same error is presented again and again.

This may seem far fetched, but it does provide a different way of looking at one's experiences. There is always hope, because nothing is finished with forever. Mistakes can be corrected. In our patriarchal model of time, the past is irretrievable, and there is no chance to undo errors. But if we look at Nature, the cyclic view of existence is clearly illustrated. Plants, animals, people die, but the constituent elements continue to form new life out of the death of the old. It does not have to be physical death, of course. A caterpillar "dies" to become a chrysalis, then "dies" a second time to emerge as a butterfly. We undergo psychological "deaths" of all kinds during our physical life. The child becomes an adult, the virgin becomes a mother. What is worth conserving from each stage is retained, yet growth continues. All that happens is that the fundamental energy which is the source of everything changes form.

The cyclic view of existence has another profound implication for our lives. A linear view of progress through life and time severely limits us. There is a beginning and an end, so we become goal oriented. Many religions reflect this. The end in view for most Christians is to become "perfect," and go to Heaven as a result. In Eastern religions, the objective is Enlightenment. The goal is impossible, of course. As we move towards it, someone moves the goal posts, and changes what is defined as "perfection," because society itself never stands still. Even if we take the sacred book of a particular religion as defining perfection, interpretations will differ, and new slants on the material will occur to forward thinkers.

If we see instead, that there is no end, and that we are always changing, always in the process of becoming, there can be no ultimate fixed goal. We can of course have short term ones, towards which we move because of our desires, but we will realize that they are not fixed for all time. The energy locked up in who we are at any given moment can be transformed i.e. it can change form, and this can go on indefinitely.

The Major Arcana of the Tarot pack takes us through a cycle of change. There is order in that change. Just as you cannot run before you can walk, so you can't learn some truths before others. Though each of us has an individual curriculum of personal development, we can still generalize about the nature of the lessons to be learned by humanity as a whole. What form these take, however, varies from person to person, because we are unique. Those who learn only through pain, for example, will experience painful events designed to allow them to move away from a particular way of perception. Those who learn through joy, in contrast, will move towards what will provide happiness. Learning to tell the difference between the two is a fundamental task for all human beings.

In order to understand the Tarot cards from the viewpoint of the paths of the god and Goddess, we have to pair them, one male card and one female one. The World card, which is nominally the last one, is twinned with the Fool card, the first one, which joins the cards into a circle. The Fool card is thus a beginning and then another beginning, forever, because it cannot be separated from its twin.

Before the beginning, and at the end, if we are thinking in time, comes the World card. It shows a nude woman surrounded by a plaited wreath in the shape of a vagina. She appears to be stepping forward, signifying that she is being born from the Great Mother. Surrounding the wreath are the figures of an angel, bird, bull and lion. These represent our three-dimensional world, which traditionally is said to be formed from the four elements of Air, Water, Earth and Fire. Air is Aquarius, the angel, Water is Scorpio, the eagle, Earth is Taurus, the bull, and Fire is Leo, the lion. Part of the woman's body seems to be draped with a cloth, and in each hand she holds two small rods. The cloth is a partly unrolled scroll, showing that there has been a beginning to the logical or intellectual mind. It covers her sex organs, fulfilling the same role as the fig leaf in the Biblical story of Adam and Eve. Although animals live in the same way as they were created by the Great Mother, and act instinctively, already humans are trying to "improve" what She has given them. The cloth symbolizes the beginnings of individual creativity.

The other card of the pair is the Fool card, the male one. Whereas the woman seems serene and at peace, the young man in the Fool card appears confused, with little comprehension of what is around him. He is very badly dressed, giving the impression that he is barely able to look after himself, and he carries a small bundle on a stick. It could almost be a packed lunch prepared for him by his mother, because he has decided to explore on his own for a while. His only companion is a small dog. In later packs, the Fool is depicted walking off the edge of a cliff, but in the medieval one, he is simply starting to walk down an incline. It is downhill all the way on his path away from the Great Mother, but he has to go, and wants to go, to see what it is like being separate and independent.

The next card is Number One, the Magician. Since he is far better dressed than the Fool, it implies that man is now more able to look after himself. In front of him is a small table, on which are various items he has either made or is selling. Here is a person who thinks more than the Fool, and sees himself as quite clever or resourceful. He seems to be coping quite well without the assistance of the Great Mother, and has both ideas and creations which do not directly come from her.

The Priestess, Number Two, is the twin of the Magician. If a priest is the mediator between god and man, then a priestess is the link between Goddess and Man. At this stage of evolution, women are still almost totally instinctual, and well connected to the Great Mother's wisdom. The Priestess stands between two pillars, and carries a scroll on her lap, signifying that she is part of, and controls the status quo. Human society is still largely dependent on her, although men are beginning to move away from the Great Mother and from their intuition. The Magician, in his attempt to gain personal, or ego-consciousness, is losing contact with the Great Mother, but he is not yet able to survive on his own. He is reliant for advice and for knowledge on the Priestess, who instructs him in every area. We know from recent research that it was the women in Neolithic times who grew the crops, threw the pots, and practiced animal husbandry. Men had to learn these things when they wished to become independent of women's guidance. Eventually they appropriated control of them, or diminished the status of such activities. The Priestess represents the level of consciousness of society when it was peaceful and harmonious for century after century. Man had the time to evolve his conscious mind without harming others, since it was women who ruled, and he could not implement any new ideas without their cooperation. Their wisdom saved him from bringing in changes which would disrupt the balance of society.

Card Number Three is the Empress. The parallel card is the Emperor. Man has now reached the stage where he has sufficient confidence in his abilities to oppose the collective will of matercentric society. When we look at the Empress card, we see her seated in a wheat field. In the background is a forest and a stream, signifying that she is part of all Nature, and not apart from, or superior to it. The Emperor, however, is seated on a elaborate throne, on a high plateau. In the background are mountains. The Emperor has set himself above others, thus creating the first hierarchies. The mountains represent the position of the god in this pecking order. He is in the mountaintops, or in the realms of the sky, not the fields and streams. He is remote and therefore unknown and to be feared. The Great Mother, in comparison, is within us all, as she is in the whole of Her creation. There can be no superiority or inferiority in being a particular part of Her creation. We are all equal, yet uniquely valued and cherished by Her.

The next card is the Hierophant, Number Five. When the Emperor began to control society, he discovered that although he could rule through the use of violence and fear, society collapsed under those conditions, into chaos and disorder. For a while, it seemed that there were only two alternatives; the rule of women, which was harmonious, but unexciting to a patriarchal male, or the rule of men, with its resulting turmoil and fragmentation. A new figure emerged, who used fear in a different way. The male priests, who at first worked with the priestesses, gradually took over their role within society. Gods were invented to compete with the Great Mother. Women, being largely unconscious, offered little resistance to this, and slowly, the gods became preeminent. New goddesses were invented, since the memory of the Great Mother was still there, but they were inferior to the gods. They represented qualities which were in line with men's wishes for women's new role in society. They were caring rather than powerful. Women by and large accepted this, and became submissive to the propaganda of the priests. Fear of the invisible god and his retribution for breaking the rules of the priests became a way of controlling them.

Because men at this stage of evolution were fundamentally both selfish and irresponsible, and could not see another's point of view, the Father god which was created by the priests had to be very strict about what was and was not allowed. This was enshrined in codes of religious behavior, and as quickly as possible, incorporated into the law of the land. Since the priests could not watch everyone who might be transgressing these commandments, the god was declared to be omniscient and omnipresent. If he didn't punish you for being disobedient to his rules while you were alive, it was because he had something even more awful in store for you when you died. Hell. The propaganda worked. Men who could not be controlled by violence, feared the wrath of god. Not all of course, but enough so that society ticked along without collapsing in a heap at frequent intervals. In some countries, particularly Eastern ones, the figure of the Emperor was combined with the god. He had a large enough ego to wield the power of life and death over his subjects, and see himself as divine. His belief in himself, plus widespread conditioning, meant that many of the people accepted his divinity as a reality.

This use of fear produced the first manifestations of guilt. People could never be as perfect as the priests said the god wanted them to be, and they were encouraged, especially if they were female, to feel unworthy. They could try and try, but since the Fall of man, they were doomed to be sinful. This made the gap between a perfect god and human beings even wider, and man began to feel terribly lonely as well as fearful and guilty.

The invention of a Father god had another interesting spin-off for the Hierophant and the Emperor. The propaganda could be extended indefinitely into areas which the rulers did not wish other men to go. If the god was seen to disapprove of wealth, for example, and you couldn't go to heaven if you were rich, this left the field clear for the rulers to accumulate property and power without the opposition of true believers. If we scrutinise our own belief systems, we will find that this propaganda is deeply imbedded in us. Often, we aspire to be "spiritually evolved" by following the rules laid down by patriarchal priests many years ago. We have to repeat that there are no rules, only Love. Behavior which arises from fear of displeasing a deity, or in the hope that it will bring favors from him, does not spring from love, but external rules and belief systems. We must find our own way to our own truth, by listening to the voice of the Great Mother. Sometimes it may be found in books, religious codes or the words of gurus, but all must be filtered through ourselves, to see whether the teachings are relevant to our own path.

Card Six, the Lovers, shows the figures of two women and a man. One of the two women, who appears to be older than both of the others, seems to be pushing the man away; the younger woman is holding on to him. The man is looking back towards the older woman. Above is Cupid, whose arrow is pointed towards the younger woman and the man.

This card symbolizes the changing status of women as patriarchal society begins. The man no longer has the opportunity to marry a wiser and older woman, but has to have a partner who is inferior to him, for the sake of his growing ego. He selects a patriarchal woman, who will defer to his wishes, and see herself as his servant. Usually, this will mean that she is the same age as him, or considerably younger. Such a woman cannot mother him except in a very limited way, and he cannot learn from her intuitive wisdom, since he is supposed to be superior to her. Though he suffers the loss of guidance from the matercentric woman, and looks back longingly towards her, he needs the younger, patriarchal female at this point in his evolution. Her passivity, obedience and ignorance will force him to grow, and become independent of both the matercentric woman and the Great Mother.

The next male card, is Number Seven, the Chariot. We are now seeing the patriarchal society in full flower. A man stands in a chariot pulled by two horses, which he is making no attempt to steer. There are no reins for the horses, and the man has his hands unconcernedly in his pockets. On each of his shoulders there is a face, each looking in opposite directions. These represent the intellect and intuition of the man.

Patriarchal man likes to believe that he is guided by his intellect, and that his society's rules and laws reflect this. As far as he is able, he denies the place of emotions in the world, and sees them as generally messy, especially if they are "negative" ones. He is unhappy with the idea of intuition, since it clearly can't be controlled, and sometimes gives him ideas and impulses which are radically different from those allowed to him by patriarchal society. If he believes himself to be clever, he insists that his intelligence comes from the development of his intellect, and that all of the improvements he makes to the world are logical and rational.

At first sight, it would seem that the man should be in conflict, that the two forces, of intellect and intuition, will pull him in opposite directions. But the horses are not running wild; they are moving in harmony, without the guidance of the man. The two faces on his shoulder appear to be ignoring each other, since they are looking in opposite directions, but this is just at the conscious level. Underneath, the man is following the will of the Great Mother, and is not entirely motivated by his mind, as he fondly supposes. Though he insists that the Great Mother does not exist, and ignores and denies his intuition, this is for the sake of his ego, which needs to feel all powerful at this stage in his evolution. In reality, the underlying harmony of the world continues, unaffected by the beliefs of his limited mind.

Card Eight, which is Justice, is unusual in that it depicts a woman representing this concept. Throughout the patriarchal era, the administration of Justice has been controlled by men, either formally, in the shape of courts, judges, tribal leaders etc, or informally, through the advice of wise old men. Only recently have we seen women judges, lawyers, politicians and priests. The introduction of Law and Punishment only really began within a patriarchal society, along with ideas about Justice, so how come a female figure represents it?

The answer lies in the different forms of what we choose to call Justice. In a male dominated world, the ideals of truth and justice are never realized, especially for women and disadvantaged men. Laws, by and large, are designed to protect those who have from those who have not, and maintain the status quo. It is easy to see that under such conditions, fairness, equality before the law, and the meting out of true justice cannot easily happen. Even when judges attempt to be fair and equitable, they cannot succeed, because they are applying their limited minds and their social conditioning to judging people who are largely different from themselves. A judge, moreover, is never likely to be appointed to this position unless he whole heartedly agrees with the rules of the patriarchal game, and has played them for many years.

So when we see a woman as the figure of Justice, we know we are talking about true Justice. This is not the end of the story, however, because we are far enough into the cycle to be meeting a patriarchal woman in this card. In her right hand is a sword, which is man's version of how to achieve justice, through violence, punishment and fear. She has accepted this. However, in her left hand, the hand of the Great Mother, she holds a pair of scales, which indicates that she has not forgotten true justice for all. Throughout recorded history, many women have attempted to achieve true justice, using whatever powers patriarchal society has allowed them. Only recently have they been acknowledged, and named in our history books, instead of being dismissed or forgotten by the chroniclers. A good example is Lady Godiva. Her story as it comes down to us is quite trivial. She is remembered vaguely as the woman who rode naked on horseback through the streets of Coventry, covered only by her long hair. The "peeping Tom" who dared to look at her was struck blind for his audacity. In actual fact she was a strong minded woman who insisted that her husband relieve the common people of extremely burdensome taxes. He jokingly agreed to do this if she would ride naked through the streets. Such was her courage that she agreed, despite the effect this might have on her in such a narrow minded society, and her husband capitulated. It is interesting that all we have left of this story concerning such a daring and concerned woman is the fact that she was naked.

This card also shows the beginning of conscious suffering for women. Having very little sense of self, she would be oblivious to her own pain, but keenly aware of the suffering endured by others, particularly children, the sick and the poor. It would be this awareness which leads her into seeking justice, even if she is impotent to achieve it. The difference between her and men who are asking for justice at this stage, is that they want it for themselves, but she seeks it for others.

Card Nine is the Hermit, which suggests a man who is alone. Though he has forgotten the Great Mother's existence, he has no consolation from the god. He has seen through the propaganda of the priests, and no longer believes in a divine father. As far as he knows, he is the only intelligent life in the universe. The Hermit holds a lantern, which represents the small and limited light of his intellect. He looks old and world weary, almost in despair because he cannot throw enough light with his tiny lantern to dispel the darkness around him. When he looks into his own light, he sees himself as a god, but if he looks into the darkness around him, he feels impotent and ignorant. The darkness holds many terrors for him. It contains the Great Mother, whom he thinks he has abandoned, and he fears punishment for this at an unconscious level. His dilemma is acute. The light makes him feel safe, but he has realized he must enter the darkness if he is to be cured of his suffering and despair. To see in the dark, he must put out the light of his intellect and abandon self-control. This requires both courage and trust. The Hermit card is about man on the verge of surrendering to the Great Mother. He may remain in this position for a long period of time, summoning the courage to enter the darkness, but his movement is inevitable because he has nowhere else to go.

Card Ten, the Wheel of Fortune, represents the state of mind of women who are at the same stage as the Hermit. They have accepted the beliefs of patriarchal society up to now, and worshipped the father god. When man began to reject the father god, and turn to atheism, women reluctantly followed. Now they have nothing to believe in, but too little ego to see themselves as masters of the universe, as men do. Women can only now believe in Fate, that whether things go well or badly is a matter of luck, not divine order. To them, as well as to men, the universe is a soulless mechanism, which neither knows nor cares about their existence. Since they are far away from consciousness of the Great Mother, the voice of the intellect is stronger than their intuition. They are beginning to develop self-awareness, which involves suffering, because they become aware of all the pain involved in a patriarchal society. The next step for women is to stop surrendering to men, and gain self-awareness. It is as difficult a task as the Hermit's, but like him, they have nowhere else to go. One of the factors which will assist them is the inevitable "fall" of man from his position as lord of the universe. On the card we see the royal lion, which symbolizes the individual male ego, looking fearfully at the chasm he is about to be toppled into. Although change is inevitable, he does not wish it, and because he has lost his sense of spiritual purpose, he can only be afraid.

The next female card is Number Eleven, Strength, which is paired with the Hanged Man. On it we see a woman holding open the jaws of a lion. Later versions of the Tarot often depict a Herculean man on this card, because of patriarchal attitudes, but it is interesting to note that many recent versions have reinstated the female.

The strong woman is someone who has developed enough of an ego to be authoritative within male dominated society. More and more, we can see this type of woman emerging in our own world, because our Western society is largely at the midpoint of the cycle, where this card is placed. Although this type of woman is assertive and powerful, she still has many patriarchal ideas. She has observed the methods used by men to get their own way, and is copying them. What she wants for herself is also largely dictated by patriarchal values, so she is likely to seek for wealth, power and status, using her new found strength. Later on she will discover what it is she really wants. As she looks around at patriarchal females, she is likely to be angrily dismissive of them, because this has been her past for millennia. She will almost see herself as a man, and avoid choosing anything which smacks of traditional female roles. She is likely to be even more ruthless and competitive than the men around her, so she cannot be called a matercentric woman, but she may be seen that way by herself and others.

The Hanged Man, Number Twelve, parallels the Strength card. He is a Hermit who has finally abandoned his intellectual striving, and hangs between matercentric and patriarchal society. His enigmatic smile shows he is no longer suffering, but he is still not sure who he is. His conscious mind has relaxed its rigid grip, allowing messages, fears and long buried taboos to emerge from the darkness of his unconscious, but he is not yet a matercentric man. He has reversed his direction, and no longer aspires to "heavenly" patriarchal values, but the rope holding him shows he has not yet surrendered to women and the Great Mother. Though he is submissive, he has very little awareness of the Great Mother, and no idea what his next step might be. In his confusion, he may become a substitute patriarchal female, as the woman on the Strength card has become a substitute male, and behave in what he sees as a "feminine" way. Or he may become what patriarchal society deems a "wimp," a dropout, "hippy," "toyboy" or "New Ager." All these negative labels show he is no longer identifying with his traditional role as a male, and as far as patriarchal society is concerned, he is going backwards.

Card Number Thirteen is the Death card. It is the card which represents the Twentieth Century as a whole. In simple terms, this might be because we have the capacity and will to bring death to huge numbers of people, and because vast numbers have died through famine, war and ecological disaster. We have the wherewithal to destroy all life on this planet with our weapons of war, and the byproducts of our civilizations are killing the biosphere.

It is also, however, the card which denotes the death of patriarchal society. It has almost completely discredited itself; people no longer believe naively in "Progress" through Science, or that politicians and religious leaders have a premium on truth, so the old ways must die to make way for the new. This will not be an overnight process. Many people are still firmly patriarchal, and will require much more time before they are ready to become totally disenchanted with death, war and suffering. The ways in which they will choose to accept the death of patriarchy are manifold. Some will require an event of great magnitude before they are willing to change; death from starvation, or in some other highly painful and dramatic scenario. We will feel great pity for those who ask for such suffering, but it is entirely their choice, and must be respected. If we can help them, and they wish to accept our help, we can alleviate the suffering, but we cannot forcibly change their consciousness to ours. We can only point out that their way brings pain, and maybe there is a better one. If we do this, we must also remember that we do not have all the answers, and that we too have a great deal to learn.

Other people may "die" to patriarchal thinking in an apparently gentler way. The realization that they no longer wish to live in a world of conflict comes gradually, on an internal level. They may not know how to change what they see around them, but they do know that they are no longer in support of it. If they use violence to effect change, then they are still partly patriarchal, but there is essentially no necessity for this. It seems impossible, but all changes can be made inside, and then come into being in the external world. We can, for example, dream of a happier world, in which there is harmony. If we believe it can happen, it will happen, and if enough of us believe it, the whole basis of life on the planet will change. We still have to face the long buried pain which we have hidden from ourselves, believing we had no option but to live in a world of fear, but we do not have to meet any more suffering "out there". Those who have realized that they have brought suffering to others can also move into a happier world without the necessity of punishment for their "sins." There must be complete willingness for change to occur, and for the benefits of selfishness, insensitivity and "superiority" to be relinquished, but it can happen. What is required is forgiveness, of self and others, for all the mistakes that have occurred, and an acceptance of the Great Mother. This may occur in many forms, because we are all so different, but the content is the same. Love.

Card Fourteen, Temperance, shows an angel pouring liquid from one vase to another, equalizing the masculine and feminine forces, and bringing them into balance. No one would argue that a balanced world is what we are all now seeking, but we differ not only in the ways we wish to achieve an equal society, but in our definition of what it is. Our limited minds theorize about it, but our concepts are based on our present thinking. We look round and see what we think is wrong with present society, and devise a Utopia which will rectify its mistakes. Our ideas about positive aspects of a "perfect" world are also a product of our present consciousness, and must also be limited.

There have been many strides in achieving a "fairer" world in recent times. Men and women have looked at the position of disadvantaged people, such as the slaves in America, or the industrial poor in England, and poured their energies into achieving reform. More recently, there has been the Women's Liberation Movement, and pressure groups to eliminate oppression ranging from Apartheid in South Africa to the imprisonment of dissidents by repressive regimes. These reflect growing matercentric values, but as yet we have only just begun. We cannot stop at superficial changes, and we won't, because as our consciousness changes, even more ideas will occur to us. One of the icons which will inevitably fall is the simplistic concept that equality involves the power, wealth and opportunity which is available, being shared out amongst all people. This is not going to give us the spiritual growth we require. Not only does it decide for us what we might want a fair share of, based on patriarchal values, it looks at the world from a highly mechanistic and material viewpoint. We must abandon these ideas as anything other than temporary ones, and see that it all has to go in favor of disadvantaged people like women, and what they might want, before the balance can be restored. We realize that this idea will be opposed by many. Some, because they have been the "haves," not only fear the loss of their advantages, but the revenge of the "have nots," who will now be in what they see as a position of power over them. Their projection of their own behavior patterns onto others will not allow them to see that there is no necessity for the same abuses of power to occur. But to the extent that they both fear it, and welcome it as some sort of "atonement," it will happen.

The "have nots" may accept the idea of equality for a while. If you have had nothing but deprivation and cruelty for millennia, the prospect of half of whatever is going will seem attractive. If you add to that, the conditioning they have received from the rulers and religious leaders about "fairness," then they are even more likely to accept that equality is a good idea. It allows them to feel moral superiority over the "haves", which is good news for their growing ego.

However much people want an "equal" world, it is not an imminent proposition. At the level of our spiritual evolution, we must complete our cycle. This involves the restoration of the Great Mother to our consciousness, and experience of whatever it is that we have not yet learned. Men need the opportunity to serve others unselfishly, and feel the universe from a position inside its wholeness. They have had the opposite experience, of being served, and of seeing themselves as separate from the rest of creation. Women need the experience of allowing themselves to be loved and served, and of perceiving themselves as separate beings. They already know about the unity and interdependence of all life, and the subjective experience of this is familiar to them. Now, they require the view from outside that unity. Eventually, balance will be restored, and we will be able to achieve true equality, but for now, we have many lessons still to be learned before it can happen.

Card Fifteen is the Devil, the female card paired with the Tower. Normally, we think of the Devil as a man, but the figure in this case is clearly a woman, since she has breasts and wide hips. At her feet are two small females in bondage. Later Tarot packs often depict the devil as hermaphroditic, or show a male and female figure beneath her. The devil has clawed feet and bat wings, showing she comes from the night side, from the Great Mother. Her talons are those of an owl, which is not only a night creature but associated with Lilith, the first woman in Jewish mythology, who was replaced by Eve because she refused to be subservient to Adam. Many commentators on the Tarot claim that the devil/Lilith is imprisoning the humans, and that it is the "sins of the flesh" which bind them to the devil. This is not so. The human females on the card are true matercentric women. They are nude, so free and unrepressed by taboo and dogma. Lilith is also matercentric, but represented as the Devil because this is how patriarchal society sees her. Any woman who fails to assume the role given to her by patriarchal men must be evil incarnate, fit only for ostracism or death.

The Devil carries a sword in her left hand. It is to cut the bonds of the matercentric woman, and set her free. To begin with, because most of society is still patriarchal, the freed matercentric woman will appear to be very "devilish". She will seem selfish, undutiful and immoral, because she is able to put her own needs first some of the time. Society will fear her, and attempt to bring her back into line, using a combination of tactics including violence, disapproval and the fostering of guilt.

The Tower is card Number Sixteen. Usually it shows a tall building struck by lightning, but in the medieval pack, the sun is the agent of destruction. Patriarchal society, seeing the god as light and sun, has attempted to reach him by the use of the intellect. Their tower has risen so high that it has been scorched. Those at the top are the ones destroyed, and we see them falling to earth. The individual and collective egos of those who have aspired to rise above the Great Mother, and have travelled the furthest distance from her, are the first to have their carefully built hierarchies shattered. They have placed themselves above others, and looked down on them, but their systems have become too massive and unwieldy to sustain. They may not see their "fall" as a productive experience, but it is.

The sun and Tower also represent the imbalance between male/female, light/dark, conscious/unconscious in our society. Patriarchy has reached towards the light of consciousness until it has become unstable. The values of striving, achieving and conquering have been over valued, and we must re-orientate ourselves to include intuition, passivity and cooperation, the gifts of the Great Mother.

If we look at the Tower as a model of the way our society is structured, we see that it has become impossible to sustain. At the Tower's foundation are those people who are lowest in the pecking order. Most of them are either direct producers of goods and services, or, like mothers, essential to the continuation of human society. As we rise up the Tower, the people become more important, both to themselves and others, but they are not producers, however widely we define that term. They have little contact with the foundation of the Tower, either in terms of the people down there or the earth itself. Theirs is an intellectual, financial or power centered height, which divorces them from the rest of existence in an artificial way. The aspirations of most people are towards these elevated positions, because they have more status, power and financial reward attached to them. No one on the path of the god wants to be at the bottom, because it is seen as failure, so they either drop out of the system, or spend energy on "clawing their way to the top." The base becomes smaller and smaller, unable to sustain the growing numbers of those higher up, until it reaches the point where it can no longer support the Tower. It is too unstable and inflexible and has reached so high the sun has burned it.

Those who fall are rejoining the Great Mother, here pictured as the earth. If they are willing to see this as necessary for their own growth, they will turn onto the path of the Goddess. If they do not, they will try to climb the Tower again, using all the skills they have acquired in previous attempts. Eventually the penny will drop, but they may cause themselves unnecessary suffering before it does. The picture of failed financiers jumping from skyscrapers during the 1929 Crash is a potent image of this. Some will choose death rather than surrender.

The Star, card Seventeen, shows us a true matercentric woman living in a matercentric society, because she is nude. She holds two jugs, containing liquid which she is pouring onto the earth, healing it from the scars caused by its misuse during the patriarchal era. In the background is a tree, which was something revered by former matercentric societies. It symbolizes a new appreciation of the way in which Nature sustains us.

The Star represents the Great Mother, because it is only at night, when stars appear, that we can see the whole of the Universe. During the day we are blinded by the sun, the light of the intellect and the conscious mind. These are important, but equally important is our view at night, when the sun has disappeared, and we can use our night vision; our intuition and our sense of the wholeness of all creation.

The male card twinned with the Star is the Moon, card Eighteen. In it we see the return of the dog which was the companion of the Fool. If you reverse the spelling of "god," you get "dog." Man believed himself a god towards the end of the patriarchal era, but that world has now been destroyed. His status is reduced to that of a dog within a matercentric society.

The nature of man and dog are very similar. Both use a pecking order in which the strongest control the weakest. But a well trained dog is also the most loyal, friendly and hard working companion you could imagine. If it is badly trained, however, it can be vicious, an uncontrolled liability within a household where neither the dog nor the people are happy. Man is the same. If left to his own devices, he quickly begins to display aggression, and can be very harmful. Trained, especially through a wish to please his female "owner," he can be a magnificent creature; helpful, loyal and happy.

The presence of the Moon on this male card shows that man is now using intuition. He has allowed himself to be immersed in the waters of the unconscious, and returned to a relationship with the Great Mother. One of the dogs is shown handing some writing to a lobster which is emerging from the sea. Since the seas are controlled by the Moon, and both are symbols of the Great Mother, this suggests he is relinquishing the fruits of his conscious mind, in the shape of the writing, to Her. The last details on the card are the small buildings flanking the dogs. These represent the final remnants of patriarchal society. Unlike the Tower, they are low and insignificant, and later Tarot packs often show them as ruined. There is almost no trace left of the mighty world man constructed while he was on the path of the god.

Card Nineteen, the Sun, shows a small child on a horse. He is not attempting to control the animal at all; it can go wherever it wishes. We are now seeing the truly matercentric man. He is utterly content to be guided by his intuition, and has no need to exercise control. Patriarchal man felt it necessary to restrict and control everything around him, because he feared that chaos and loss would ensue if he did not, but this did not make him happy. He was afraid to relax his tight grip on the world and enjoy life. The child on the Sun card, however, is joyous, able to allow both himself and others total freedom. He is in the state Jesus Christ referred to when he said that we could not enter Heaven unless we become like little children.

The Sun shines down on this laughing child. Until now, the sun has been associated with the conscious mind and the intellect, and seen as the province of men. In a matercentric world, however, it is the man who is intuitive and passive, and the woman who is developing her intellect. So the sun which is giving such warmth and joy to the child is the matercentric woman. Man is happy to be guided by her, since she is more balanced in the use of her intellect than he was. She tempers everything with intuitive knowledge from the Great Mother, whereas he ignored it, and took society to the brink of destruction. The whole scene is one of growth and contentment, symbolized by the sunflowers blooming around the child.

The Day of Judgement is card Twenty. In order to understand it, we have to free ourselves of patriarchal thinking. What we read in the Bible about Judgement Day is orientated towards the punishment of "sin," and the rewarding of true believers with a place in heaven. We hear about the graves opening, and all souls being judged according to the rules of the god. Those who have broken the rules face a terrible fate. They will burn in everlasting flames. They are the "chaff," or the "goats." The "wheat" and the "sheep" will be with God. Though many Christians no longer believe in this scenario, others still do, and are hopeful of being "good" enough to escape Hell. Even those who consider themselves progressive often still accept the idea of a "sorting out." They may see Hell as a state of mind, or the flames as some sort of purification, but the idea of judgement remains. Some are "better" than others, and an external force i.e. the god, will decide which is which. After that, there will be rewards and punishments.

In a matercentric world there can be no judgement of this kind. We may make mistakes, but we can't "sin." Nor can we be judged by something outside us, since there is nothing outside us. We are all interconnected with each other and the Great Mother to form a whole. Only in a world of separate, disconnected parts, could anything outside us both judge and punish us, whether it's our fellow human beings or the deity. In the transition to a matercentric society, we may still continue to punish ourselves, or subconsciously give permission to others to do it, but by the time we have reached the level of development shown by this card, we will have gone beyond all such notions.

At the bottom of the Tarot card are three human figures. One is standing in a box, which symbolizes our material, three-dimensional world. Above is an Angel, who appears to be blowing a trumpet. We are being called to leave the earth to explore new worlds and new dimensions, because we have all, both men and women, resolved the paradox of personal and universal love. We feel and know that we are part of the universe, yet we are still individuals within its wholeness.

Card Twenty One, the World, and its male twin, the Fool, both end the cycle and begin a new one. Hopefully we have learned from our experiences, and can move on into new growth, new creativity. Though there is indeed "nothing new under the sun," we will be more aware of our unlimited nature after a completed revolution. The woman returns to the Great Mother, fully conscious that she is both part of the Great Mother and also separate from Her. The Fool is now aware that he is a fool.

INTUITION:
THE CHANNEL TO THE
GREAT MOTHER

The scientific world likes to believe that new inventions and ideas arise from logical thoughts, using the accumulated knowledge of the past as a bridge to reach further. The towering geniuses of the present stand on the shoulders of those who have gone before them, and apply their intellect to climb even higher.

To a certain extent this is true. Those who open the way before us allow us more freedom to build on their ideas. But they can also limit us by what they have chosen to explore. Over time, the areas they have researched become well traveled roads, which makes it difficult for others to even think about a different route, let alone begin the job of clearing away the entrance to a new way. Eventually we come to believe that the only paths are the ones we habitually use, and ignore all the others because we are unaware of their existence. We may feel that people who try to show us another road are mad, because we have closed down all our options except the ones "everybody" accepts.

One of our mind-sets is the belief that we solve problems and originate new ideas using our intellect. The education of scientists focuses on this, and ignores emotion and intuition as at best, irrelevant or peripheral, and at worst, harmful to the clarity of the logical approach. But the intellect can only work with the old, by laboriously reorganizing accepted wisdom—rearranging the furniture, so to speak. To bring in something completely new requires intuitive genius, which takes no time at all. As long as there is desire for an answer, it can arrive "out of the blue," usually when the logical mind is inactive. This process has been chronicled many times. Information is received in a dream, while listening to music, or walking in the countryside, when the intellect is not focused on the problem.

All of us, not only scientific geniuses, use our intuition in this way. When we are relaxed, we loosen the constraints of our "logical" mind. We can observe a stream of thoughts arising spontaneously, and moving through our minds in an uncontrolled way. We make connections, lead on from one image to another, without there being a sensible or logical thread between them. Most of these thoughts seem to be nonsense, and some are so disturbing that we immediately censor them, but others allow us occasionally to tune into new possibilities, plucked from the unknown. We may not feel that this kind of "daydreaming" is important to us, and see it as a holiday from the real work of our intellect, but it is in fact an avenue to growth. The feelings, images and ideas which come to us in this widened state of consciousness are a mixed bag of fears, speculations and creative explorations. If we compare the brain to a radio receiver, then this state allows us to tune into new stations; instead of constantly listening to Classical music, we dip into a little Hard Rock for a change, and see whether we like it enough to try some more. We can also contact those parts of us which are heavily judged against by the conscious mind, and become aware enough of our fears and hatreds to begin the process of reintegration. If we are not yet ready to do this, we slide away from such areas with the ease of constant practice, and may not even know we have encountered them.

Where do these inner images and thoughts come from? There are many theories which explain the source. In many societies, both "bad" thoughts and inspiration came from supernatural deities, and were seen as external. Christianity used The Devil to explain the inner temptation to evil deeds, and the god as the force for good. Both influenced man in a kind of spiritual tug-of-war, and both used rewards and punishments to influence him. Although these ideas have lost ground in Western society, there are still many people who excuse their "bad" behavior on the grounds of having been influenced by evil entities, and give the credit for "good" things to Angels, spiritual guides and the god.

Jung postulated the existence of a level of awareness below our personal unconscious which is a communal one, and called it the "collective unconscious." If we see our conscious mind as the part of an iceberg which is above the water, and our personal unconscious as the rest of the iceberg, the collective unconscious is the sea in which all the icebergs float, and from which they were all made. It contains the history of the Human race in it; all human vices and virtues, talents and inadequacies are part of us, through our link to the collective unconscious. In esoteric thought, this same idea is envisaged as the Akashic Records, which contain a memory of everything which has ever occurred.

Using this concept, we could explain all new ideas and impulses as having come from other people, who are cross fertilizing with us all the time, and allowing us to take relevant information from the collective pool. It would explain why new ideas appear simultaneously in different parts of the world, without any visible communication between people, and why we can observe phenomena like Fashion and mob violence, which are collective agreements to behave or dress in a particular way. It can even explain possession by "evil spirits" or "bad" thoughts, since at a deep level we may be vulnerable to their influence through our connection to the collective unconscious. However, it doesn't give a convincing explanation for the genius in Art, Music or Science, who is not re-synthesizing old knowledge, unless we accept that the individual manifesting such talent is merely expressing for us all what has been collectively produced by the whole human race.

The atheist scientist likes to think he is the only intelligent life in the universe, which is a depressing outlook when you see the mistakes made by scientists over the years. If we were to rely on them to get us out of the messes we have recently created, we would have very little hope of survival, despite their cleverness. According to the scientist, everything is an accident, a random mutation of the body or mind which promotes the survival of the species. New behaviors and ideas are products of our desire to adapt to and manipulate our environment, and are retained only if they do not threaten this. So our geniuses are variations from the norm, who may help us to survive better, or who may be of no use at all. The same goes for the imaginative ideas of the ordinary person. They are randomly generated by the brain, for possible future use in surviving biologically, which is our only imperative.

The patriarchal idea of a father god offers us an equally cheerless picture of the world. Here is a deity who is perfect, omniscient and omnipotent, yet he creates a life form in his own image which is so imperfect that it needs rules and punishments to keep it in line with his will. On top of this, the father god somehow allows an evil deity, the Devil, to exist which seduces us from the straight and narrow road to heaven, then blames us for listening to it. We become the battleground on which the opposing forces of good and evil play out an unending war, and we can never trust ourselves in case some of our ideas come from the wrong side. If we are on the side of "good," then we worry that our intuitions will cause harm to others, and sacrifice our impulses to be more than we already are in the name of "love." If we are on the "bad" side, we suppress any input which might cause us to lose out in the battle for our own personal survival and gain. Either way we are stuck, because we do not allow the free flow of information to help us move from our current position.

Intuition is a gift from the Great Mother, a glimpse into unlimited possibilities from which we can choose according to our will. This is not a reward for being good, though we can look at it this way if we choose to. The gift comes without conditions, and will not be withdrawn because of failure to meet some rules laid down by Her or Her representatives. If we do not want it, we can block it out, but it is always available if we allow it to reach us. Nor is the Great Mother a deity entirely outside us, as unlimited and unconditionally loving as we are limited and unloving. She is who we all are, collectively, when we do not place boundaries around us to fence ourselves off from the rest of Creation. That part of us which believes itself a completely separate individual fears Her, because it sees connectedness and unconditional love for others as leading to sacrifice and loss for the ego. It is afraid it will lose the gains it has made for itself alone.

Allowing love from the Great Mother to reach us through our intuition is not a trivial exercise. If we loosen the bonds of our conscious mind, we will experience many changes, as a result of the flood of information coming to us from the Goddess and from our repressed emotions and thoughts. For some it will be the way to a total transformation. The person they were will die, to be replaced by a larger self. If this happens quickly, or in an situation where there is no understanding or help available, the result can be what society defines as madness. Many geniuses have been regarded as insane because of the constant flood of ideas reaching them via their intuition. Often they had no way of slowing this flow once it began. They made manic attempts to act on it all, or attempted to pass the information to other people, who either did not understand it or were frightened by it. Or they mixed intuitive knowledge with personal desires and fears. Having experienced, however briefly, a sense of a self which was larger than the everyday one, they became convinced they were a god, or perhaps a reincarnation of Mohammed, sent to save mankind. They did not realize that if they were god, so is everyone else, because their ego wanted to believe in their supposed unique divinity. This, we have to quickly say, is a completely different story from actually being a clear and powerful channel for the Great Mother, though it may look similar from the outside.

When we venture into the dark underworld of the unknown, we meet ourselves. We encounter the Great Mother, who is unconditional love. Since we are part of Her, our bliss when we feel Her is a recognition of how it used to be when we were in paradise, still strongly connected to Her and to each other. We feel no barriers, no fear; only joy and happiness. Even a transient flash of this reconnection can act as an amazing catalyst in someone's life. Having felt love from the Great Mother, they can never be quite the same again. They may interpret their experience in terms of the particular religion they follow, and see visions of people and deities from it, but the form is irrelevant. However briefly, they have opened up.

The unknown also contains those parts of us which have been eliminated from our consciousness, because they have been judged against. We have judged against the Great Mother too, of course. We may believe that we are inferior beings, unfit to be anything other than what we already are, yet still unconsciously yearn for Her. But there are also forgotten longings, guilt and fears in the darkness.

If we live in a patriarchal society which forces us to behave in particular ways, and brainwashes us into "correct" behavior, our impulses to be different from this do not disappear. They go underground, and we may not be aware of them at all. A man, for example, who has been told that he must not lie, steal, kill or rape, may behave in an extremely law abiding way. His fear of punishment prevents him from either acknowledging his desires to do all these things, or from acting on them. He may believe himself to be a paragon of society, destined for Heaven when he dies. He will probably also be highly judgmental of all those who do not behave as he does, but "give in to" their antisocial impulses. If he is in a position to do so, he will punish transgressors in an extremely emotional and angry way. They are bad and he is good because he controls himself, so they must suffer as well as be prevented from harming others.

Such a man, who still has individual desires he has not fulfilled, needs the voyage into his personal underworld to meet them. If he does not do this, he merely postpones the inevitable. He represses his desires, but they are still there. It's something like sitting on a large monster in a sealed container. Only by remaining vigilant can the man ensure that the monster does not escape and wreak havoc in the world. Many tightly controlled men are convinced that this would happen if they allowed their feelings free expression. Unleashed, they would kill or otherwise harm everything in their path. They experience this as further pressure to control themselves.

If all of us stopped sitting on our own personal monsters one day, it's possible that there would be total mayhem. Some of our feelings and desires are pretty angry about being shut in a dark cupboard for millennia. They might overwhelm the conscious personality and run riot. Other feelings would not rush out, but huddle fearfully in the darkness, because any previous attempts at movement have been met with violent subjugation. They would require substantial evidence that the same thing was not likely to happen again. We can see the same phenomenon in everyday life. A child who has been repeatedly beaten by adults does not respond with instant acceptance when given help by a kinder person. She is likely to fear that this is a temporary lull in her misery, and be very wary. In time she may completely lose her fear, but it is a slow process. So it would be if we were to allow some of our hidden desires to emerge, because of our painful memories.

If we do not relax our conscious control and contact our own hidden parts, the monster does not remain patiently in the container. It tunnels underground, and pops up in our life as other people. They home in on us, exhibiting behavior designed to trigger off our release. John Smith, for example, is an entirely worthy individual; a regular churchgoer, successful businessman and faithful husband. He has no inkling of the monster. When he finds that his brother-in-law has two mistresses, he is apoplectic with fury, and bans him from the house. His strong feelings are a message to him that he should look at himself a little closer, but he doesn't. As far as he is concerned, his brother-in-law is "bad" and he does not realize that his self-righteous fury is in direct proportion to his unconscious fear that this is something he might wish to do, or has been guilty of in the past. At a conscious level, he feels safe from ever behaving in this way, but his anger shows us that it's not quite so simple. He may be exhibiting "the fanaticism of the recently converted," or refusing to see that deep down he too would like two mistresses.

We react to the people in our personal life drama as if they are completely outside us. They are not. We are all interconnected. Those relationships and situations we need for our growth have a habit of catching up with us, whether we like it or not. We have an impulse to grow, to extend ourselves because of our very nature as children of the Great Mother. This involves us in an urge to explore the unknown. For each of us, that has a different form. Most men will be required, by their own unconscious desire to return to the Great Mother, to explore unconditional love for others; instead of looking ever outward for the answer to the riddle of creation, they will look in. They will have to begin the process of redeveloping their intuition, and respond to their increasing desires to help and serve others. Most women will have to accept their inner drive towards individual free will, after millennia of feeling that to desire anything other than the happiness of others is selfish and unwomanly. For all of this we require trust in the Great Mother.

How do you tell whether an impulse coming from within you is the voice of the Great Mother, or whether it is the ego's? This causes problems for people who wish to "do the right thing," and worry that they can't tell the difference between impulses for "good" and mad, bad or dangerous ones.

If we consider that it is equally valid to have a sense of a separate self and an awareness of being part of All That Is, then it is not "bad" to be spoken to by the ego. We have to acknowledge all the parts of us. To deny individual free will is not necessary. Nor must we deny our connection to the Great Mother. If we balance those two voices inside us, that of the ego, and that of the Great Mother, then we become whole. So we can listen to both. Men, by and large, have paid attention only to the promptings of the separate ego, and ignored the voice of the Great Mother. This has led them into self-centered behavior, and produced a capacity for cruelty which can only come from blocking out awareness that the rest of creation is linked to them. They see people and the planet as wholly outside them, so it becomes acceptable to hurt them. Women, in contrast, have largely listened to the Great Mother, and not the ego. They feel their connection to others, thus diminishing their willingness to cause harm.

Once we move onto the path of the Goddess, there will be change. Men who have oppressed both other men and women will find that the voice of the Great Mother is impossible to ignore. Though the ego will still speak to them about loss if they listen to Her, its voice will become weaker as it realizes that no sacrifice is involved. The man will be reassured by his experience of joy when even small movements are made towards unconditional love, encouraging him to listen even more. Women will find that the catastrophes they imagined would happen should they refuse to remain slaves, never materialize. Although they may take time to lose fear that men are suddenly going to switch back to oppressing them, they will find that men's new responsiveness to them is here to stay. This will encourage them to continue to develop their individual free will without the terror of the past being recreated.

There are no rules about these inner voices, just as there are no rules about behavior. If we listen to what their message is, we will eventually become whole, though we may not act on what they suggest. Just because I have an impulse to steal does not make it the right action for me, but I must accept that part of me feels like doing this. It is the suppression of desires and feelings in the first place which has caused us difficulties, even though it may seem the only possible action. A man on the path of the god, for example, may be forced to obey laws which give the women around him some freedoms. In his heart of hearts he feels they should be his slaves, but he has to hide this, both in his behavior, and from his conscious mind. He does not really know he feels this way. Eventually the pressure of his need is too great, and he becomes a secret rapist, terrorizing women while in his "normal life" he is a devoted husband. It would have been better for him to acknowledge his desires and allow himself to feel his anger at having to suppress them. Perhaps he could have found a woman who still wished to be a slave, and avoided the horrendous build up of denial which resulted in violence.

A woman who is changing paths may experience difficulties if she denies her inner drives. She may wish to be treated as more than a second class citizen, yet still be in a largely patriarchal society. She tells herself that her desire is not possible, but she still secretly possesses it. Underneath her surface rationalizations, which enable her to operate as a patriarchal woman, she is burning with anger and despair. Because she is unlikely to turn outwards with these emotions, and attack men, they fester inside her, leading to depression, and diseases like cancer. If she had acknowledged and accepted her desires, without guilt and fear, this would not have happened. Eventually she would have been totally sure that it was what she wanted, and reality in her vicinity would have changed to accommodate her wishes. Her unconscious denial that what she wanted was possible or "good" had prevented her dearest wishes coming true. Once the denial disappeared, because she unreservedly accepted her desires, consciously and fully, life supported her, and granted them.

It cannot be said too strongly that we must allow ourselves to be who we are. Many thought systems encourage us to have desires and goals which do not fit us. We may aspire to ideals of nobility and selflessness which are contrary to some of our feelings. Not only does this produce repression of those parts of us which refuse to go along with these aspirations, it also leads to projection of these parts on others, inner unhappiness and what we might call evil. As Buddhists say, we must be in "the Now." This involves acknowledging all parts of us, and accepting them without condemnation. Only external morality tells us these aspects of us are "bad," which implies there is only one way for everyone to behave, only one way to grow. As long as we allow others to decide which side of our personality is "light" and which is "dark," we will continue to hide bits of us from ourselves. Like Hercules, we must drag the many headed Hydra into the light of consciousness, where it will die, as the fear of our "dark" side will die when we allow it to surface, and listen to its needs with compassion and love.

Once we have begun to reclaim ourselves, listening to and feeling with our lost parts will bring us closer to balance and wholeness. They may be angry or in pain, so it is not merely a cerebral task. It will take time, for most people, but it will eventually bring harmony and joy. If we accept help from the Great Mother, and open to intuition, the process becomes easier. She is always ready to assist us, but we often refuse to ask because we fear what might happen as a result. As we have said before, those who have given most space to the ego fear personal loss; those who have given little space to the ego fear that they will lose the love of others, and become "selfish" or tyrannical. These fears should not be ignored, but felt and respected until reassurance comes. Then we can act without internal conflict.

Although we parade logic and reason as being the best guide to behavior, we do not use them as often as we think we do. Emotion, particularly denied emotion, plays a large part in our decision making processes. If we add to that, our belief that we live in a hostile universe, in which conflict is inevitable, we can see that our lives are anything but "reasonable." Our House of Commons gives us a superb example of how decisions are made. Firstly, we have a Government and Opposition, which means that most of the time, a Labor M.P. is never going to agree with a Conservative M.P., whatever the rationality of the situation. If we add to that, the fact that politicians are as interested in power as in making a sound decision, we move even further from logic. Self interest does not make for unbiased decisions, especially when an election is on the horizon. Individually and collectively, the Members of the House of Commons are riddled with prejudices and fixed ideas which have nothing to do with objective fact, however cleverly they argue their case on that basis. They also lack full knowledge about a particular issue, partly because their minds refuse to allow them to consider all that could be relevant, and partly because they are not objective thinkers, but seekers after power.

This does not make politicians in England "bad" people. They are only as limited and muddled as the rest of us. But they have chosen an occupation in which they make decisions affecting millions of lives. Though they may vary in their altruism and perceptiveness, they still feel that somehow they are capable of making "the right decision," for us all. We in our turn allow this to happen.

We have other beliefs which prevent us from seeing clearly, most of which we have acquired from our parents and society in general. Some of these we may never question. Others are replaced as we outgrow them, but we never lose the need to surround ourselves with ready-made explanations of how the world works, to impose a structure on it. The model of reality in this book is no exception. Infinity is too much for us to comprehend in its entirety, so we select a chunk and call it the whole. We replace true, intuitive Knowledge with faith and belief. If some of our beliefs rest on shaky foundations, we use our intellect to search for information to support them. This is quite easy to do, because there is a vast amount available. We are able to pick out facts that support our beliefs and ignore the rest. The truth is that we do not arrive at our beliefs by looking clear eyed at the facts available, and reaching a sensible conclusion. Our beliefs often fly in the face of evidence, and are the motivating force for selecting information, not the other way round. We hang on to them for safety, and only relinquish them when our inner consciousness is ready to change. Our beliefs evolve as we do.

Politicians, religious leaders and scientists trade on our need for beliefs by which to structure our life. They offer us a ready-made package which we can "buy." This removes the uncertainty about what is right and wrong in a given situation, and they assure us that if we follow their guidelines we will be in heaven, whether that is a spiritual or material one. A world without structure and rules seems frightening to most people. Often they will fall into the hands of a rigid system because of that fear. New religions which regulate every aspect of life have mushroomed in recent years, as new matercentric ideas of free choice permeate society and frighten some people. Those who join such sects are comforted by the certainties of the guru or leader, and are willing to sacrifice everything for this kind of security, even their families. Societies in which everyone knows their place and keeps to it offer the same kind of safety. The known and explained is preferable to free choice, even if your life in such a world is a relatively unpleasant one. You know where you are.

We seem to be contradicting ourselves here, because we have also said that the speed of change, and of life in general within a patriarchal society is unhealthy. So why are we not endorsing rapid change as a way of effecting the breakdown of patriarchal structures and rigid belief systems? Again, form is irrelevant, and content is all. Change imposed from outside is different from change brought about by a new willingness to grow. In an ideal world, no one will want to force alterations in behavior on others, or judge them because they wish to be different. The movement towards the Great Mother will produce inner change, which will reflect in the dissolution of fixed systems that have outlived their usefulness. Those who still wish to join together in clinging to them, will not be allowed to force them on others who do not want this. If we find that others can still make us do things we do not wish to do, then we will have to go inside to find out why, and ask for help from the Great Mother in eliminating our denials.

Bill: My own life has taught me the mistake of believing that decisions are intellectually based. I used to think of myself as a thinker, an intellectual sort of person, until one day it dawned on me that I often argued points which couldn't be sustained logically. My beliefs and opinions had very little to do with logic and reason.

My family—my father in particular—and my society, brought me up to be what can only be described as a male chauvinist pig. It was an attitude I never questioned, even when it led to the breakdown of the first serious relationship I had as a young man. By chance I then read a book called The First Sex, *by Elisabeth Gould Davis. I can't say that it was a wonderful book, and it certainly showed no intellectual brilliance, but the content appealed to something very strong within me. My views on women changed overnight, and I began to read Women's Liberation books. None of them contained what I was looking for; nor has any book since that time. I realized that if I wanted to read the book I was searching for, I would have to write it myself. Once I found Pamela was as interested as I was, it became possible.*

Reading through the reams of material on the subject of life, the universe and everything, I found that certain ideas excited me and others left me cold. Pamela says that a true statement goes "boing" inside her in the same way. It has nothing to do with the intellectual rigor of the argument, and everything to do with some other way of discriminating, a different kind of intelligence. I began to realize that something below my conscious awareness was guiding me, directing me to certain books, and using this feeling of "truth" to show me which ideas would assist me on my own path. Obviously, other people would be directed to concepts which are right for them.

This guiding intelligence, I eventually realized, is my intuition, and I have followed it all my life, though not all of the time. Any occasion on which I have allowed my intellect to make decisions, has always led to disaster. When I was a child, it caused me some unhappiness, because what it told me was different from the views held by my family and society, but I was stubborn enough to listen, and follow its guidance. It always proved itself correct for me.

The intuition is the "still small voice," referred to in the Bible. In most people, it is swamped by conditioning, until we almost believe it does not exist. But it is the voice of our Creator, the Great Mother. This produces a paradox for religiously inclined people. We are supposed to live our lives according to the wishes of our Creator, yet the channel that lets us contact her is feared, ridiculed, or seen as nonexistent. We are told by people like ourselves what it is She wishes us to do, and threatened with punishment if we do not obey. Only since matercentric ideas have begun to change the rigidity of patriarchal religions, have any ideas filtered through that we are all part of the Creator, and can contact "him" ourselves. Such notions, believed by various sects like the Cathars in medieval times, led to their wholesale extermination by the Catholic Church on the grounds that they were heretics. The real reason they were killed, of course, was that they threatened the temporal and spiritual power of the Church hierarchy. Power was seen to come down from the god, via the Pope, to the lesser ranks of the clergy. You were not allowed to marry, be buried, or be christened etc., without the offices of a priest. Nor could you worship alone. You had no opportunity to find your own way to your own truth, because it had already been decided for you. Even minor variations from the norm were forbidden.

Despite all this, the Creator can still influence us and our religious leaders by imparting Her wisdom disguised as dogma. When we allow it, our religious beliefs evolve to become more in tune with unconditional love. If this did not happen, we would sink into a black hole of negativity, with no hope of escape.

None of us has ever left the Great Mother, though we may think we have. She is still protecting us, and preventing us from becoming stuck forever in our mistakes. Much to the consternation of ruthless patriarchal leaders, they can never achieve a society in which everyone is totally obedient. Ideas always arise which reflect desire for change. If these come from the poor and powerless, they are relatively easy to suppress, but if enough people desire the change, even the most violent and genocidal ruler cannot hope to prevent it. When ideas arise within the ruling elite, then movement is swifter, since the power to effect alterations is greater.

It is a truism to say that people can be killed but ideas live on. If human consciousness desires something, it will happen, whatever the opponents of the idea do to prevent it. Though patriarchal men attempted to eliminate Wicca, for example, and killed vast numbers of women as witches, they were not successful. The practice of the Old Religion lived on, secretly, until such a time as it could gain wider acceptance. The same is true of other ideas. After the First World War, Germany was subjected to the humiliating Treaty of Versailles. This in no way crushed the desires of many to expand "The Fatherland," and added feelings of anger to those of failure. It is no exaggeration to say that the figure of Hitler, who sought to conquer other nations, represented the collective will of those Germans who wished to see their country achieve European domination. The systematic extermination of the Jews, who were the scapegoats for German problems, and representative of "the other," to Germans, were again killed by this collective will, which was strong enough to ignore the will of those who disagreed. Because most of the genocidal activities took place in secret, it does not mean that Hitler and his immediate colleagues were solely responsible; at an unconscious level, Germany accepted and condoned this activity. We are not saying this to sit in judgment on Germany, but because the denial of collective responsibility leads to further suffering. Given the same situation, we may have behaved in exactly the same way as Germany. Its behavior is a mirror for us to see ourselves and learn valuable lessons.

This is a particular example of a truth which has universal application. Our personal and collective past must be acknowledged and allowed to bring itself up to date. If men, for example, begin to lose their desire for enslaving and suppressing women, they may find it difficult to cope with the backlog of pain then presented to them by women. If they say simplistic things like—"that was in the past, it's different now," they will miss out on a vital step in their evolution. One of the things they must do is to learn to respond at an emotional level. An individual woman is not just herself. She represents all the oppression, pain and suffering experienced by all the women she is in emotional contact with, which crosses racial, age and time barriers. She may be enjoying "equal" treatment, yet feel strong ties to those she reads about in books, who did not enjoy her freedom. The man, in his turn, represents the men who have inflicted this pain. If he is in a relationship with a woman who wishes to release this reservoir of human pain and suffering by empathizing with it and talking about it, it is something he has chosen. He can help her and himself in a way which transcends time, by becoming emotionally responsive to the material she gives him. As we have said before, time is not as simple as we think it is. Through his unconditional love for those he has oppressed in the past, man undoes his mistakes. One man is all men. Whether we explain this by saying that the man has had past lives in which he was cruel and selfish, or whether we look to the collective unconscious for an explanation, doesn't matter at all. A man needs to feel love for those who did not receive it in the past. Listening to and responding with the emotions of a woman who is in contact with past pain is vital to him. In this way, he unravels time, and allows himself to move on. If he refuses, saying that he does not want to hear, then he slows his movement towards the Great Mother. This is currently a popular stance with many men, who do not wish to acknowledge the past, or who do not have the emotional capacity, as yet, to respond. Their impatience when a woman wishes to talk about past injustices, or the suffering endured by women in other countries, is a clear indication of this. Nor are men the only ones who are unwilling. Many women have also cut themselves off from the past, and are not yet ready to process these emotions. At this point, we have to reiterate our perennial reminder about form. Not everyone who wishes to discuss past oppression is using this to clear emotions and grow. Use your intuition to guide you as to what is really going on. Some people have the trick of "bringing up the past," to engender guilt, punish someone for their "sins," or in order to eliminate the present time from their lives.

The Bible states the necessity of integrating the past quite clearly. It talks about the sins of the fathers being visited on the sons unto the seventh generation. Patriarchal religion interpreted this as punishment from the god which was so vindictive that it didn't stop at the guilty, but punished innocent descendants as well. If we look at it again, we can see that it shows once again our interconnection, in this case, through time. The repercussions of our actions from the past can be "visited on" i.e. released, by the present generation. Parts of the human race which live in what we see as the past, i.e. they're long dead people, are still connected to us. Giving them the chance of release, through our current empathy and connectedness, frees all of us, since we are all in contact. This seems a complicated and improbable idea, but it is nevertheless true. If we think of time as a place, it makes it easier. We can envisage responding to the plight of slaves in the country of Ogagnol, who are suffering now, because we feel that there is something that we can do. We don't feel that way about societies and people who have crumbled into dust. Yet they still exist and can be helped, because time does not cut us off from them in the way we think it does. It lives in us still, in ways we do not fully understand. We can undo the past mistakes of humanity if we choose to, just as we can rectify a fault in a house we built ten years ago.

Our Creator gives us the truth we need now, through our intuition. This may be something which is for us alone, for a large group, or for all. We need different beliefs at different stages of our evolution, not because we are stupid or inferior to others, but because we are unique, and need to evolve in a way which best fits us. Although we criticize patriarchal society, we know that it is pointless to attempt to change people's attitudes by argument. We can disseminate information to those who wish to hear, and hope it will be of use, but we have to recognize that our ideas will not appeal to everyone. The people who listen to what we have to say will be those who are already converted, or ripe for a change. Many patriarchal people are perfectly willing to die rather than relinquish their beliefs, and in some cases would like everyone else to die as well. Despite the fact that this causes suffering for themselves and others, they are not likely to abandon their ideas until they realize that pain is unnecessary. This may take a long, long, time.

The fact that truth is not the same for everyone causes confusion in society. Many people believe that a belief system which works for someone else will work for them, and we see fashions in ideas which are both helpful and unhelpful. The helpful aspect is that we are given more choice. The media present us with so many new ideas every day, that we have the opportunity to select in a way which was impossible even twenty years ago. Dietary systems, health care, political ideology, spiritual ideas; there is so much on offer that sometimes we feel like a small child in a sweet shop, unable to choose from the glittering array. This is not helped by the fact that patriarchal values infiltrate many of these ideas. We are told, as we were by the Christian Church, that only this truth is true, and all the others are false. This produces the same old fears. If I don't eat this way, think this way, dress this way or behave this way, I am "bad," incorrect, stupid, or just plain old fashioned. When the desire for change arises, we may run around from one new philosophy to the next, despairing of ever finding the one which is "true," and which will do to us what its authors claim—the "This book will change your Life" syndrome.

It's great that there are so many new ideas, and that the world no longer insists on total conformity. But we are in danger of doing the same old thing—looking to someone outside us to make our decisions, and feeling guilt and fear because we are different. The new orthodoxies are no better than the old if they look down on those who disagree, and insist that they have a premium on goodness and truth. A medieval Christian, who tells you that it is evil to dance on a Sunday, has the same consciousness as a modern day vegetarian who despises all those who eat meat. There has only been a form change. The spirit of condemnation and superiority, and the idea that there is one "right" way to be, is the same.

There is a truth for us all, though we may share it with others. We may need to try on a fair number of the new ideas before we find one which fits us. If it feels right, and comfortable, then it is right. The person next door may have chosen something completely different, which is right for him. Only our patriarchal thinking stops us from seeing this, and we impose our views and beliefs on others as if they are the only ones which will work. All of us need the freedom to choose who to be, and the right to take the consequences of our choices. It is our only way to learn and evolve.

Life in patriarchal society is much easier if you share the same belief system as everyone else. Being "different" is lonely and often dangerous, because of intolerance and fear. You need to be courageous if you are to trust your intuition enough to deviate from the norm, because so many people have been persecuted, murdered, incarcerated or ostracized for their beliefs. For this reason, many parents socialize their children into acceptance of the status quo, not because they particularly like it, but because they fear for their fate if they are in any way "odd." This perpetuates the cycle of conformity. Some groups take pride in their ability to brainwash children. The

Jesuits, for example, are reputed to have said, "Give us a child until he is seven years old, and he will be ours for life."

We feel unable to throw off our conditioned ideas for many reasons. It is difficult, for example, to cope with constant persecution for a particular belief, and we may abandon it for a quiet life. But subtler pressures are just as tough to resist. Since we need other people, it is doubly difficult to accept love and help from them, yet refuse to conform to their wishes. Sometimes, we can feel ourselves the only sane person in a madhouse, and despair of ever finding someone who thinks and feels as we do, or is willing to love us as we really are. Our pressure on ourselves and each other to fit a narrow mold has driven us crazy, but since we are all mad, no one really notices.

One of the effects of allowing people more freedom to follow their intuition, rather than dogma, is that children will become happier as we change to a matercentric society. At present, although society pays lip service to the importance of mothering, it regards it as one of the lowest status occupations. Mothers have traditionally had no rights and massive responsibilities. They had to accept the dictates of the male god, male-oriented rules, and the superiority of the father of the family. Lack of economic independence and respect from men, has given them few options when raising children. Though they usually felt love for their offspring, theirs has been an artificial situation. Their job has been to nurture children on behalf of patriarchal society. This has involved no say in the number of children they bore, and a long list of behaviors which they were supposed to inculcate in the child. Since male children are quite likely to love the mother who loves them, the process has also involved a mother in seeing that love crushed by society in the name of masculinity. A boy has been encouraged from an early age to "break free" from his mother's apron strings, and identify with the general contempt for women which society promotes. In doing this he becomes "a man." The only fate foreseeable for her daughters was the same oppression she herself experienced. Until recently, most women have not questioned their role as the servant of man and his ideas. Though they may have been unhappy about raising sons to be killed on battlefields, and daughters to die in childbirth, by and large they had internalized patriarchal values. They attempted to love their children on the one hand, yet indoctrinate them on the other.

Pamela: Coming into contact with mothers from other cultures has shown me more about past oppression than books ever could. In a Women's Refuge, I was asked to think of a solution to a seemingly insuperable problem. An Indian woman had come into the house because of violence by her husband which had nearly killed her. With her was a son of six and a daughter of four. The son was the problem. He constantly hit all the children smaller than himself. When the mothers intervened, he bit and kicked them. His own mother explained that she could do nothing to prevent his behavior, because according to the rules of her society, women were not allowed to tell men what to do, not even small and vicious boys. Although she had broken the rules of her society by leaving her husband, she could not overcome her conditioning in this area.

So her son felt free to behave in the same way as his father. We found no wonderful magic wand, I have to report. Though the European women attempted to give love and support to the boy, he interpreted this as womanly weakness, and intensified his violence. Eventually, we had to ask his mother to move, because no solution could be found other than returning his violence, and no one, understandably, was willing to do this.

When we look at present society, we see that women are generally more interested in people, children and animals; living things. Even when they move out of the home into the workplace, they tend to choose jobs which involve nurturing or interacting with people. Men, in contrast, seem to prefer inanimate things, which is why they have to structure society according to external rules and laws. Even in so-called "free" countries, the Law is more important than the person, except when an individual has enough wealth or power to sidestep it.

To make matters worse, men's lack of emotional and intuitive development means that they cannot work with others in an egalitarian way. They feel the need to know where they are in the pecking order, so that it is clear who is allowed to tell them what to do. Seeing everyone in terms of their relative status inevitably leads to power struggles, since the ego is striving to gain for itself. The only way this seems possible, is by taking something from someone else, whether this is power, status or money. These "things," some of which are intangible representations of a belief in scarcity, satisfy ego needs. Patriarchal people firmly believe that there is only a fixed amount of everything. In order to have more of what they want, someone must have less, and most of the energies of dominant patriarchal men are poured into taking "more than their fair share." This can only happen if others share their belief that there is only a certain amount of something available, and see themselves as not having enough power to get an equal portion. The world then becomes a place where you must grab what you can before someone else gets in first. When you've grabbed your bit, you must then guard it with your life against predators. Men in positions of power spend a high proportion of their time in erecting defenses as a result of this way of seeing the world. They must guard against the enemy within the organization—young men who want to topple them from their position of power—and the enemy without—anything from rapacious tax collectors to burglars.

Believe it or not. all of this comes from seeing the world as composed of dead "things," without life, growth, or evolutionary capacity. Even people are not excepted. One has only to listen to a politician discussing economic policies, to see that populations are as inanimate in his perception as the building in which he works. The employer who sacks large numbers of his work force during a recession, may feel that he has no other option, but his ability to do this is entirely based on his inner belief that people are things.

The further away he gets from his work-force in terms of the size of his organization, the easier it becomes for him. Callousness towards employees in a far flung branch of your organization is more possible than when you have become intimate with the people concerned. Of course, some men can be just as capable of regarding human beings as ciphers when they know them well. However, it usually produces a feeling of discomfort in even the most hardened of patriarchal men if they have to give the boot to Bloggs, who has a widowed mother, and is struggling to find the money to pay for a vital operation to save his child's sight. Usually they still go through with this, and push the feeling of unease away because, as they see it, they have no choice.

Nothing is a thing. Everything has consciousness, even if it is one which we cannot understand. This realization will come to men when they allow their intuition to guide them. They will see that the universe is composed of living matter, all of which wishes to be. Looked at from a position outside of creation, patriarchal men can only see the world and everything in it as external to them, without life. The ability to manipulate people and the planet comes from this perception. To an entirely patriarchal man, the only living entity is himself. Everything else must therefore be for his use. What else could it be for, since if he is all that exists, he must be god, and he must have created everything and have power over it all.

This is an extreme, of course. Very few men have lost their feeling of connectedness to this extent. Most feel the existence of people to some degree, though the most patriarchal will still regard wife and children as extensions of themselves, rather than independent beings. But there are enough men in positions of power, who regard the world as their plaything, to cause mass distress. They feel justified in their disregard for others as a factor in their plans, because they have no feelings for them. This allows them to send soldiers to certain death in battle, slaughter civilian populations, and indulge in the usual crimes of murder, rape and intimidation. The anger they feel when prevented from indulging in these activities, and the satisfaction they experience when no one can, is entirely connected to the needs of the ego. There is no point in appealing to such a person's humanitarian feelings, because they do not, as yet, exist. Irresponsible and selfish behavior springs from their inability to feel love for others, and respond to them. At the other extreme, we find those people who are so sensitive and connected to others that they never say no to any request, in case they cause pain, or they feel too powerless to resist being pushed around. Again, it is unbalanced. There is very little to be gained from encouraging such a person to choose an activity which pleases or benefits no one but themselves. As yet, they have too little ego or recognition of personal power. When both of the people in these extreme positions are ready to change, they will do so. All we can do, in the meantime, is to use our fallible systems of law and social control to even up the situation, and protect those with a small ego from those who would exploit them. We manifestly fail to do this, since we do not recognize that preventing oppression does not cure the desire to indulge in it nor the willingness to endure it.

At the risk of sounding totally judgmental, we have to point out that almost all criminals, murderers, rapists, child molesters, soldiers, muggers, secret policemen, concentration camp commanders, arms manufacturers, dictators, torturers and bigots are male. If we leave out any element of condemnation, it is clear that it is men who pose the greatest threat to happiness for most people. Though they may have the ability to organize and control people, which women have little experience of, it could be said that they couldn't make a worse job of running the world if they tried. Not only are women oppressed, but most men are too. Our beautiful planet has been ravaged by war, the exploitation of its soil and massive pollution. We have the capacity to render it uninhabitable through nuclear accidents or nuclear warfare.

So far, so good. Millions of people are talking about the problems of the environment, and the oppression still found in many countries. There is a general consensus on the part of many Western men that women, the planet, black people etc., should be given more respect and consideration. Some have fully accepted that equality for all is the goal. Division of power and the sharing of responsibility for all decisions is aimed at, with both men and women, for example, participating in all aspects of life.

This is the current "New Age" ideal; very comforting for men who have "had it all," because they go from having had all the cake to having half of it. It is also relatively unthreatening for women, who have neither the confidence to say, "my turn," nor the intuitive knowledge to see that a matercentric society is necessary for human evolution to continue. We cannot stop at some invisible middle point when we have lessons still to learn. The pendulum of change will swing past it. But men fear a world guided by women because of the way that they abused others when going through their own process of ego development. They fear that women will behave in the same way, which some may do initially, having been conditioned by patriarchal society into believing that men's way is the only one possible. Also, they cannot see how women could manage it, since so few of them seem capable of tuning their video in, let alone ruling the planet. Women fear a matercentric society too, and for some of he same reasons. They are new girls on the job, and are heavily marked by millennia of being told that they are here merely to help and serve others. They will start out wanting to be "fair and equitable" too. Then they will realize, through their connection to the Great Mother, that the best way for all is for men to be allowed to serve society and learn about love and responsiveness. The only way that this can happen is for society to become matercentric. As Jesus prophesied, the meek will indeed inherit the earth, but it will be in order to lose subservience and gain a feeling of independent value. When that has happened, we can achieve balance, because neither men nor women, logic or feelings, intuition or materialism will dominate.

This is not the same as perfection. Perfection implies lack of movement, of having reached a goal, so there is nothing more to do. It is the state envisaged by many Christians as Heaven. Consciousness will never cease evolving, so there will always be new possibilities, which of course brings in the chance of making mistakes. Integrating new ideas can be achieved without disharmony and imbalance, but only if we look at the whole, and disregard nothing. As soon as we begin valuing some people or things as superior to others, we introduce instability. Though we are free to move towards what we want, and away from what we do not want, this does not imply that some are "good" and some are "bad." The Great Mother asks us to accept all of ourselves and become whole. We can't do this on an outer level until the inner process occurs first. If we balance ourselves, then society cannot fail to follow suit. Those who refuse to grow may well choose another reality in which they can continue to be out of harmony, but we will not be part of it.

Women, unlike men, do not regard the world as populated by things. Though they have been heavily brainwashed by society into limiting their love to their immediate family, i.e. a man and his children, most still insist on caring for others. Unlike men, they do not seem to need a reward for this in the shape of status, power, money and extravagant praise. When they see a need, or feel the pain of others, they respond, and take responsibility for relieving distress in a way which most men seem unable to do. Since the world has been brought to its knees by an excess of egocentricity, and a lack of love on the part of men, it seems ravingly obvious that women would make a far better job of ruling it, even if there were no spiritual reasons for this. Women, however, are no more ready, in general, to begin guiding and leading men than men are to be advised by a wiser and more enlightened woman.

As we have pointed out several times, many women who are changing paths have chosen the route of suppressing their love for others in an effort to gain something for themselves. Out of fear that this is the only way, they have become just as unfeeling and callous as men. Though this may satisfy the masochistic needs of some men to be punished for their "sins," it does nothing overall to alleviate human suffering. Such women will relax when more men appear who are ready to surrender to powerful women. At present, since most men are solidly patriarchal, the only way to achieve anything as a woman seems to be to play them at their own game. Patriarchal men who are contemplating changing paths will respect and allow some power to a woman who has "balls," by which they mean that she is aggressive, dominating, success oriented etc. i.e. she is like a patriarchal man. Though she may have to work twice as hard as a man to achieve any recognition, and be ten times as intelligent, she can get somewhere if she sticks to the rules.

This may seem unfair, and counterproductive, since society appears to be losing the nurturing side of these women, and gaining nothing in return. But it is an improvement on the total exclusion of women from business and politics which occurred before. And since nature abhors a vacuum, the grand sum of love in society is not diminished, because men who care for others are growing in number. Few are ready to surrender to women, since there are almost no matercentric women to surrender to, but they are growing in their awareness that this is their next step.

What is to stop a complete reversal of patriarchy, a world in which women are selfish, oppressive and uncaring, and men are the devalued nurturers of women's lives? This thought may be preventing many people from changing. Men fear the possible tyranny of women, and women fear that they will have to be tyrants if they cross over into having a leading role in society. If these views are not allowed to become conscious, they operate to prevent change. Women become exasperated by men who talk about equality yet manage to find wonderful reasons why it shouldn't happen right now, and men become equally irritated by women who demand power, then back away from it with a multiplicity of feeble excuses when it is offered. Both sides, at a conscious level, are totally sincere, but underneath is fear. Women look around themselves at society, and see that power involves treading on the feelings and rights of others, even if it is "for their own good." They have an instinctive bias against coercion, unless they are suppressing unconditional love, and they can see no other way to run society, because there has been no other way for millennia. They don't wish to cause pain, or thwart anyone's desires, so they continue to hope that somehow, a way will be found to make it all better, and that everyone will become loving and caring by the waving of a magic wand. Men see the same society, where conflict and coercion rule O.K. and either feel that women do not have the necessary qualities to change anything, or that they too will have to become dictatorial and ruthless to keep society functioning.

In a sense they are not wrong. In a patriarchal society, hierarchy and domination are inevitable, because those who have power use it for personal gain, and not for the happiness of all. Those who seek to influence others have their own ego in mind when they do it. Even if they see themselves as the guardians of morality and law, they are benevolent despots, since they have the arrogance to believe that their way is the best and only way to achieve stability and happiness.

Women's link to the Great Mother cannot be totally suppressed. They know that coercion merely produces outwardly correct behavior, and does not change consciousness. Although they may initially punish men for their behavior, once they are ready to forgive, they will desire to rule by consent. Only in this way can they feel at ease with a leading role in society. When men see that no force will be used, and that women truly desire harmony, not domination, they will become passive and willing to surrender.

The desire to guide society in a way which denies no one's freedom will not arrive overnight. It seems to us that women must access the power of the Great Mother in order to develop both the wisdom necessary to be leaders, and the knowledge that no oppression or mistreatment will be necessary. They must turn away from the male god towards a female Creator, and open themselves to her love and power. Only in this way can they truly become Her representatives on earth. If they do not do this, men will not want to worship them, or accept their guidance voluntarily. They cannot respect and follow women who lack inner connection to the Great Mother. The only other option available to women who are changing paths is to ape patriarchal men, and fight for dominance and "rights," using the same tactics as men do. This will not get them what they want, except in the short term, and it will certainly not produce a happy society, for them or for others. Men will feel no desire to surrender to them, so it will be a patriarchal power struggle, with the unhappiness and disharmony this brings. Any gains will be followed by losses as patriarchal men wait for a new front to attack on. It may seem to us that women have only achieved the gains of the last few years because of their struggles with the male establishment, but it is not true. There has been no need whatsoever for the strife and violence. It satisfies that part of us which enjoys conquering and battles, but it lays up trouble for the future. Patriarchal men who have been forced to moderate their behavior towards women have not changed their inner attitudes. Given half a chance, they will rejoin the battle when women have relaxed a little, and redouble their efforts to "put them in their place."

This should not make us fearful, since irreversible change has occurred, and moved us towards a matercentric society. The inner willingness of men to change paths, and return to the Great Mother, and the willingness of women to begin the development of their own individual creativity, has produced the alterations in society, not the surface shouting and yelling. If we ask for what we want, and we have no conflict about having it, the Great Mother supplies our desire without any fuss. The anger and violence associated with recent changes has been caused by lack of certainty. A woman who feels her new desires may not be met, because of past experience, or who feels someone may lose out if she gains, may add anger, fear and justification to her requests. It seems to her, because her connection to the Great Mother has weakened, that this is what you have to do. You don't, unless you enjoy making life difficult for yourself.

Passing laws to remove barriers against women is as patriarchal in essence as laws which restrict them, though it will be some time before we fully realize this. If a man is denying a woman's right to freedom in a certain area, are we overriding his free will by preventing him from discriminating against her? We are, because we are using coercion to force him into "correct" behavior, so we are no better than he is. Unfortunately, in our present patriarchal society, we can't see a better way to prevent the abuses of power. The growing power of women, and the feeling that oppression must be curbed, leads us into solutions which fit us as we are now. We respect force, whether it is the force of the law, or some other form of coercion. Bullies notoriously abandon bullying when faced with penalties of some kind, even if it means violence is necessary. So we use it. It seems to work, but it does not change the bully's desire for a victim.

Society accepts coercion as a way of life, which allows the bully to operate, whether he is in the school playground or in charge of a multinational company. Cooperation, however, involves freely joining with others in a collective endeavor, and has no element of fear or force in it. To reach a cooperative society, we must eliminate coercion from our lives, in all of its forms, as fast as our fears and desires allow us. As always, this requires trust in the Great Mother, which develops slowly as we allow her to help and support us. Eventually, we will come to realize that no one can make us do what we don't want to, and that the same goes for everyone else. We will abandon all our strategies to persuade, cajole, and oppress others, since they no longer work, and have no desire or expectation of being restricted ourselves.

To begin with, men who are changing paths may obey women, out of respect for their power in the patriarchal sense. They know, at some level, that women are going to be the leaders of society, but they can't imagine a world in which this is achieved without force, punishment or structures. Some of them will thoroughly enjoy this stage of their growth, and seek out a bullying and ruthless woman to be the agent of their atonement for the sins of the past. Others will look for a softer version of this; the woman who is strong yet more caring than a male boss. But she will still be partly patriarchal, in her firm belief that it is her money, her decisiveness and assertiveness, or her position in society which allows her to lead. She still needs the props of a hierarchy to feel safe, and so does the man. He is not likely, at this stage, to obey his secretary if he is the boss. She is not likely to either want him to, or believe it's possible.

After the crossing of the central pillar, change becomes more radical. Men will be willing to listen to and follow the advice of women who have no status at all within patriarchal society i.e. they are not rich, young and beautiful, well educated, respected professionals, successful business women, white or aristocrats etc. This doesn't mean such women will have nothing to contribute, far from it, merely that their patriarchal status is irrelevant. What will count is that they have begun to manifest the power and wisdom of the Great Mother. Men will be able to feel that this is so, since they will have been developing their intuition for some time, and will have lost their ability to judge women's usefulness by patriarchal standards. Women, in their turn, will cease appraising men in these terms too, and begin to value the passive (i.e. receptive to them and the Great Mother) and intuitive man, who seeks to serve society with his skills. As women become valued for their wisdom and ability to guide men, their confidence will grow, enabling them to relax further into their new role. Since the guidance given by women clearly benefits society, men will continue to look to them for advice. Their growing love for all will not allow them to continue to judge and oppress others for personal gain, so the whole structure of society will change. The idea of profiting at someone else's expense will die away, as will the need for external power in its myriad forms.

Eventually, there will be no trace of man's overbearing egotism, and women's self sacrifice. Once each sex has learned from the inside, and expressed on the outside, the knowledge that we are one with the Great Mother and All That Is, yet independent creators as well, we will have completed our cycle. We will move on, to new cycles and new worlds.

The Quabalah

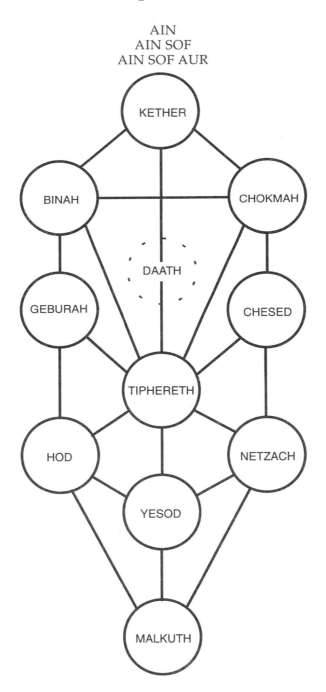

AIN
AIN SOF
AIN SOF AUR

KETHER

BINAH

CHOKMAH

DAATH

GEBURAH

CHESED

TIPHERETH

HOD

NETZACH

YESOD

MALKUTH

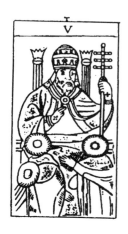

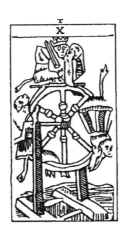

About The Authors

William Bond and Pamela Suffield reside in Suffolk, England. Pamela teaches high school full time in addition to writing and raising her teen-aged daughter. Bill is a craftsman and teaches occult sciences.

They are convinced that the Goddess brought them together to collaborate on *the Gospel* after both of them became disillusioned with the New Age movement and a variety of neo-Pagan traditions which failed to acknowledge the necessity to restore the feminine ideal as the ideal in the collective psyche. They are presently working on a new book and are available for consultations, speaking engagements and astrological charts.

ORDER FORM

Telephone Orders: Call Toll Free 1-800-247-6553.
Have your Optima, Discover, Visa, or MasterCard ready.

FAX Orders: 1-419-281-6883—Bookmasters Inc.

Postal Orders: Artemis Creations, 3395 Nostrand Ave. 2J,
Brooklyn, NY 11229-4053 (718) 648-8215

☐ I am ordering _____ copies at $19.95 each postpaid.

☐ I am ordering the *Gospel* on Audiotape at $15.95 postpaid.

☐ I would like to receive a Goddess Kali pendant with satin cord, a
$10 value, and have enclosed Proof of Purchase and sales receipt, plus
$1.50 handling fee.

Shipping: Book Rate: *allow three to four weeks.*
First Class Priority Mail: $2.50 additional.

Payment: ☐ Check $_____

Credit Card: ☐ Visa, ☐ MasterCard, ☐ Optima, ☐ Discover

Card Number: _____

Name on Card: _____ Exp. Date:____/____

Signature: _____

(Required to process order.)

☐ **Please send me** *Emotions: From Patriarchy to Matriarchy*, by
Pamela Suffield. A discussion of the patriarchal male, patriarchal female, and progress necessary to reach a matercentric model. A companion to *Gospel of The Goddess*. Audiotape. $15.95 each postpaid.
☐ **Please send information on the** *FEMINA SOCIETY WORLDWIDE.*